TRADING ON MOMENTUM

TRADING ON MOMENTUM

Advanced Techniques for High-Percentage Day Trading

KEN WOLFF
WITH CHRIS SCHUMACHER
AND JEFF TAPPAN

McGraw-Hill
New York   Chicago   San Francisco
Lisbon   London   Madrid   Mexico City
Milan   New Delhi   San Juan   Seoul
Singapore   Sydney   Toronto

Library of Congress Cataloging-in-Publication Data

Wolff, Ken.
    Trading on momentum / by Ken Wolff, Chris Schumacher, Jeff Tapan.
       p. cm.
    ISBN 0-07-137068-4
    1. Day trading (Securities)   2. Investment analysis   3. Stocks—Prices.
I. Schumacher, Chris.   II. Tappan, Jeff.   III. Title.

HG4515.95.W658   2001
332.64—dc21   2001030665

McGraw-Hill

A Division of The McGraw-Hill Companies

1 2 3 4 5 6 7 8 9 0   DOC / DOC   0 9 8 7 6 5 4 3 2 1

ISBN 0-07-137068-4

This book was set in Palatino by MacAllister Publishing Services, LLC.

Printed and bound by R.R. Donnelley & Sons Company.

This publication is designed to provide accurate and auhoritative information in regard to the subject matter covered. It is sold with the understanding that neither the author nor the publisher is engaged in rendering legal, accounting, futures/securities trading, or other professional service. If legal advice or other expert assistance is required, the services of a competent professional person should be sought.

> —*From a Declaration of Principles jointly adopted by a Committee*
> *of the American Bar Association and a Committee of Publishers*

McGraw-Hill books are available at special quantity discounts to use as premiums and sales promotions, or for use in corporate training programs. For more information, please write to the Director of Special Sales, Professional Publishing, McGraw-Hill, Two Penn Plaza, New York, NY 10121-2298. Or contact your local bookstore.

 This book is printed on recycled, acid-free paper containing a minimum of 50% recycled, de-inked fiber.

CONTENTS

Chapter 5

Chapter 6

Chapter 7

Chapter 8

Chapter 14

Momentum Investing   231

Epilogue   255

ACKNOWLEDGMENTS

We would like to thank Ela Aktay of McGraw-Hill Professional Publishing for giving us the opportunity to write this book and Beth Brown from MacAllister Publishing Services for her efforts during the production process. Without your untiring efforts, this book would not have been possible. We also want to thank Victor Jung, a fantastic partner and good friend for his remarkable efforts in the production of this book and technically on a day-to-day basis in the chat room pits. And Steve Demarest from MB Trading for his friendship and constant encouragement.

Finally, a warm and grateful thanks to the thousands of traders, both past and present that have graced the cyber halls of Mtrader.com and RealityTrader.com over the years. You have helped us create an explosive online revolution that has literally changed the way traders are educated and enter the trading arena. With your help, we have literally changed the face of online trading, helping us shift the power of trading decisions from brokers to individual traders. Your enthusiasm, thirst for knowledge, and quest for education were the reasons we wrote this book.

INTRODUCTION

The face of the stock market has changed forever. With the introduction of the online trader, the market exploded in late 1996, creating volatility and momentum previously not thought possible. From this, the spawning stocks like Qualcomm, Yahoo, Iomega, and Cisco, only increased the interest of the everyday American to join the ranks of the do-it-yourself investors and traders. Instant wealth was created and it seemed as if the market could only keep going up. No matter what a trader did, it was hard losing money as the market continued to climb to new heights every day. This added more members to the online trader ranks as rags-to-riches stories were on the news and in almost every conversation on the streets.

Then the bubble popped in March of 2000 just after the Nasdaq peaked over 5,000. Massive panic hit the streets as stocks continued to plummet and those instant millionaires saw their paper profits disappear almost overnight. When the market didn't immediately recover, this further added to the exodus, creating a downward spiral to the likes never seen in the history of the stock market.

For the everyday momentum trader, the period from 1996 to March of 2000 was like shooting ducks in a pond. Stable predictable patterns that repeated over and over again were the norm. All one had to do was find a pattern or method that worked and ride it for months on end, over and over again. After the crash in March of 2000, the face of the market changed forever. Although the market actually had more of the main ingredient of volatile momentum required for a momentum trader, the patterns and methods that previously worked for months on end, changed on a daily basis. What worked yesterday, didn't work today. This new dynamic and ever-changing market took, by some estimates, 40 percent of the short-term traders out of the market, permanently.

Those traders who learned to change tactics in this new changing market, not only survived this new market momentum, but also profited handsomely. The two required traits in the market for a momentum trader are momentum and volatility. The period after the crash in March of 2000 actually showed more of these two traits, yet the majority of momentum traders lost in what was actually a better market condition to profit in. Why? For one simple reason: they failed to change tactics and methods as the market changed. They continued to do what worked yesterday, but not today. This is the purpose of this book: to teach you the techniques and methods that actually do work in this new market, how to exploit the new momentum, and how to profit handsomely from it.

A momentum trader doesn't care what a stock will do next month, next week, or even in the next hour, only how it is currently reacting. By trading only what the tape is currently showing, it removes the guess-work of what will happen in the future. Momentum trading is unique in that it takes advantage of the predictable, repeating momentum cycles created by the vast majority of inexperienced traders and investors. These patterns tend to repeat themselves over and over again because they are caused by two very basic emotions: fear and greed. Inex-perienced traders overreact to the momentum created by news, hype, or cyclical market swings caused by these two basic emotions.

By understanding the root causes of these emotions and the ability to recognize the predictable momentum they generate, professional momentum traders exploit patterns that tend to repeat themselves over and over again. The ability to recognize the root causes and the indica-tors signaling that a pattern is about to repeat itself enables a successful momentum trader to enter a trade just as the momentum is starting, and exit sometimes just minutes or seconds later as the momentum slows and turns. By riding waves of continuous momentum, it creates opportunity for tremendous gains not available to investors or longer-term traders.

The vast majority of those who enter into the momentum trading arena end up losing in the end for the simple reason they do not educate themselves prior to jumping into the shark filled waters with other sea-soned professional traders. This book is designed to give the reader a peek into these advanced methods, the psychology, and unique tools pre-viously only available to a professional momentum trader and level the playing field.

Although Ken Wolff and Chris Schumacher use the same basic core methods, you will find that Ken concentrates primarily on Level 1 screens, using rhythm, pace, indicators, and market dynamics to iden-tify momentum shifts. Chris uses these techniques as well, but takes it one step further by discussing many of the methods available on the Level 2 screen to enhance these techniques. Many find Level 2 confus-ing and do not use it at all, whereas others say they cannot trade with-out it. So, whether you are using Level 1 or Level 2 screens, both are discussed in detail throughout the book. You will find that these two tech-niques do not conflict with each other, but build on each method. As you progress through the chapters, it is important to fully understand the con-cepts being discussed before moving onto the next chapter as each chap-ter builds on the preceding chapter.

STRUCTURE OF THE BOOK

This book is divided into three main parts. Chapters 1 through 3 cover the basic concepts of the market as well as the tools of the trading game that you must be familiar with to level the playing field with seasoned professionals. You will learn about Market Makers, online teaching forums, and order-routing methods. You may or may not want to participate in online chat rooms, but they have unquestionably become a major force in the market and can dramatically impact the movement of certain stocks. Without understanding these forces, you are playing with one eye closed to the reasons behind those moves. Finally, the advanced tools of an active trader will be discussed.

The next section, Chapters 4 through 8, is an in-depth look at momentum, its root causes, and key factors in identifying who the market players are behind it. By understanding who is responsible for the momentum and the psychology behind the forces that push and pull on the market, you will then be able to spot predictable momentum patterns. This section explores several niche patterns that tend to repeat themselves over and over again in certain market conditions. You will also learn to spot certain stocks, called *indicator* stocks, that tend to lead the movement of the general market and give you an edge on what the market is about to do. It will also give you specific methods of assigning a mathematical score to each of the major causes of market momentum, creating a matrix that enables you to determine how certain patterns will react under these different market conditions.

Chapters 9 through 14 examine specific methods, rules, and mindsets that are an absolute necessity for every successful and profitable trader. It explores how the time of day you trade is just as important as how you trade and how to create the proper mindset to ensure you do not fall for the most common pitfalls that take most traders out of the game. The section titled "The Golden Rules of Trading" spells out clearcut rules that I have spent years developing. If you read nothing else, read these rules.

The book concludes with a discussion on what I call momentum investing, a unique form of trading that takes the best of two distinctly different forms of trading: momentum trading and investing. No matter what your form of trading is, this section will enable you to capture the explosive gains of momentum trading while participating in the slower, longer-term trades of investing.

1
CHAPTER

THE BASICS

This chapter will discuss the genesis of the stock market and provide you with a quick background of the different exchanges and the players who control it. Without this understanding of who controls the trades and their motivation behind the scenes, traders cannot fully participate in the market with open eyes. An in-depth discussion in Chapter 3, "Tools of the Trade," will explore the different brokerage and execution services available. The last topic covered will be the type of equipment required to participate in the new electronic trading world.

THE START OF IT ALL

When individuals asked how the market was doing many years ago, they were referring to the Dow Jones Industrial Average. The Dow Jones Industrial Average, or Dow, is a basket of 30 stocks that is perceived as indicative of the stock market as a whole and its relative strength or weakness. The index includes stocks such as Alcoa (AA), Boeing (BA), Caterpillar (CAT), General Electric (GE), and Walt Disney (DIS).

The Dow Jones Industrial Average was introduced by Charles H. Dow in May of 1896 and at first was not widely followed. Charles Dow began with 11 stocks to try to apply a visualization of the market short-term trends. It was a very simplistic approach and one that we may scoff at in current times. However, it was a key building block to how we view the markets today. In 1916, the index was expanded to 20 stocks and then in 1928, to 30 stocks. Periodically, stocks are removed and replaced with new ones, but they are all leaders in their industry and are widely held. Later in 1929 came the Utilities and the railroad average was renamed Transports in 1970.

With the advent of the Internet age, the Dow has seen some changes in its lineup. In the latter part of 1999, Intel Corporation (INTC) and Microsoft Corporation (MSFT) ousted Union Carbide (UK) and Chevron (CHV) and were the first two Nasdaq-related issues to be included in the Average. Many new indices are available now such as the Russell 2000, Nasdaq, Wilshire 5000 Total Market, AMEX, and Standard & Poor's 500. Basically, each analyst follows a different spectrum of the market and each of these indices represents a more specific set of sectors or stocks that are included. For example, the Russell is a measure of small caps, whereas the Wilshire is representative of the entire marketplace.

With the explosion of online trading in the past decade, many market participants are now keeping a close eye on the Nasdaq and the S&P 500. The Wilshire 5000 has also been watched as a close indicator as it is suggested to be representative of the whole market. Today, when someone asks how the market is doing, we need to clarify which one as each one tends to have a life of its own. One day the Dow may be up 120 points and the Nasdaq down 150 as each has its own character and different types of stocks it represents.

These indices are all made up of stocks that are traded on exchanges. Several exchanges are available, but the two most notable are the *New York Stock Exchange* (NYSE) and the *National Association of Securities Dealers Automated Quotation* (Nasdaq). The NYSE registered with the U.S. Securities and Exchange Commission in October of 1934 as a national securities exchange. In 1971, the Exchange was incorporated as a not-for-profit corporation.

The NYSE is an open auction system located in a 36,000-square-foot facility. Institutions and retail investors are represented by Exchange members in which they call out bids and offers for stock in specific locations on the physical trading floor. The laws of supply and demand govern the price for stocks in this Exchange. The NYSE uses a market specialist whose job is to keep a fair and orderly market in the issues that he or she has control over.

Orders to buy and sell are sent directly to the specialist either electronically or from the agent representing institutions and retail investors. The benefit to having all order flow to a single specialist is the presence of liquidity. This ensures that prices do not fluctuate in a less than orderly fashion. This is intended to provide the individual with open access to several potential buyers and sellers to get the best price that you can for your transaction. In contrast to the specialist system, the Nasdaq marketplace uses a totally different system.

The Nasdaq opened to the world on February 8, 1971, in response to Congress asking the Securities and Exchange Commission to conduct a study of all securities markets in the late 1960s. The SEC, after finding the *Over-The-Counter* (OTC) securities markets unknown and fragmentary, offered automation as a solution. This challenge was set forth to the *National Association of Securities Dealers, Inc.* (NASD) for implementing the program.

Throughout the mid-1970s and 1980s, several key enhancements were made to the Nasdaq system. Inside quotations were displayed that offered the best Bid and Ask prices visually. This narrowed the spread (difference between the Bid and the Ask) in the majority of the 2,500 Nasdaq stocks at that time. The *Small Order Execution System* (SOES) was introduced to automatically execute small orders against the inside prices. Finally, in 1997, the SEC approved the Nasdaq's request to begin quoting stock in spreads as narrow as ¹⁄₁₆ to produce better prices. Whereas the NYSE is an actual trading floor, the Nasdaq is a huge computer network that has fueled the trading frenzy that has emerged over the past 10 years.

MARKET MAKERS

In the Nasdaq marketplace, instead of specialists providing liquidity and orderly pricing, Market Makers assume this role. Market Makers are independent dealers that actively participate for order flow. They display quotations that are indicative of their willingness to buy and sell at certain price levels. Over 500 market-making firms provide the needed liquidity in the Nasdaq marketplace.

This liquidity provides investors with supply and demand to enhance an immediate and incessant trading atmosphere. Market Makers participating in this type of trading are required to follow basic rules set forth by the SEC. They must provide a reasonable two-sided market in the issues that they make a market. They do this by disclosing their buy and sell quotations. They must honor their quoted prices against liability orders and report the trading in a timely manner per regulations. They must also display both quotes and orders according to the regulations in the Order Handling Rules developed by the SEC.

Basically, four types of market-making firms are available. They are retail, wholesale, regional, and institutional. Retail firms employ a retail brokerage network that caters to individual investors. They tend to facilitate order flow for their clients to provide liquidity for the price of the stock to ensure stability. Wholesale firms exist to trade shares for institutional clients. They also act as an agent for broker-dealers that are not registered Market Makers in a particular issue but need to fill an order in that stock for their own clients. Wholesale firms tend to be an important facilitator for the other three types of firms.

The institutional firm provides service to pension funds, mutual funds, insurance companies, and other types of money management entities that want to execute large block orders. The regional firm tends to focus on only companies and investors in a certain region of the country. This allows them to provide more in-depth analysis of companies in that area for their clients.

Since 1971, the Nasdaq market has split into separate markets. The Nasdaq is now made up of the Nasdaq National Market, The Nasdaq SmallCap Market, and the OTCBB (OTC Bulletin Board). The National Market lists over 4,400 companies. This National Market contains issues such as Microsoft (MSFT), Dell Computers (DELL), Intell (INTC), Cisco (CSCO), and other large and widely known companies of the world. The SmallCap Market has about 1,800 securities. The less established companies are usually found in this market until they can meet the more rigid requirements of the National Market. The OTCBB lists a group of stocks that tends to be issues that traders stay away from, as their future is uncertain at best.

ELECTRONIC COMMUNICATIONS NETWORKS

In the Nasdaq Stock Market, we have two groups of market participants. The first group we talked about already, the Market Makers. They provide the liquidity necessary to keep stock prices stable and orderly. The alternate group is made up of *Electronic Communications Networks* (ECNs). An ECN is a private trading system and is a relatively new addition to the Nasdaq marketplace. ECNs simply match buy orders to sell orders. If the order cannot be matched, the order is placed to the respective ECN order book until such a match can be made. In 1997, when the SEC order handling rules were implemented, ECNs were incorporated into the structure. ECNs are required to register with the Nasdaq and are required to follow NASD Regulation to participate in the marketplace. ECNs are basically order books that match orders at specific price levels. There is no human intervention with ECNs. If the order on the book is matched, it's executed, sometimes with price improvements.

At the time of this book, nine ECNs are currently registered. They are Archipelago L.L.C. (ARCA), Attain (ATTN), B-Trade Services L.L.C. (BTRD), The BRASS Utility (BRUT), Instinet Corporation (INCA), Island (ISLD), NexTrade (NTRD), Spear, Leeds & Kellogg (REDI), and Strike Technologies (STRK). ECNs became more prevalent as the online trading explosion occurred. Institutions and Market Makers use ECNs to provide themselves with anonymity when entering orders for stocks at price levels. One of the advantages of ECNs is that active individual traders can utilize ECNs to bypass Market Makers in the attempt to get a better price when Market Makers are not present at inside price levels.

ECN orders are routed in a way that they are first matched against a pending order. If the order is unable to be matched immediately, it is posted to an order book on the quote screen until either the individual cancels the order or a matching order executes against it. The primary choice of active traders in the past few years has been the ISLD ECN. The amazing amount of volume that ISLD constitutes on a daily basis has prompted some desires to have ISLD become its own exchange. What started out as a quotation-driven market has evolved into a quotation- and order-driven marketplace for investors and active traders.

In the NYSE, stock symbols are comprised of one, two, or three letters. For example, Agilent Technologies has the symbol A. Boeing Co. has the stock symbol BA. Caterpillar Incorporated has the stock symbol CAT. In the Nasdaq, symbols are either four or five letters. For example, Microsoft Corporation has a stock symbol MSFT. Nasdaq stocks that have a fifth letter usually have a meaning associated with that fifth letter. You can find what these definition symbols mean at **http://www.nasdaqtrader.com/trader/defincludes/sdDefinitions2.stm#nasdaq issues.** An example would be on a stock like IRIDQ. IRID is the symbol for Iridium and the Q is defined as a company in bankruptcy proceedings. These fifth letters are especially important to traders as you want to avoid stocks with uncertain futures. Those that are delinquent with their filings or in bankruptcy are stocks that have clouded futures at best and are not worth our time.

We spend a lot of time talking about the different exchanges, but momentum traders primarily concentrate on stocks traded on the Nasdaq. These stocks tend to be more technology oriented, and by using the Market Makers and ECNs, they produce more intra-day momentum. Momentum traders do trade stocks on the other exchanges, but they tend to be larger and more stable, which leads to less volatility and momentum. Momentum traders do not care whether or not a stock is moving up or down; all that is required is movement and momentum and as such we concentrate mostly on Nasdaq stocks.

THE ESSENTIALS

Traders often ask about hardware, software, and data requirements when they are setting up shop in their homes or offices to begin trading. With the introduction of online trading through brokers such as E*TRADE and Ameritrade, the Internet has placed the power of information dissemination at the trader's fingertips. This not only empowers the individual to make his or her own trading decisions, it allows us access to applying our decisions to market participation in real time. The explosion of online trading is a by-product of the increased efficiency in data distribution and the personal desire for self-directed decision implementation.

Many brokers are offering lower commissions and complete data packages to pull traditional investors and active traders away from high-priced brokers. Many commission rates are under $20 per trade and depending on the level of activity or size of one's portfolio, the data package is free. What was once available to us only through our broker is now available to us with a few clicks of the mouse. At face value, we are on a more level playing field. Obviously, the public is still the last to know in some areas, but we certainly have more access to more information than ever before.

We are in a stage of technological advancement when hardware that is bought today is obsolete within a year. Processing speeds are faster and more user-friendly functions are enhanced. One year ago, 5 gigabytes of hard-drive space was more than enough to store most of our applications. Sixteen megabytes of RAM was enough memory to allow our computer to function efficiently.

The first component that one must have is at least one computer. The computer that you choose should include at least a 500-megahertz processor. It should also include at least 128 megabytes of RAM as you will be pulling a lot of data down into your computer and it needs to be processed and displayed as fast as possible.

The monitor that comes with your computer should be at least 17 inches. Advanced traders often find themselves with limited screen space and would gladly pay for a larger screen. With recent deals and rebates through some of the larger computer stores, a brand name computer can be bought for as little as $500.

Many advanced traders like to have at least two computers or monitors when watching stocks throughout the day. Some have elected to network their systems to provide more efficiency through their data feeds. Although this may seem like something that is beneficial, beginning traders should start small and build as they progress. There is no reason to go out and buy two or three computers and monitors if, in six months, you decide trading is not going to work for you. It's best to keep your capital for trading and as you begin to profit over time, expand your systems with your portfolios.

The most important component a trader needs is a fast connection to the Internet. Traders have often joked about using carrier pigeons to send in their orders because their connection to the Internet is slow. Although a simple phone line with at least a 56K connection is minimal, you should research at least three more efficient routes, depending on what is available in your area. First, your local cable company may provide cable modems.

RoadRunner is probably the most familiar Internet cable access service. This can provide speeds up to ten times faster than a normal 56K connection. Other options include DSL, ADSL, ISDN, Satellite, and Frame Relay that may be open to you in your area. When you look into these options, find out how much the up-front capital requirement is, how much the service costs per month is, and how fast the optimal speed is when comparing it relative to price.

You don't need a T-1 line to trade stocks, but if you are going to put out an extra expense for something, get the fastest Internet hookup you can afford. With a 56K modem, inexperienced traders may not notice it, but when the volume of trades is heavy in the first few minutes of the market, it tends to backlog your quotes. This forces you to trade on information that is sometimes minutes behind what is really happening in the market. A solid, fast cable hookup will alleviate much of this and help level the playing field.

2 CHAPTER

GETTING STARTED

This chapter will examine the different education and teaching forums both available on the Internet, pointing out some of the benefits and common pitfalls and traps that await you. It will teach you how to develop a proper trading mentality and identify realistic expectations of gains and losses. Finally, it will teach you to do the one thing most traders fail to do: paper trade until your methods are successfully creating high-percentage gains.

EDUCATION

Many of the traders that came from the explosion of online trading see the market as a game that is to be played, rather than a business to be learned. It is precisely this reason that we see such a high turnover rate among aspiring traders who want to make trading a career. A lack of education and preparation is clearly the number one reason why traders lose money and are forced out of the game.

Many of today's active momentum traders actually stemmed from the explosion of the stock market in 1999. They saw the phenomenal gains in stocks like Qualcomm (QCOM) (see Figure 2-1) and Yahoo (YHOO) (see Figure 2-2) and were simply dissatisfied with the meager returns they were getting from their money managers and professional portfolio managers. They saw the huge gains others were making and they wanted a piece of the action.

This opened the public's eyes to the gains that can be made by properly exploiting the market. The potential capital to be made is in fact huge, but nothing comes without risk. You can reduce this risk by realizing that education and a disciplined approach should be two of

F I G U R E   2 - 1

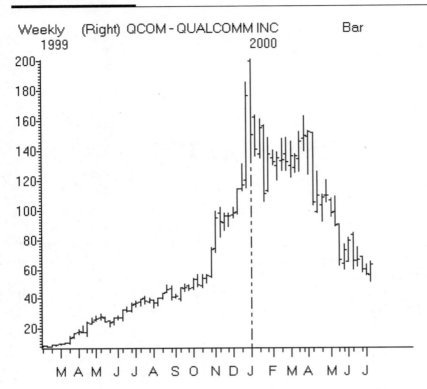

Weekly   (Right) QCOM - QUALCOMM INC   Bar

your top priorities. Too often, traders jump in feet first without rhyme or reason or even a basic understanding of the market, tools, or methods required. Do not make this mistake—it is a costly one.

Investors will spend literally hundreds of hours researching stocks for their investing portfolio, but jump right into the mix when learning to daytrade without understanding even the basics. You need to look at trading as a business, and with any business, there are startup and education costs. Taking losses while you are learning is part of the game, but your number one objective during this period should be capital preservation.

Historically, the market has found a way to weed out the undisciplined traders and end their careers abruptly. Just as you would listen to your broker for investment advice, you should have a disciplined approach to studying the stock market to gain a basic understanding of key fundamentals. From this foundation, aspiring traders can move

FIGURE 2-2

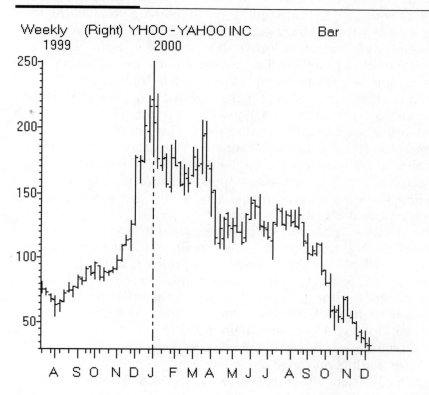

along with a consistent progression until they feel that at some point they are ready to make a living from trading. The key to effective trading is developing your *own* disciplined approach and methodology.

You can develop these methods by several means. First, you can find a mentor who is an active, successful trader and learn by example. Play follow the leader; trade when he or she trades and fully explore the logic behind each trade. This is the best method, but unfortunately the hardest to do as successful traders who are willing to spend the time teaching on a day-to-day basis are hard to find. Secondly, you can embark on a self-education process by reading many of the good trading books currently on the market. This gives the new trader a basic background on methodology and technique but lacks the real-time, live trading experience. Lastly, you can find a mentor or teacher who leads and teaches groups of traders online. Several online services are available such as Mtrader.com or RealityTrader.com where this type of education can be found.

Before you embark on this journey, you must identify what your goals are. Is your goal to trade full- or part-time? Are you looking for a career or simply a way to increase your odds in the trading world?

Granted, each trader's objective differs; some want to make a living at home trading from their living rooms, while others simply want to learn trading as a hobby. Some want to make trading a disciplined career, while others are looking for that age-old quick buck. Whatever the reason for one's desire to be a market participant, it must come with an acceptance of responsibility. That responsibility lies within the understanding and need for education, cautious progression in a disciplined trading program, and finally the implementation of a comfortable trading system. If any of these steps are skipped, trading becomes more akin to gambling. Over the years, gamblers tend to lose the majority of their money on unsound decisions or methods.

When traders first begin trading, they need to find a method that works for them. Numerous systems and methods are available to trade on the stock market. There are methods for options, futures, derivatives, currencies, bonds, equities, and so on. If speculation is involved, there is a system somewhere for it. The trick is to find the method that best fits your financial status, risk tolerance, and learning curve. Obviously, buy low and sell high is the common method that makes money. Knowing when to buy and when to sell is the key component to trading.

To learn trading, one must study a theory and be able to apply it to trading at a consistency rate that allows for gradual profits over time. Those that expect huge one-time gains in trading methods are also setting themselves up for big one-time losses. Normally, over time, one cannot continuously make huge gains without a few huge losses to complement them. These get-rich-quick schemes almost always end up in failure. The market doesn't allow for consistent get-rich-quick methods. It finds a way to take from the undisciplined eventually.

ON-SIGHT TRAINING

Over the past five years, with the explosion of online and daytrading, many educational services have evolved to help traders with their progress in this business. Although some of these services are nothing more than just stock picking sites, some very good educational sites are available that correct a lot of misinformation about the marketplace and provide a reasonable forum for professional discussion. Most of the systems or methods are different, however, and therefore must be reviewed by the individual before making any choices about which one to pick. You should review many things when ascertaining an opinion about where you want to learn.

First, beginning traders need to choose whether they want to learn from on-site training or if they feel comfortable enough with straight online discussion. Both have advantages. In discussing the on-site training, the major advantage is obviously being able to speak face to face with professional traders. This type of training requires that you travel to their facility, but they are not cheap and can cost anywhere from $1,000 to $5,000 for a week's worth of training and personal guidance. They will take you on a crash course for one week on the A to Z's of trading. They will work with you on an individual basis to provide you with a basis of trading that is a starting point for where you need to start relative to your trading experience. The traders who are teaching are accredited in their fields and have a working knowledge of key components such as Level 1, 2, and Time of Sales. They can pick out price action and point out key points of interest to you onscreen where everyone can participate and ask questions regarding their examples. It is simply a more personal approach to learning to trade.

The main disadvantage that one should know when choosing this route is that the expense for the crash course may not be worth it. Trading for a living is not something that can be learned in a week's time. The costs can add up when you include expenses such as a hotel room, food, a rental car, and plane tickets. This tends to scare many beginning traders early when thinking about this avenue for their learning process. The alternative to on-site teaching has therefore become the online teaching forums.

ONLINE TEACHING FORUMS

Online teaching forums have reduced fixed overhead costs. Many of them pay for the servers for the site, a few licenses for data transfer, possibly a news service, and then salary to the employees and professional traders. When compared with the facility and upkeep of on-site training, the costs are much lower. These cost savings are passed onto the traders. Whereas a week of training at an on-site training course will cost you $1,000 to $5,000, an educational service may only cost $200 a month. This is the major advantage to on-site training. You can test the waters to see if the methods being taught suit your needs before you lay down a large payment.

This gives you five months' minimum with most educational services versus one week of a crash course at some on-site training facilities. For around $50 a week, traders have access to the service instructor's expertise and knowledge. They are encouraged to ask questions and participate in a professional manner that enhances a trader's progress. Most educational programs are not stock picking services because their function is to provide reasoning behind the methodology, rather than just alerting the room to entry and exit points.

Everybody is looking for the cure for cancer, the easy fix in the world of trading, but it simply doesn't exist. If you limit yourself to a room that only offers simple stock picks, promotes buy and sell calls for entries and exits, you are doomed to failure. If you are in a trade just because some room guru says it is a good trade without knowing the logic and methods behind it, you will lose in the long run. You may make a few good gains, but over time your losses will take you out of the game. We have all heard the old saying, "if you give a man a fish, you feed him for a day, but if you teach him to fish, he is set for life." It could not be any more true in the world of online trading rooms. Many times the fish you are being fed are not healthy and are never in the quantities promised. The only way to truly succeed in trading is to learn the methodology yourself and make your own trades after you have educated yourself.

The disadvantage to on-site forums is the personal approach where one does not interact face to face with the room leaders and instructors. This provides a sense of uncertainty behind the service as traders are skeptical about who is running the room. Primarily, this skepticism stems from the media coverage about those room leaders that have never traded a stock in their life but are deeming themselves as experts. It also stems from those reports that room leaders are front-running their alerts in the room and then selling to their members. The trick for aspiring traders is to develop a trust with their instructors.

Trust is usually developed by the information that is provided and the guidance that one is willing to give. Most offer a free week or two of trial services to evaluate. I have seen educational services with great and true information to traders, but no guidance through the learning process in terms of key issues like money management or stop loss risk. I see some services offer information on these key issues but then berate the clients in the room if they ask what the room leader deems to be a stupid question. If someone is genuinely trying to learn the business of trading, he or she should seek out a forum that will continuously provide a supportive atmosphere where any and all questions can be asked without fear of attack or retribution.

When reviewing educational services, you need to compare the cost of the service versus the benefits that are most important to you. With varying degrees of trading expertise, some traders may find some services too advanced or simple relative to their knowledge base. If the cost includes items that are not needed by the traders for whatever reason, then they need to weigh those aspects.

The most basic of rooms should at least provide a forum by which one can follow along on trading alerts with the room leaders to gain an understanding of the methodology. As you become more advanced, you will require the understanding of morning preparation, daily classes to go over key trading issues regarding methods and topics of confusion, and individual help from room instructors. Some services are offering free online seminars, weekend seminars, trading universities, after-hours discussions, and much more. The key is to find the average cost of these services and weigh it against the benefits of the room relative to your needs. If the methods presented by the individual traders do not fit your abilities or learning curve, then finding a system that works well for your style is crucial. Otherwise, frustration sets in and progress is halted immediately.

Methods are simply the theory behind the trades. Whereas one trader can earn a living off one method, another trader can starve following the exact same method. It is not the method that is the key to success. It is the ability to follow it in a consistent manner and adjust what is working while weeding out what isn't. If a trader is reviewing a site and likes the methodology and service, then he or she has a basis for trust. If the method is not liked or profitable, then moving onto the next service is a viable option. These services usually don't require a contract for a specified time period of membership and most offer at least a free week trial to evaluate how the room works and assess its effectiveness in trading and instruction.

Although I think that on-site teaching has its value and may work for some traders, obviously I am a big fan of online teaching forums. Many of the online forums simply offer stock picks, when to buy or sell. If that is what you are looking for, plenty of services are available that offer this. In fact, most of the services do not offer education at all, only buy and sell calls. I find that the best online forums offer the education to teach you how to develop your own trading programs. Simply following the leader into and out of trades is never profitable over time. A good online service prepares the members for the coming day, identifying stocks that are expected to be in action and laying out a rough plan of attack. Without a pre-market plan, simply too much data needs to be absorbed and traders tend to get overloaded and chase after anything moving. Once the market opens, staff traders offer real-time market commentary on what is happening and why it is happening. Real-time education is the key to successful trading for both on-site and online education services. Once the action slows down, traders on the staff examine every aspect of the market, what happened, what did well, and what didn't do quite so well. At some point during the trading day, structured daily class sessions teaching the core methods or topics that warrant attention should be discussed.

HYPE

I spend a lot of time discussing the topic of hype in this chapter because I have seen literally hundreds of traders lose their entire portfolios due to it and I want to ensure that you fully understand what can and is happening out there. One of the main complaints I hear about online services is that a lot of hype and misinformation tends to be given. This occurs primarily in the free chat rooms but occurs in some of the fee-based services as well. A service you pick should be absolutely free from hype. Although free chat rooms have their value, they are a cause for concern.

The upside is that a room moderator usually tries to weed out the misinformation on stocks or comments presented in the room and warns those who are posting misinformation to refrain from doing so. Although this upside is nice to see, the opposite side is that the room moderator could be simply using the appearance of a single or a group of room leaders to tout his or her own stocks with a large audience.

I have seen this occur far too many times. The fleecing of traders by these so-called room leaders is what first brought me to the education of aspiring traders. I did this in hopes of protecting them from such forums of misinformation and hype. The most common hype that I see is when a room leader is going to give out a "special stock pick" at some point during the trading day. Many of these rooms have hundreds of members simply because it is free. When these picks are given, it can create a very large momentum move if the stock generates interest from a large portion of these room members.

When the room leader is ready to announce the stock pick, the traders are waiting anxiously in anticipation. This type of momentum is called channel momentum. When the leader finally announces it, depending on the stock, it can move up a point or more when the traders in the room follow the leader into the trade. However, the room leader entered a position in the stock before the announcement was made. As the stock is propelled up, he exits his trade safely, selling his shares to those room buyers who are anxiously bidding the stock higher. Room leaders normally pick low-volume stocks to tout because they can move up quickly on low volume.

Unfortunately, they turn and drop twice as fast as the rest of the traders scramble to exit their trades all at once, leaving them holding a losing trade. They end up selling the stock in panic or holding the stock hoping for the stock to return to those heights so they can exit the trade with little or no loss. Usually, the stock never returns to those highs and the trader is left wondering what to do next and takes a bigger loss. I have seen too many traders lose their entire portfolios falling prey to this type of hype. It is a self-fulfilling prophecy; the more the leader calls trades, the more people follow him or her, the more the picks go up, and the better his or her reputation gets for calling winners every time. Traders need to be careful about finding out what the best entry point is on the alert, and if it's too far away from where the stock is currently at, they need to look for a possible re-entry or let the trade go.

Another common form of hype is when a room leader touts a stock that receives positive news of some sort. We call these news alerts. This happens when a company will issue a press release for an FDA approval or maybe an alliance with a strong company like Microsoft or Intel during the trading day. The room leader will then immediately enter the stock and then push the stock to the room. You will see comments like, "This is *great* news and the market will reward it by pushing it up to new highs."

The room leader will continue to hype the stock as the majority of his room continues to bid the stock higher. Meanwhile, he is once again selling his position to these traders who are bidding the stock higher, and maybe even shorting it at the highs as he is calling the trade over and done with. More often than not, several free forums are touting the same stock at the same time. In fact, I have suspected for years that some of the room leaders are in many rooms at the same time under different names. This creates an added momentum to the stock as now we have three or four free rooms touting the same stock with nearly three to four thousand members. The initial reason for the stock entry is based on a room leader's unaccountable hype. The exit strategy is now based on hope. This is a sure sign that this trader will not be trading for very long as a career.

When an individual hypes a stock, he or she is attempting to move the stock in a quick manner that enables the person to exit the stock to those late buyers that are bidding the stock higher on excitement. The process usually looks like the following dialog:

"Hey, is the news that MSFT is in a deal with company ABC with a $50 million investment out yet?"

"Yes, huge news! $50 million! This stock is going to the moon!"

"I'm buying on any weakness. This is a 10-bagger, no problem!!"

"It is up-ticking. This is your last chance to buy at these levels."

"There it goes. It is flying!"

"Oh yes, I love this stock. This is a *huge buy*!"

"If you aren't in now, you had better get in or you will miss the opportunity of the day."

"Look at that volume. There is definite institutional backing on this stock. Smart money is buying this one like crazy."

"Gooooo ABC!"

"Here comes the first pullback in this stock. I'm adding to my position *big time* on any weakness."

These are just a few of the comments that can constitute a hype of a stock. The catalyst for the momentum is the news that Microsoft is investing $50 million into the company. Although this news is certainly favorable for most companies that were going to do a deal with Microsoft, hopefully you can see the underlying hype that was created with these comments. The first sign of hype is the exclamation points after sentences. If you see exclamation points, the person is very adamant about his or her viewpoint of the stock. When you go a level deeper into these comments, we see some very interesting information about these people. To do this, let's assign value to company ABC.

Assume that ABC is trading at a level of $10 a share. Then as the news comes out, most experienced traders will enter the stock anywhere from 10.01 to 10.02. Bidding the stock at 10 will certainly not ensure you an execution because there will not be much selling to the bid at 10 to fill your buy order. Now, as traders enter at no worse than 10.02, they begin to shout out these comments in the room. The first thing to realize is that these chat rooms have thousands of participants. If one or more of these forums is touting the same stock, namely ABC, then some very sharp upside momentum to the stock can occur. The primary traders, those in at 10.01 to 10.02, will be the ones hyping the stock first. They will attempt to bring in other buyers so that the stock continues to rise.

Once traders begin to enter at 10.25 to 10.50, they will add to the hype of the stock, shouting their targets of $15 and $20 a share attempting to bring in more buyers.

Eventually, the stock may go over 10.50 to near 10.75 where the hyping begins to die down. The reason the hype dies is that those primary hypers who successfully tried to get the stock over 10.50 from 10 are now selling the stock to the late buyers. As the stock pauses, those late buyers see the stock dropping and desperately try to keep the hype going. However, these late buyers are fighting a losing battle because the stock hype is now over and there really is no institutional backing of the stock. More often than not, the stock will move back down near the price that it was at when the stock was first hyped. In this case, it would settle down somewhere near 10¼ or lower as those that bought the high are selling in panic and frustration.

The underlying point to this scenario is that those who are hyping a stock are usually already in the stock at a lower price and are trying to create excitement for you to buy at higher levels. They will use these exclamation points. They will post the news over and over again. They will post the whole story of the news and they will continue to mention the stock over and over to draw attention to it. They will use any catch phrases that signal a strong move to get the unknowing excited enough to buy the stock and bid it higher. Meanwhile, they are selling the stock to those late buyers. More often than not, you are buying near the high of the move and will get caught in selling and have to take a loss. Be very cautious of stock hype.

When looking back at these comments, a person will realize two things. First, the comments made in the room are never posted to help others, but rather fulfill a need or desire of the individuals. Second, their claims of price targets or accountability have no basis if they are wrong and someone loses money because of it. Often, we will see chat room leaders and bulletin boards make outlandish comments or offer almost impossible price targets to those reading them.

This serves two purposes for them. If they are correct, they tout themselves as geniuses because they knew it was going to happen. A few people have received rich lives in big predictions that actually came true. However, when these people are wrong, there is no retribution for your loss. They are anonymous people hiding behind a screen name that place the blame right back at you for your losses because you did not research the trade or the company enough. I hear the following comment in the trading room from room leaders when a loss is made.

"Geez, you didn't stop out of that stock already? It clearly topped. Why didn't you exit? I exited hours ago. You should do your own homework if you are going to trade."

Meanwhile, if someone checked the daily log of the chat room, more often than not, the room leaders will post their entry, but we will never see an exit price, especially if it is a loss. Then if they do post their loss and a room member challenges the room leader, the member is scolded for not doing his or her own research. This doesn't seem like a productive way to learn does it. If we follow the leaders' advice and they have a winning trade, they think they are the smartest people in the world. If we follow their advice and they are wrong, then it is our fault because we did not do our homework. Either way, they come out as winners and we are still sheep because we haven't learned anything. Unfortunately, learning what is good news and what is hype only can come with experience of watching stock action relative to what traders are saying. If the stocks tend to do what they are saying, maybe they have credibility. If they do not and often go in the opposite direction, maybe it's time to re-evaluate.

Again, avoid rooms that have instructors, room leaders, or even members who are hyping stocks, touting gains, mentioning the same stock an over again to attract attention, ridicule or berate their members, and offer no sound trading advice. These room leaders are simply not out to help anyone but their own bottom line and provide no basis for trust. Their ambiguity is astonishing to read sometimes in how they approach the trading and the comments that they make include no discernable information from which to make a clear trade or learn a high percentage method. Review and compare and make an informed decision.

Several years ago I suspected that this type of manipulation was going on and sent my staff into these rooms to monitor. My suspicions were confirmed when I saw room leader after room leader calling entries into trades at certain prices when there was no possible way to get the trade at that price. Then I would see them hyping the stock to no end and call an exit that was unattainable. I even saw the same calls being made in several rooms at one time using the exact same verbiage, which confirmed my belief that not only are they hyping individual rooms, but multiple rooms at the same time. Be wary of hype; it is real and it is out there; and if you fall prey to it, you will lose some or all of your portfolio before you know what happened to you. Good rooms have a moderator who doesn't hype his or her stocks, his or her own trades, and talks in a sane and professional manner. They do not talk of conspiracy theories or other external information that is out of the control of the trader.

This being said, I still believe that free chat rooms have value if you understand the dynamics involved. Free chat rooms should be used as a source of supplemental information, but I look at every bit of it with a suspecting eye and never believe it unless I see it myself. Chat rooms also help to judge the overall daytraders' interest in a stock and can be used as a source of news just in case I missed a good news release on my news-scanning service. This does not happen very often because I have a full team of news readers on staff using the latest scanning software packages as well as our members, 450 sets of eyes diligently scouring the news for gems that cause momentum. Chat rooms are a great source of information with highly professional traders that are all looking for the same set of trading parameters from which to trade. This way most stock activity is noticed and if a trade is valid, the room will find it.

TRADING MENTALITY

Simply put, trading stocks for a living is not for everyone. It takes a certain type of mentality and personality to succeed. Before you enter into this profession, you must assess yourself and take a good long honest look at yourself to see if you have what it takes. The rewards can be phenomenal and the freedom is like nothing else, but if you do not have the tools internal to yourself, you will fail. Books have been written on this one subject about trading psychology. Let me just reiterate that trading is a large part of how you think about the markets and unless you deal with who you are and can be honest, you will not make it no matter how hard you try.

You must have the ability to admit when you're wrong and not let ego interfere with your decisions. Trading is a very mechanical process, weighing the rewards and calculating the risks. If you do not have the ability to admit when you're wrong, you let emotion enter into your trading decisions and you are destined to lose in the long run. You must be disciplined. Traders who cannot stick to a disciplined approach tend to take more chances, chase after bad trades, and are more apt to veer from what works to what they hope will work.

Hindsight is the number one enemy of a trader. I hear the following two phrases constantly:

"I should have held that stock. It is up 10 points from where I sold it."

"I could have bought that stock when I saw the news."

Hindsight is a killer to many traders early in their learning process. It is a killer because it shows what you should have done and leads to a straying from the discipline that you need to survive in the long term. It is very easy to see what one should have done after the fact. It is not that easy to participate in the present. When I see traders continually beat themselves up over a missed opportunity, I fear they are headed for big losses. Here is an example of why.

I see traders in the beginning rationalize their trading so that each loss was not their fault and each gain was due to their intelligence. Assume a trader buys a stock at $45 a share with expectations for $50 a share where he wants to sell it. As the stock rises to $50, the trader sells the stock at his target for a nice $5 per share profit. The trader is excited because his expectations were met and his intelligence was proven right. However, minutes later, the stock is at $60 a share and the trader has a conflict. He was intelligent enough to sell at his target, but now he sees himself as stupid because he didn't hold for an extra $10 a share on his trade. It is not stupid to take surest profits when expectations are met. The stupidity lies in allowing hindsight to dictate your trading. Allowing this to happen leads to big losses. Let's elaborate.

Suppose the trader takes his $5 per share gain on this stock and enters another one at $60 a share. His expectation is for $65 a share. As the stock hits $65 a share, he decides that the last time he sold, he missed out on a $10-per-share gain by selling and decides to hold. Now the stock moves up to about $70 a share and the trader is confident that he did the right thing. However, now the stock begins to drop to $65 again. The trader figures he still has $5 in profit in the stock and he is not going to sell on this profit-taking. Shortly after this, the stock trades at $62. Now the trader sees the stock up only $2 a share from his entry instead of his $10 in profit just minutes earlier. He decides he wants to get it back and holds the stock. Eventually, the stock is trading at $55 and then at $50 a share due to market nervousness or whatever. The trader can't stand it anymore and sells at $50 a share for a $10 loss.

When reviewing this trade, he let hindsight turn his $5 dollar per share expected profit into a $10 loss per share. He saw one stock run another $30 per share and assumed this one could do the same. Stocks move in an independent fashion relative to historical data in these examples. No correlation suggests that because my last stock went up another

$30, this one will too. The next mistake that was made was the rationality that he was up $10 and now only up $5 a share and that he should hold it to regain his missed opportunity. This all occurred because he let hindsight in one trade affect his decision making in another. Trades are not related from one to the next. Hindsight is killer. Don't let it allow you to stray from your discipline.

The second hindsight comment serves to feed the egos of those who were proven right by their speculation. Many analysts, room leaders, market timers, and financial powerhouses are guilty of these comments. To take this to a micro level, let's focus on room leaders or members in a chat room. Many times you will see comments such as these:

"Did anyone catch my call on DELL at 40? It is at 45 now. I hope someone got it with me."

"Oh yeah! This stock is up 45 points from where I alerted it. I always get them early."

"Congratulations to those that bought this stock at 10 when I alerted it. It is at $20 now. Can I call the doubles and triples or what?"

Hindsight alerts stem from several things. One reason is that members want to feel the need for appreciation. They wouldn't mention the hindsight trade otherwise. Hindsight statements provide no benefit for anyone because the trade is already over. It only serves to inflate the egos of the people making the statement and their need for attention. Moreover, many of these statements you will see are only the ones that were profitable. Notice how the big gains are mentioned but none of the losses. You hardly ever see the following comments:

"Hey, sorry about that trade at $50 a share. It is at $10 a share. I hope no one rode this down with me."

"I was wrong about this stock at $50; it has never gained momentum, so I am dumping it right now at $45."

I tend to have more respect for those who post their losses or admit their shortcoming in public forums. One way to stay in touch with (or realize) your losses is to post both entries and exits to your trades in real time as you are making them. We monitor the attainability of these trades to ensure they are accurate because it serves no purpose other than hyping a stock if they are not real time. We use posting our entry and exits as a learning experience to our members instead of a vehicle to hype egos and trades as you will see in many other places. It educates our members to the value of stop losses and highlights the educational part of trading. Trading the stock market is not as easy as some make it out to be, and showing only the gains and none of the losses tends to break the confidence of those watching and shatters their disciplined approach when they find they are not making the same phenomenal gains as everyone else is touting. To post real-time entries for yourself either in a forum or by yourself, simply write down the time you made the trade and at what price, and keep this journal handy. Some even have a trading buddy that they share these journal entries with so that they have accountability.

EXPECTATIONS

Many traders' favorite question when they start is how much can they make? This question is very hard to answer because trading the market is very difficult and everybody's abilities are not the same. Many have very steep learning curves and lack the knowledge or willingness to put the time in to educate themselves properly. They are looking for the cure for cancer, the easy way out. When this lack of education is coupled with the fact that they are trading against the best traders in the world, with deeper pockets, the odds are stacked against them right from the beginning. Although I have seen gains of over 700-percent by one trader, I have seen losses that have forced bankruptcy proceedings. The question is not easy to answer as it depends on many factors and the following aspects of choosing trading as a career should be taken into account.

First, identify your expectations. For example, do you expect to get rich quick? Forget it, trading is not a get-rich-quick scheme. Trading is about learning how to create a stable uptrend in your portfolio over time. If you expect to make easy money in a few short trades, I can guarantee you the biggest surprise of your life. Keep your expectations sane and realize that you have a rough road ahead.

Then you need to determine if you have enough starting capital to give yourself a reasonable chance at success. I have seen figures reporting that 70- to 80-percent of all traders who enter the game consistently lose money and are forced out. The difference between the winners and losers is education and a disciplined approach to trading. Those who educate themselves properly and stick to a disciplined approach emerge over time as the winners; those who don't, lose and leave.

When figuring out how much money is needed to start trading, it is important to take a big overall view of your current financial situation. The best thing to do is develop a basic business plan. This should include at least six months' worth of planning that entails living expenses, initial capital outlay for equipment and data, portfolio size, and unforeseen events. Everybody is different, and I have seen several great traders make a very decent living off of $12,000 to $15,000 portfolios, pulling $5,000 in profits every month to live on. But not everybody is or can be a great trader. The best thing to do is not strap yourself in the early stage financially. Figure out how much money you need to live on a month and how much risk capital you are willing to lose during the process. If the risk is too great, then active trading may not be for you. If the risk is possible to incur, then you have a better foundation to move forward.

You can certainly learn to trade on much less, and many learn with a portfolio between $5,000 and $10,000, but it will not feed the family while you are learning. A portfolio of $25,000 to $40,000 is ideal. This amount does a few things, but most importantly it enables traders to make small mistakes over the period of the 6 months while learning. Small mistakes will not break the bank, but it will let you evaluate after 6 months if this is worth sticking with or not. I have seen traders with $500,000 decrease that by half simply by trading a huge amount of shares and taking big losses on each trade without adhering to strict stop loss principles.

The idea that the more money a trader has, the easier trading gets is dead wrong. Having more money can distract traders from discipline because they feel that they can afford a few big losses and feel they can easily make it back later on. This gives them the feeling of being invincible to big losses due to the large amount of initial capital. Having to $40,000 gives many traders the ability to trade most of the momentum stocks each day with enough shares for profit potential. How they progress from their capital base depends on their ability to learn and apply theory to practice.

The learning curve of trading is large for several reasons. The primary reason is preconceived ideas of the market's functionality. Their investing acumen is a far different approach to momentum trading. Many have been weaned on the buy and hold mentality that has rewarded many investors for the last few decades. However, in the realm of daytrading, the buy and hold approach is seriously detrimental to one's long-term performance. This mainly relates to the fact that momentum traders often are focusing on shorter horizon time periods for gains. Therefore, their profits per trade are much smaller.

If one were to take smaller profits and larger losses over a period of time, then his or her ability to sustain the bigger losses would be greatly jeopardized over time. Even if one trades at a 90-percent success rate, it will only take one large loss to offset those gains. I have one student who told me that over a period of time he took 80-percent of his losses on only two trades. This is not a disciplined approach and an inability to stick with a safe stop loss program can seriously do mental and monetary damage.

When I first began to teach, I had a star pupil who was very aggressive and traded at a very high percentage. It seemed as though her trading got better with each day and she was very excited about her future because trading was her passion. One Monday we went long on a stock that was down over 20-percent from the previous day's closing price. We got stopped out of the trade as the Nasdaq went into a tailspin to a record low. She failed to keep a stop loss on the trade and lost around $10,000 and it scared her so much that she drew into a shell. I could not get her out of it as she allowed the trading freeze to disable her trading talents. Her husband would even stay home from work and try to force her to trade my intended targets, but she finally dropped out of the trading scene.

Losses are a problem for many traders as they can't seem to find the strength to turn a small loss into reality. This often leads to making a small loss a large one. You must have the strength to adhere to stop loss principles or your account will look like a roller coaster. Every trader has losses; it is a part of the business, but large losses will end your career before it even starts. Keep them small.

Undisciplined traders tend to allow emotions to be a big part of their trading. They tend to view each trade as a life and death situation in their trading career. This approach to each trade clouds decisions of when to enter and exit. Many feel that trading is a reflection of their personal self. They tend to think that all losses reflect a loser and that all profits reflect a winner. This is far from the truth; trading is inherently difficult. We have said previously that active traders go up against the best in the business and they have deeper pockets. Everybody takes losses in trading; our job is to limit the losses and maximize the gains. Losses are part of trading. When a disciplined trader exits a trade with a loss, he or she does not get upset and refer to the loss in a negative way; the trader should think about that trade in a positive light. Traders do this because they prevented a small loss from becoming a larger loss. This protects trading capital and allows them to continue to learn how to trade over a longer period of time.

Small losses certainly do not guarantee success over time, but they give the trader a longer time period in which to study the market and learn from their mistakes. One large loss can easily take a trader out of the game. I'd much rather see a trader take 10 small losses so that he or she has experience with more trades to learn from. One huge loss simply does not give active traders experience.

If one can approach the trade with an indifference to the trade, removed from emotion, then he or she can focus more on the price action and understand when it is time to exit the trade. If traders exit the trade with a small loss, then they do not get frustrated or upset. If they exit the trade with a profit, they do not get jubilant or excited. They are neither losers nor winners. One trade does not make a successful trader. Profits over time in a consistent and disciplined manner are the key to long-term success. One large loss will not allow this possibility to occur.

If you entered this business to make a killing overnight and get rich quick, leave now and save yourself time, money, and frustration. With that attitude and approach, you will be leaving sooner or later; it's just a matter of how much money you will have left when you do. The successful traders who are at it year after year don't make overnight killings; they earn their profits one trade at a time. With a disciplined, unemotional approach they can and will add up.

PAPER TRADING

No matter what your experience level is, when learning or trying new methods, paper trading is paramount. Too often traders see the phenomenal gains being made by other traders and jump right in before they are properly educated and have tested the methods. This usually is at the cost of a large chunk of their portfolios. Paper trading will do three things for you: first, it will protect your capital; second, it will build your confidence; and lastly, it will prove to you that you fully understand the methods and that they work.

Paper trade until your winning percentages are 90-percent; then throw real money at the trades once you are satisfied you can make money. It only makes sense to not throw real money at a method or a trade until you can prove to yourself that the methods are working and profitable. Otherwise, you are simply gambling, and as with any gambling, the odds are in the house's favor.

To begin paper trading, simply watch the stock setup, write down the price that is most honestly attainable when the setup occurs, and then the exit price of where you would exit the trade. You need to be honest with yourself. Cheating with entry and exit prices doesn't hurt anyone but yourself. You aren't out to prove anything to us, just yourself. Use realistic prices for entry and exit to judge how well you understand the system.

The biggest transition problem that traders have is from paper trading to real trading. It is very important that one understands and learns the theory behind each method that he or she chooses to utilize. The theory simply provides the foundation to trading. Ideally, this method provides reasoning and discipline behind each trade. Active traders approach their learning phase in different fashions. Some traders do very well with the theoretical portion of the methods.

Some traders just jump right in before the basic foundations are learned. Maybe they understand how to read tops and bottoms and maybe even understand a basic function of order routing. They can paper trade these methods at a degree of 90-percent or better. They feel they can move to the next step of the trading process, use real money, and trade with live shares. Then as they begin to trade real money, the theory and discipline goes right out the window. They hesitate to enter trades and fail to exit at stop levels. Their 90-percent suddenly falls to 60-percent or worse and they become frustrated.

When I began my learning experience in the stock market, I would sit and paper trade until I found a system that would repeat over 90-percent of the time. I would get really excited thinking I had unlocked King Tut's tomb. I would begin to trade the pattern, only to be disappointed as it changed on me, and then go back to paper trading until I found another unlocked secret. The same thing would occur and be very frustrating until one day I saw the same old pattern repeat itself. I was able to take advantage of an old friend and make my money. It was then that I learned about repeating patterns that always come back sooner or later and when they did, I would line my coffers with profits. Without good paper trading techniques, I would never have solved the repeating pattern mystery.

Paper trading is a far cry from live trading. In paper trading, all price levels are attainable. An execution for a certain price is never missed. Therefore, each trade is much easier to enter and exit and offer the chance for profitability. Moreover, traders begin to use hindsight in their paper trading. They begin to look back and tell themselves what they would have done in that situation. They fool themselves into thinking that they are able to trade in a would-have fashion. The market does not offer second chances in a trade. The trade either ends in a profit or loss. There are no do-overs. Many traders feel that they can just fix their exit and entry points to bring out that smaller loss or reasonable profit. In real trading, each trade must be entered and exited with the same indifference described previously and without hindsight telling you what you should have done. There are no second chances.

The transition from this paper trading to live trading manifests the hesitation in early trading. Traders who were entering and exiting stocks with ease in paper trading begin to hesitate to press the enter button. They do this because they begin to fear loss; after all, this is *real* money now. They know that they can't do a would-have trade and hesitate to enter the position for fear of loss if they are wrong. The other reason is that they are afraid that if they do enter the position, they won't know how to minimize the loss as it pertains to execution routes if they are wrong.

Although it is easy to enter and exit stocks on paper, the functionality of trading as it relates to order routing is much more difficult. This fear of not choosing the right execution route to exit, especially if the stock is moving against them, causes hesitation to enter the trade. Although a trader may make nearly 100 trades a day on paper, his or her trading now becomes closer to five trades a day or less when the trader first starts trading with real money.

As traders begin to move more into live trading, I recommend that they do so with smaller shares. This allows them to gain a sense of how each order route works without the fear of large losses if they are wrong. While they are learning a more experienced approach to order routing, including entering and exiting positions, they are developing this indifference to each trade that is very important. Although their trading may move to a lower percentage of successful trades early, they are gaining the necessary knowledge on the difficulty of entering and exiting trades. This allows them to judge which stocks are within their abilities to trade and which are not.

Knowing how to read a stock, find the opportunity price levels, and then capitalize on that opportunity with the right execution method is the ideal process by which to trade. Each component of the process takes a fair amount of time to learn. The learning curve is steep for this very reason. Learning the reasoning and theory of the method takes time. Applying this theory to a simulation of trading takes time to ensure that the method is working for them. Finally, trading with real money and increasing share size as they feel more comfortable with executions take the most time.

The trader who has the ability and time to move through each phase has a greater advantage over those who simply jump into the market with both feet and no reasoning or methodology to their trading. When you decide to become an active trader, give yourself enough time to fully learn the theory of the method. Then allow yourself enough time to apply that theory to simulation trades.

Finally, when moving to small shares with real money, enter trades with indifference. A profit does not make you successful, nor does a loss make you a failure. It is simply a learning process. Continue to progress through each trade in a separate way so as not to let the previous trade dwell on your thinking and cloud judgment in the current trade. They are mutually exclusive. One trade has nothing to do with the next. Approach them in this manner. After one has enough confidence in trading with small shares to gain a sense of execution and price action functionality, they can begin to increase their share size per trade to offer themselves a chance at better profits over time.

I have found that some of the best traders are pilots. Why would that be? Pilots have a very methodical way at looking at procedures and emergency procedures. When an engine catches on fire or a hydraulic pump fails, the pilot immediately goes into a series of emergency procedures. If *a* happens, then the correct steps are *b*, *c*, *d*, and *e*. Little emotion is involved; they cannot wish or hope the emergency will go away or fix itself. They let the events of the emergency dictate their actions. Traders should do the same. Don't let emotion enter into a trade; follow procedures. If the procedures work over time, changing them because you have a feeling this time it will be different will only lead to losses. This will only reinforce poor trading habits and allow the hindsight monster to trample your disciplined trading program and eventually decimate your portfolio.

DECISION TIME

I have talked a lot about the pitfalls of trading, hype, hindsight, chat room traps, and maybe even trimmed some of your expectations down a bit. I do this on purpose early on because as I said, not everyone is cut out to be a trader. It is time to take a deep look inside yourself and see if you have what it takes to press on. If you don't, there is no shame in turning away from something that will not work out for you. If you take a good honest look and decide it is not for you, you will save yourself a lot of frustration and money that could be better used elsewhere.

That being said, I hope your look did reveal that you do have what it takes to trade. The rewards can be fantastic and the freedom you experience by working for yourself, on your own time, and own pace is parallel to none.

3 CHAPTER

TOOLS OF THE TRADE

This chapter will go into the advantages and disadvantages of online brokers and direct access brokers. Order routing methods are a trader's edge when trading against thousands of other traders and Market Makers for the best prices available when your system says to take action. Using the wrong route in certain situations can mean big money losses if not learned properly. We will also discuss the available tools that will aid traders in their progress to seeing and participating with the market on a daily basis. This includes charting software, hardware, and software requirements just to name a few.

TRADITIONAL AND WEB-BASED BROKERAGES

Since the explosion of active trading by the general public, numerous brokerages have developed their business plans to tailor to these individuals. Web-based and traditional brokerages such as E*TRADE and Schwab & Company do offer interesting advantages for the trader. The major advantage is to the newer trader because the trader does not have to learn a wide assortment of execution routes required by *Electronic Direct Access Trading Firms* (EDATs). He or she simply has to put an order in, including the ticker and number of shares, and the order routing method is chosen for him or her.

Although this looks attractive at first, it has several disadvantages. The biggest disadvantage is the speed at which your trade is executed and your order confirmed. With a traditional broker, you must identify a trade, call your broker on the phone, and verbally give your order to your broker. This can take some time and by the time you reach a real live broker, especially in the busy periods, your trade has already come and gone in many instances.

Web-based brokers are a step quicker, but speed is still an issue. Although they are constantly improving their execution speeds and confirmations, it still is not quick enough for momentum traders in all cases. Many times you only have a few seconds to enter a trade after you make your initial entry decision before the stock moves on. When E*TRADE first came out, it seemed that they were the next best thing since sliced bread, but since then, a newer and faster service emerged. If you're not playing with the quickest service available, others are beating you to the punch.

In order to understand the disadvantages to the active trader, we need to discuss the basic functionality of the majority of online brokers. Using a Web-based broker in active trading has no advantages. They are too slow. When we discuss *online brokerages* (OLBs), we are talking about firms such as E*TRADE, SureTrade, Ameritrade, Schwab, and Datek. These firms work very well for the investor or the trader who makes a few trades a year. However, for the active trader, this system puts a trader at a disadvantage due to the order routing system. The system process progresses in the following manner. When a trader wants to buy 1,000 shares of a stock, he or she must first move around the Web site to the Transaction or Order Placement portion of the site. The trader will then see several options for intentions. He or she will have the option to buy, sell, short, or cover a position in the stock.

For this example, let's use a buy option. A trader enters in his order for 1,000 shares in the *Size of Order* box. He then clicks the box marked *Buy* and enters in the stock symbol for the stock he wants to purchase. However, he must still decide some more options. He must decide if he wants to buy 1,000 shares at the market price or a limit price. If he chooses the market price, he will have his order executed at the best available price when his order comes up in the order queue. If he chooses a limit order, then he is subject to his set price or better. This ensures he never pays more for the stock than what he has set in his limit box. The other side of this is that he may never be filled at that price if he is late with his order, and the market has risen in price on him for that stock.

Let's assume that stock XYZ is trading at 50 on the bid and 50.01 on the ask. This means that the price to buy the stock is 50.01. If we were to turn right around and sell the stock immediately, we would sell at 50. This would result in a net loss of .01 for the trade. Because we bought and sold 1,000 shares, we would multiply .01 by 1,000 shares and lose $10.00 on the trade plus commissions. The next screen is a confirmation for the order asking the individual if he is sure this is the order that he wants to place. He then presses the *Yes* button again to send the order to the market. He now has a live order sent to the Nasdaq marketplace. This is where using a Web-based brokerage gets interesting. When the trader sends his order to the marketplace, he is in essence sending an e-mail message to the brokerage company.

If the order is a market order, then this company sends this order to its respective Market Makers of choice to execute the order at the going price. If it is a limit order, then it is no worse than 50.01. If the Market Makers cannot execute the limit order, they hold the order until that price becomes available.

The process of manually entering the information into the data fields on the order page, sending the order, confirming the order, having the order sent to the Market Maker, having the Market Maker take the other side of the order, and then having a delayed confirmation is not the ideal situation for the active trader. The process can and has taken up to 20 minutes during the open of the trading day. I remember trading a stock called MZON with E*TRADE. I entered in my order to buy the stock at a certain price. I was asked to confirm the stock order and I did. The order was sent to the market and I waited. I watched the stock move up 4 points, then down 10 points, and back up 4 points before I knew I had confirmation of the buy order and at what price. I had gone from up $1,200 to down $2,000 and ended up taking a loss of nearly $400 before the trade was over. This time delay is simply too long for the active momentum trader.

This inefficiency may be suitable for the investor who buys and sells a few times a month but is much too long for the active momentum trader whose trades sometimes only last a few minutes. This void in efficiency created a need for an even quicker, more reliable execution service, which was filled by *Electronic Direct Access Trading Firms* (EDATs).

ELECTRONIC DIRECT ACCESS TRADING FIRMS (EDATs)

EDAT firms are companies that cater to the active trader. In comparison to Web-based and traditional brokerages, EDATs are much more efficient in the way orders are placed and confirmations are given. I feel it is irresponsible for online brokerages to offer active trader tools while still being inefficient in order placing and confirmation times. Several EDATs are available to active traders. A few examples of EDATs can be found at MBTrading.com, Castleonline.com, and CyBerCorp.com. I personally use MB Trading for both my data feed and execution services. I simply find them the best overall in speed as well as technical and customer support. Interestingly enough, Charles Schwab & Co. recently acquired CyBerCorp.com. This tells us that the acknowledgment of the need for such efficiency was clear. So let's see how EDATs work and why they are more beneficial to the active trader.

EDATs provide a direct link to the markets by using several execution routes. These routes enable traders to place orders against liability from Market Makers or Electronic Communications Networks (ECNs) in individual Nasdaq stocks. Placing a *Small Order Execution Service* (SOES), SelectNet, or ECN order provides this direct access to the Nasdaq market. These services also enable us to place orders for listed issues through the SuperDot system.

As we discussed earlier, listed issues are handled by one specialist who is responsible for keeping an orderly market for the stocks he or she provides liquidity for. The SuperDot is a system by which we can enter orders directly to the specialists. The specialist will then match the orders on the order book and execute the trade, fill the order from his or her own inventory, or place the order in the order book until he or she can match the order. If the order is filled, the confirmation report is then sent back to the individual stating how many shares were filled and at what price the trade was executed. If the order is placed to the order book, then the individual must wait for a confirmation of execution. No messages stating "your order is still pending" will be sent back to you.

The SuperDot system can distribute an order up to 99,999 shares for an individual listed stock. This system, because it is much more efficient in the way orders are handled and can reduce the cost of doing business, translates to lower commissions for the active trader. Lower commissions are necessary for active traders to reduce the cost per order. Many traders tend to trade for small profits and if commissions are too large, the majority of the profit is eaten by commissions. Those who are investing for the long haul or are paying brokers/managers to manage their money are paying higher commissions, which are sometimes a necessary evil for the peace of mind that they can't trade their money themselves. Therefore, lower commissions aren't as necessary for those who can't watch their portfolio and make rapid-fire decisions on a daily basis. For the active trader who does a few trades a day, lower commissions are necessary to keep more of the profit in the account. Orders that are placed in this fashion are generally executed within seconds during normal trading operations. The confirmation times usually are just as fast.

Times of abnormal activity, such as when a listed stock is added to a new tracking index, may take a few minutes due to the increased order flow and matching of orders on the order book. Because many smaller exchanges are competing for shares in the same issue, many of these are willing to execute orders at the inside price (best price). This provides the necessary liquidity that is desired by active traders. It gives a representation of an automatic execution system that is beneficial for traders who want to trade quickly at the inside price or better.

The main advantage that a direct access firm can offer to the active trader is a direct link to these market participants by SOES, SelectNet, or ECN access. This prevents these firms from selling order flow as well as trading against your position. You are not sending your order to a brokerage that in turn sends your order to the markets. You are skipping the middle step by executing your orders directly with the market participants. The disadvantage to having the ability to participate more efficiently is that you must learn to route your own orders to these market participants. Most Web-based and traditional brokerages take care of the order routing for you. With direct access trading, you must learn how to route your orders and know which routes work best in which situations.

This becomes the biggest obstacle to traders as they move from their learning phase to their live trading phase. Many individuals fear that once they are in a trade, they will not have the execution ability to exit the trade. This occurs more often when a stock is moving fast against them and they do not know how to get out with minimal loss. It is not as easy as pressing the *Sell* button with a Web-based brokerage. With direct access, traders need to know who the market participants are, how much liability they are showing, and what the best route is in that particular situation. We will discuss each route with its advantages and limitations.

ORDER ROUTING METHODS

At the time this book is being written, new rules are being proposed that will alter the functionality of the SOES and SelectNet systems. This new paradigm is being referred to as SuperSOES and I will be discussing this intermittently as it pertains to active traders. We will not go in-depth on the subject as much uncertainty surrounds its final guidelines.

SMALL ORDER EXECUTION SYSTEM (SOES)

The first route to discuss is SOES. SOES stands for Small Order Execution System. Many have heard about SOES because it was instituted after the crash of 1987. At the time of the 1987 sell-off, brokers were unavailable by phone due to the shear volume of trades. Brokers were not taking orders from individual investors and many felt helpless that they could not freely participate in the liquidation of their shares. SOES was to change this by providing traders with access to Market Makers' liability sizes. This allowed them a greater ability to enter and exit stocks without having to wait for their broker to answer the phone.

With the institution of SOES, the playing field was leveled between the institutions and the individual traders. Equal access to the markets was now possible. As SOES evolved, it has provided the trader with a greater access to market participation, but it also has some limitations that you must be made aware of.

First, to use the SOES route, a stock has to be SOES-eligible. A few stocks on the Nasdaq SmallCap Market are not SOES-eligible. EDATs have key components in their execution software packages that enable a trader to know if the stock is SOES-eligible or not. The next aspect of SOES is tier size. Tier sizes refer to how many shares are able to be SOES-eligible in a particular order. The three tier sizes currently are 200, 500, and 1,000. This means that if a stock has a tier size of 200, then a trader cannot enter a SOES order for more than 200 shares. If the tier size is 1,000, then a trader can enter an amount up to 1,000 shares.

SOES provides instant executions against Market Maker participants at specific price levels. This is the advantage for the active trader when wanting to execute an order in a fast and efficient manner. The order can be a market or limit order. This means that a market order will be executed at the best available price when that order has its turn in the SOES queue. A limit order simply states that the order must be executed at a specific price or better. If this limit price is not attainable, then the order will not be executed and the order will be sent back to the individual placing the order. SOES orders are prioritized by time. Therefore, a limit order or market order does not have a preference other than the time the order was placed. It is first come, first served in the SOES queue.

A disadvantage to SOES is that ECNs are not executable against using SOES. They are not SOES-eligible market participants. Therefore, if two ECNs are at the best price and you enter a SOES order for the inside price, the order will be rejected. In relation to the tier size of a SOESable stock, when the Market Maker fulfills his or her liability to the size quoted, the Market Maker has 17 seconds in which he or she is not obligated to fill anymore SOES orders. Those orders remain in the queue until the Market Maker fills the order, refreshes his or her quote, or moves off the best price. Any unfilled orders are then sent back to the individual placing the order as non-executed.

Two proposals to SuperSOES that are interesting in this matter are the decrease of the time constraint and the maximum size changes also. The Market Maker will now have only five seconds to decide his or her next action. Second, the maximum size will move from 1,000 up to 9,900 shares for auto-execution. If Market Makers didn't have to show more than 100 shares, this would not be such a big deal. However, the new rules will state that any quote showing 1,000 or more shares must provide access to the reserve amount that the Market Maker is willing to trade. If a Market Maker has reserve, then he or she must display at least 1,000 shares on the quote as well. Anything below that share size will move the Market Maker off the inside price once the liability is executed against. The implications of this are still unknown because we are not able to trade with this system until at least mid-summer 2000, if not later.

SOES is a system that registered market representatives and NASD broker-dealers are unable to utilize. When one wants to short a stock using SOES, one must abide by the tick rules for shorting. This states that a stock must be on an up-tick Bid for the SOES system order to meet requirements. This rule was mainly instituted for market stability because no one wants to see stocks being sold off or shorted, providing added selling pressure to a stock that was already falling on fast pace. When Market Maker participation is active at price levels, SOES is a great tool. When the participation is limited, using SOES can cost traders more profit if they are unable to recognize the scenarios that limit the effectiveness of SOES.

Two points to discuss regarding SOES market orders have to do with *Initial Public Offerings* (IPOs) and stocks that are moving fast in either direction. Initial Public Offerings tend to be very volatile on the first day. The pace of the stock and market participation is very fast and usually hard to read as the float tends to be limited and Market Makers have plenty of client orders to fill. When placing a SOES market order for such a stock, it will more than likely be executed at a price that is very far from where you wanted to buy it. If the stock is falling, this may please you. If the stock is rising, you may be paying anywhere from $1 to $5 more per share depending on the IPO. This is a highly risky and inefficient manner by which to trade IPOs.

When a stock has little Market Maker participation and the stock is moving fast, using a market buy order is highly risky and inefficient as your price may be much higher than what you wanted. However, on the sell side, a market SOES order is telling the market that you just want out, no matter where the price is. This should be a last resort scenario. With a fast-selling stock, no magic exit button is available. A trader could easily face an extra $1-per-share SOES execution if the stock is fast and has limited Market Maker participation at each level. When learning executions, be sure to understand its functionality and decide on which scenarios SOES works best. If plenty of Market Makers are at tight price-level spreads, then SOES is reasonable. If Market Maker participation at each price level is small and the pace of the stock is fast, then using SOES will generally provide an execution that will be worse than what you originally wanted.

SELECTNET (SNET)

Another route that EDATs provide for is SelectNet. SelectNet is a negotiation system that is used by Market Makers to fill orders via the Nasdaq marketplace. Instead of using a phone order, Market Makers simply enter in a SelectNet order to another Market Maker in a faster and more efficient manner. When using the phone, traders have to go through the steps of using a phone. They pick up their phone, dial, and wait for an answer. With SelectNet, the order is sent immediately. Many Market Makers prefer this efficiency and ease of use. SelectNet works in a manner so that a market participant will receive a message that another market participant wants to buy or sell a set amount of stock at a certain price. Currently, the limitation for SelectNet is an order no greater than 99,999 shares. This price can be at any level. It does not have to be at the inside prices. To facilitate this action, most EDATs offer two choices for SelectNet.

The first is a SelectNet Broadcast order. You may see the abbreviation that reads SNET BROD. SelectNet orders that are sent by broadcast are sent as an order that can be seen by all Market Maker participants on their workstations. Because the order is a broadcast order and not directed to anyone specific, no legal obligatory action must be taken by any Market Maker. The Market Maker can elect to fill your order or leave it alone. Therefore, you may or may not receive a fill and get a response back regarding your order. I have found that in cases where stocks are trading at a relatively fast pace, SNET BROD orders tend to be overlooked for executions. This makes sense for the most part for a stock that is generally moving fast in one direction. Market Makers are not willing to accept non-liability orders for a stock that they may be able to execute at a better price once the action in the stock slows to a more reasonable level of activity. This isn't always the case but provides a reasonable example for why SNET BROD orders are not to be used if you want a fast execution in a fast stock.

The other type of order is a SelectNet Preference order. You may see this abbreviated as SNET PREF. These orders are directed to specific market participants at certain price levels. Instead of all Market Makers being able to see this order, the only person who can see this order is the market participant that you preference. Many EDATs simply enable traders to click on their Level 2 screen (which will be explained later) and the SNET PREF order is automatically entered into the execution software. This is a benefit for traders who want that extra second in execution ahead of the rest of the traders. Every second counts.

When a Market Maker receive a preference order, he is now legally obligated to respond to your order. He has three options: he can accept the order and execute it, he can decline it, in which case your order will be sent back to you, or he can fill a part of the whole order. This is referred to as a partial fill in trading lingo. A trader can also use SelectNet to match orders against ECNs. To do this, he simply enters in a SNET PREF order to an ECN for any size up to the amount shown by that ECN and it is matched and auto-executed assuming no liability trades were ahead of him. For example, if I wanted to buy 1,000 shares from Instinet (INCA), I would enter in a SNET PREF order to INCA for 1,000 shares and, assuming no orders were ahead of me, I would receive my fill almost instantly. Some Level 2 software and execution packages offer you the ability to just click the INCA line at the Ask and it is automatically placed in the execution for you; all you need to do is send the order. Again, every second counts.

SelectNet orders are received and executed by time priority as well. This means that if you want to buy 500 shares of a stock at 10 and the Market Maker is showing that he or she is willing to buy 500 shares, your order will be executed, assuming no order for 500 shares came before you. If there were orders for 100, 200, and 100 and then you entered yours into the queue, the Market Maker would be obligated to fill 100, 200, and 100, and only 100 shares of your 500-share order. This is a partial fill. The Market Maker then has the right to fill the rest of your order, change the size, or move off the Ask. The problem arises when the Market Maker has SOES and SelectNet orders coming at him or her.

The following is a recent example of a stock that I missed executing because of choosing the different route. A news alert was given on a stock. I entered in my SOES order at the inside Ask as the Market Maker was showing me enough size and I didn't see any volume ahead of me. As I was entering in my order, I saw trades (prints) occur at the inside Ask, but I was not being filled. I still had my SOES order live and still saw prints at the inside Ask. The Market Maker then lifted his Ask price

and my order went unfilled. What happened was that he filled his liability obligation and I was back in the SOES queue. He then filled his
SelectNet orders manually and lifted off the Ask. I remember beating a
trader in the Mtrader chat room to the execution time, but he chose to
SelectNet Preference the Market Maker and was filled first. I had a SOES
order and was not filled. This is just one example of when different routes
will give you different results.

The disadvantage to SelectNet occurs when a stock is moving fast.
Just like SOES, your chances for an execution are much more unlikely
when a stock is moving fast. When traders send a SelectNet order to the
market, it must remain live for 10 seconds before they can cancel it manually. On the other side of the trade, once the Market Maker fills his or
her liability, he or she has 30 seconds to respond to pending orders. If a
stock is moving fast and you are hanging around for 30 seconds for a confirmation, this can feel much longer than 30 seconds. Also, if those 30 seconds pass and you are not filled, this can cause a bit of frustration,
especially if you are trying to exit a stock.

Finally, one point to consider is that a trader can enter in an *all-or-
none* (AON) or ANY order. Suppose that I wanted to enter a stock at the
best ask for 1,000 shares. If I placed an AON order at the Ask, then a
Market Maker would not be allowed to execute that order unless he or
she was willing to fill the whole amount. If I entered in an order as ANY,
then a Market Maker could fill any lot up to 1,000 shares that he or she
wanted to. The Market Maker has the ability to fill none, some, or all of
that order, assuming his or her liability has already been exhausted.
SelectNet can be a useful route when used in the right situations.

ELECTRONIC COMMUNICATIONS NETWORKS (ECNs)

The use of ECNs enables market participants to post orders anony-
mously. INCA is famous for institutional firms executing their orders
through this ECN. They offer the ability for institutions to mask their
intentions by placing liability size on the order book through INCA.
Traders never know if it is Goldman Sachs (GSCO), Fleet Securities
(FLTT), or one or more of the other Market Maker firms that constitute
size in the INCA quote. This provides an advantage to those firms that
do not want to be giving away possible intentions while taking advantage of the liquidity in the order book. With ECNs, traders are afforded
the ability to bid for stock and offer stock out at the Ask. This is a great
advantage to those traders who want to buy into selling and exit into
strength. When we discuss a few methods later in the book, we will show
why this is beneficial.

The first rule about an ECN that must be known is that ECNs are not SOES-eligible. Therefore, if an ECN is at the best Ask and I want to buy stock at that price, I would have to use a route that utilizes SelectNet or a matching ECN order if I have access to that ECN route. For example, if I want to buy 1,000 shares of DELL at 50 and the only market participant is ISLD at 50, then I would have to place an ISLD order for 1,000 shares at 50 or use a SelectNet Preference order to ISLD for that amount. Assuming I was first in the order, I would be auto-executed at that price for that order. I would not be able to enter a SOES order at 50 for 1,000 shares because ISLD ECN is not SOES-eligible. With the new SuperSOES rules due out in late 2000, ECNs may participate for SOES eligibility, but currently, they are not.

With ECNs, I have to accept partial fills as a part of the game. I remember getting a fill for one share of a stock on ISLD before. Although someone may ask why someone may trade one share of stock, the explanation is relatively easy. Some traders, when they are figuring out how much stock to buy, will divide the price of the stock by how much money is in their portfolio. Therefore, if a stock is trading at 9.99 and I have $100,000, I would be able to buy 10,010 shares of stock. When this person goes to sell this stock, he or she may get a fill for 10 orders of 1,000 shares and one order for 10 shares.

INSTINET (INCA)

The two most frequently used ECNs are Instinet (INCA) and Island (ISLD). Instinet was implemented in 1969 for the purpose of allowing institutions to display bid and offers in listed and Nasdaq stocks for other institutions to execute against. As Instinet's popularity grew, brokerage firms were allowed access. Individuals have recently been granted access to the INCA order book and routing capabilities through brokers like MBTrading.com. The major advantage to the trader is increased liquidity to route orders as well as having an order represented via another route. The disadvantage to the trader is that traders are trading against positions that are being shown via INCA, and they don't know if they are retail orders or a Market Maker masking intentions with greater reserve than what is being shown.

Although some EDATs provide access to Instinet, they are not directly executing against the order book, but rather sending the order to an Instinet representative who places the order to the order book for you. Not having utilized this method personally, I am unaware of how efficient this process is. I simply SelectNet Pref an order to INCA if they are at the price I desire, but I have never placed an order to the INCA order book. Instinet trades 24 hours a day and many wonder when the rest of the market will follow suit. When trading against an INCA order, many brokerages charge an extra fee for doing so. Currently, this cost is .015 cents per share.

ISLAND (ISLD)

Island (ISLD) was introduced in 1996 and has exploded since that time. The system is affordable and extremely liquid. The access to the order book is also an advantage to traders as they can see how much participation is at each price level on ISLD. The book can be seen for free at www.isld.com. With ISLD, traders have been given the ability to make a market in this stock. They can buy at the Bid and sell at the Ask if they so choose. They can also split the spread with an order if the spread is wide. We will discuss how to in a bit.

For an ISLD order to be entered, traders must designate this route as their choice in their execution system. However, you should review some important points regarding its functionality. First, you cannot use ISLD to match an order against another ECN or Market Maker. ISLD orders are only matched against other ISLD orders. Luckily, we don't have to worry about locking or crossing the market anymore as the rules have changed already. Before, when an ISLD order was entered to buy the stock at a price that was equal to the best Ask, the Bid order would be locking the market and would be rejected. The order must be at least .03 below the best Ask for it to not lock the market. If one were to bid for the stock at a price above the best Ask and no ISLD matching order was present to execute against, then the stock order would be deleted as crossing the market. Locking a market and crossing a market violated Fair Market rules set forth by the NASD. As of now, this no longer is true. One more important point to note about ISLD is that it is by limit order only. Market orders are not available with ISLD.

ARCHIPELAGO (ARCA)

The last route that I'd like to discuss is ARCA. ARCA is both a routing option and ECN. ARCA is the abbreviated version for Archipelago. ARCA, as an ECN, functions much like ISLD in that one is able to post orders to the order book and then to the Level 2 if the order is not matched against. ARCA's order book is now available to the public. If you have ARCA, your Level 2 will show several separate orders labeled ARCHIP. In chat rooms and bulletin boards, they are referred to as *chippies*. You will see a comment like "chippies are lining up to buy this stock."

If you do not have this access, then you are only seeing the aggregate amount of shares available on the Level 2 screen next to the ARCA symbol. Those without ARCA access will need to SelectNet Preference an order to the ARCA ECN to match an order, much like we do with ISLD and INCA, as described previously.

For those with ARCA routing capabilities, the route acts as a *smart route*. This means that the route uses an algorithmic system to execute as fast as it can at the inside prices. The way ARCA works is by first trying to match the order against the liquidity in the order book. If not enough liquidity is present, ARCA looks for available ECNs at the inside price to match. ARCA does this with SelectNet. If enough size is available from ECN participation, the order is auto-executed at that price. The problem lies within the situation when the ECNs are not present with enough size. The ARCA program then looks to the Market Makers at the inside prices and identifies the most active participant. After the system identifies this participant, it preferences this Market Maker. ARCA will continue to work the order until the market moves away from any remaining shares or until the next Market Maker at that price level fills the order.

Because ARCA continues to work this order, the ability for market orders as well as limit orders is presented. If the price moves outside the limit of your order, then you are posted to the Nasdaq Level 2 again for any remaining shares. The major disadvantage with ARCA is when the stock is moving against you and ECN participation is limited or nonexistent. Remember that ARCA utilizes SelectNet, and Market Makers, after filling liability requirements, have 30 seconds to decide on remaining orders. While the stock is moving against you and you are waiting for that response, your frustration level grows. Eventually, you are either declined or you cancel and try again. Meanwhile, the stock continues to fall and you are continuing to chase the stock lower. ARCA developers are aware of the liability requirements so that if a Market Maker does not respond in 30 seconds, they move to the next Market Maker. However, by this time, who knows where the stock will be? One final point is that ARCA will not accept odd lots. ISLD allows for orders of one share. ARCA must be in rounded multiples of 100.

These four routes (SOES, ISLD, SNET, and ARCA) are generally the most used routes by EDATs. Some offer added features such as other smart routes or other ECN access, but generally an EDAT service will provide a trader with SOES, ISLD, SNET, and, more often than not, ARCA. When choosing an EDAT system, be sure to find out about which routes they are offering for access and what fees are involved in utilizing each system according to price-per-share fees on ECNs and possible multiple partial-fill transactions.

There is a lot to absorb when it comes to order routing, but this is what separates the professionals from the amateurs. If you fully understand the routes available, you are more apt to use the right tool for the right job and get quick and better fills for your orders. It is well worth the time to learn each routing system fully.

ADVANCED TOOLS OF AN ACTIVE TRADER

Now that you have a basic understanding of order routes and the functionality of why EDAT systems are functionally better than Web-based systems, let's discuss a few more necessities of the active trader that are offered through most of these brokers. Many EDATs will offer a data package that comes complete with a Level 1 screen, a Level 2 screen, a Time of Sales Ticker, Charting, and News services. The fee for the varying degrees of information that one needs is up to the individual to assess. However, I suggest that one starts small and upgrade services as needed.

There is no reason to tie up capital in software enhancements that you may not use. At the very least, a trader should have access to a Level 1 and Level 2 screen. The Time of Sales Ticker is also important for seeing the prices at which trades occur. Charting is a must for technical type analysis, and news services are a plus because they tend to be the catalyst for momentum.

LEVEL 1

The Level 1 screen is the screen that displays the current real-time market data that you mostly see on media and Web site tickers. You can set up your Level 1 screen in many different ways (see Figure 3-1).

The most common setup for traders utilizes the following columns from left to right. They are Symbol, Net Change from Previous Day's Closing Price, Percentage Change from Previous Day's Close Price, Bid, Ask, Day High, Day Low, Volume, Last Price, Last Price Volume, Open Price, and Close Price. This information gives a face value look at the market activity for a particular stock. Any stock with a ticker symbol can be placed into a Level 1 screen to derive the information. Let's discuss some of the columns to gain a better understanding of exactly what we are looking for with a Level 1 screen.

First off is the stock's ticker symbol. Each publicly traded company chooses a stock symbol to represent their company. As we discussed

F I G U R E   3 - 1

Level 1

Symbol	Change	Bid	Ask	High	Low	Tot. Vol.	Last Price	Trade Volume	Open	Hist Close
DELL	-.70	25.63	25.74	27.17	26.13	20569400	26.21 S	500	26.61	26.91
JNPR	-2.77	27.50	27.54	30.65	28.43	10475400	28.50 S	300	30.52	34.27
CIEN	-2.49	33.60	33.65	36.36	34.32	16196400	34.54 S	200	36.11	37.03
ADPT	-.13	9.25	10.80	11.10	10.54	2079800	10.77 S	100	10.86	10.90
JDSU	-1.06	11.20	11.24	12.55	11.58	19064700	11.61 S	100	12.48	12.67
MSFT	-1.96	67.80	67.99	70.72	68.44	24634200	68.51 S	100	70.22	70.47
ORCL	-.84	18.47	18.51	19.91	18.90	29051400	18.93 S	1200	19.38	19.77

earlier, stocks with one, two, or three letters are listed stocks. Stocks with four or five letters are Nasdaq-related issues. We place the ticker symbol in the Level 1 screen to derive the information that we need to arrive at an assessment for where the stock is trading. The Net Change from the Previous Day's Closing Price represents how strong or weak that stock is on that particular day. If the stock is showing a negative number in this column, then the stock is trading lower on the day. The same applies conversely if the column shows a positive number.

The Percentage Change from the Previous Day's Closing Price calculates the percentage that the stock is up or down relative to yesterday's closing price. We want to see this to gauge possible predictability as traders react to 5-, 10-, or 20-percent price movements, depending on the price of the stock. The Bid column represents the price that we traditionally sell at. Market Makers and ECNs are found at these levels. They stand ready to provide liquidity and buy the shares that you are willing to sell at the Bid price. We learned previously that we can also participate to buy at the Bid if we so choose.

The Ask column is traditionally the price at which we buy our stocks from Market Makers and ECNs. Again, they stand ready to sell you shares that you are willing to buy at the Ask price. Additionally, we can also function to sell our shares with an ECN or SelectNet order as well.

The next two columns are Day's High and Low. This provides us with an intra-day range that will give us a better understanding of possible potential for traders. Stocks generally do not end the day at their highs or at their lows, but rather somewhere in between. This is what provides the active trader with potential as stocks move off bottoms and fall off tops of intra-day prices. The next column is volume.

Volume indicates interest in a stock. The more interest that is there, the more predictable a stock generally becomes. I see many low volume stocks that offer traders less predictability for the following reason. In a stock without traders' interest, Market Makers tend to widen spreads to compensate themselves for the added risk of providing liquidity. Whereas a few large share buys can make the stock move up in bigger increments, a few large sell positions can do the same. This makes entering these kinds of stocks more tricky. More importantly, exiting these stocks can be dangerous as they drop just as fast as they climb. In some instances, low-volume stocks do offer potential, and we will discuss when these are safe and when they are not later in the book.

The Last Price column simply shows the price at which the last sale of the stock occurred. Again, prices at the Bid side are generally sell orders, whereas those at the Ask are buy orders. It is by the Last Price column that many traders can ascertain the direction of the stock by the number of buys and sells. The Last Price Volume column is important to show us if any block trades are being executed. We will explain the importance of block trades later on in the book as well. The Open and the Close columns simply add information to get a measure for where the stock is trading currently relative to these two prices. We tend to use this as the market opens to gauge potential after the first moves in the market occur.

In the morning, traders will gather their news momentum stocks and possible favorites and place them in the Level 1 screen so that they can watch the action on several stocks at a time. I currently use two Level 1 screens with about 75 to 100 stocks on them. Many of these stocks are simple sector leader stocks that enable me with a generalization of the macro view of the market by sectors. The rest are the momentum plays that are created by news or unusual activity that either the market or I may not be fully aware of. The Level 1 screen is the starting point for watching stocks and understanding basic market price action.

LEVEL 2

The Level 2 screen is an important part of the process for the active trader. Level 1 quotes show the first level of the quote system, but Level 2 enables traders to see the Market Maker and ECN participation at each price level.

If a trader is going to route his or her own orders, then Level 2 is the map for how to best execute decisions. On the Level 2 screen (see Figure 3-2), a trader will find several price levels with market participants at these levels. The market participants will show us at what price they are willing to provide liquidity at and how much size they are willing to offer or bid at that price level. We will be discussing the functionality of the Level 2 later on in the book. For now, realize that an active trader with an EDAT execution system will have trouble seeing the underlying strength and weakness of a stock, as well as how to place orders to market participants without a Level 2 screen. Although traders have been without it in the past, the complexity of the current market participants and routing orders to them make Level 2 an essential part of an active trader's toolbox. Many Level 2 systems have a Time of Sales Ticker built into them.

TIME OF SALES

A Time of Sales Ticker is a visual representation of the trades that occur at price levels. This is the same information that a trader sees in the Last Price column on the Level 1 screen. The last sale on a particular issue is

F I G U R E   3 - 2

Level 2

DELL		43 1/16	↓	-9/16		200	Ot	16:
High	43 7/8	Low		42 1/8		Acc. Vol.		28358900
Bid	↓ 43 1/16	Ask		43 1/8		Close		43 5/8

	Name	Bid	Time		Name	Ask	Time
L	DKNY	43 1/16	09/0	L	GSCO	43 1/8	09/0
L	GFIN	43 1/16	09/0	L	SLKC	43 1/8	09/0
L	HRZG	43 1/16	09/0	L	ISLD	43 1/8	09/0
L	KCMO	43 1/16	09/0	L	REDI	43 1/8	09/0
L	LEHM	43 1/16	09/0	L	DKNY	43 3/16	09/0
L	MONT	43 1/16	09/0	L	JPMS	43 3/16	09/0
L	PWJC	43 1/16	09/0	L	FBCO	43 1/4	09/0
L	SBSH	43 1/16	09/0	L	FLTT	43 1/4	09/0
L	SHWD	43 1/16	09/0	L	MADF	43 1/4	09/0
L	REDI	43 1/16	09/0	L	MASH	43 1/4	09/0
L	INGC	43	09/0	L	MSCO	43 1/4	09/0

reported to the tape and is listed on the Time of Sales Ticker (see Figure 3-3). This scrolling indication of buying and selling gives the active trader a better historical visualization of how much buying and selling is happening in the stock. The Time of Sales Ticker will post the time of the sale, the amount of shares transacted, and at what price the sale was made. Many of these software programs color-code these sales as well. Many fix buy orders as green and sell orders as red. In-between trades, which are trades that occur between the inside Bid and Ask prices, can be seen as white or purple with some software programs.

The Time of Sales Ticker is a key component to watching the pace of buying and selling to determine the strength of the trend in that stock when trading momentum. It is an essential part of a trader's arsenal as it provides the actual trading prints of where stocks are trading.

The Time of Sales Ticker has one drawback, however. At the open of each trading day, the enormous volume that comes down the Nasdaq information pipeline includes market orders and limit orders from pre-market trading, as well as newly entered orders as the trading day opens. This event creates a funnel effect by which individual trades have a hard time making their way to our computers in a real-time manner.

F I G U R E   3 - 3

Time of Sales

|—DELL COMPUTER CORP—————

Date	Time	Price	Volume	Exch	Type
9/01/2000	15:12	43 5/16	500		Trade
9/01/2000	15:12	43 5/16	2500		Trade
9/01/2000	15:12	43 5/16	200		Trade
9/01/2000	15:12	43 5/16	300		Trade
9/01/2000	15:12	43 5/16	700		Trade
9/01/2000	15:12	43 11/32	100		Trade
9/01/2000	15:12	43 11/32	100		Trade
9/01/2000	15:12	43 5/16	100		Trade
9/01/2000	15:12	43 5/16	900		Trade
9/01/2000	15:12	43 3/8	200		Trade
9/01/2000	15:12	43 5/16	900		Trade
9/01/2000	15:12	43 3/8	200		Trade
9/01/2000	15:12	43 5/16	3000		Trade
9/01/2000	15:12	43 5/16	400		Trade
9/01/2000	15:12	43 5/16	1000		Trade
9/01/2000	15:12	43 11/32	700		Trade

This is a bottleneck that begins at the Nasdaq and has nothing to do with individual brokerage systems.

With the huge volume each day, it is unfortunately a necessary evil that we have delayed Time of Sales information at the open. I have found that within 10 to 15 minutes after the open of the trading day, my quotes seem to move in tandem of where my Time of Sales prints are showing trades that occur. Many ask how we can trade when we can't see the trades that occur at the open. The answer will be explained later on in the book when we get to our methods sections and how we approach each individual day.

CHARTING SOFTWARE

Charting software is helpful for those who use intra-day charts and technical indicators to enter and exit stocks. Some are as basic as just having a three-month chart with a 50-day moving average line and a 200 day moving average line. Some go as deep as a one-minute tick information chart. The basic idea behind charting is to identify technical areas of support and resistance. Numerous charting patterns are available, ranging from extremely basic to extremely complex and expensive. The idea is to find charting software that does what you need it to.

Most traders will use charting programs offered through MBTrading.com, ATFI.com, or Qcharts.com. Other ideas for more in-depth views would be programs like Metastock. These systems enable you to add filters to search for definable setups through parameters created by the user. Basically, traders are using charts to identify trends and counter-trends in the market. They can use pivot lines, Fibonacci indicators, Bollinger Bands, and so on to aid themselves in doing so. Just be sure to subscribe to what you need in the beginning. Don't sign up for information you aren't ready for. Added bells and whistles are neat, but if you do not need them, why pay for them? It just ties up trading capital.

NEWS SERVICES

Finally, news services are beneficial for the active trader. You can collect this type of information in several ways. Many news providers are offered through your broker or at least they will give a referral to someone who has a reasonable cost for what is offered. Generally, access to business wires such as Dow Jones, Reuters, PR Newswire, and Comtex is enough for news momentum candidates. Real-time news is obviously the optimal situation as fresh news generally provides the best momentum moves. However, as we have seen many times, even old news can move a stock if it is under a different headline. A trader can subscribe to these news services for a monthly fee (see Figure 3-4).

F I G U R E   3 - 4

News Scanner

DJ	09/03 16:39	DJN:	AWSJ:	DaimlerChrysler Talks To Mitsubishi In Japan
DJ	09/03 16:38	DJN:	AWSJ:	Heard In Asia:Politics Dim Hopes For Rally In Malays
DJ	09/03 16:38	DJN:	AWSJ:	US Labor Day Holiday Polls May Dictate Election
DJ	09/03 16:38	DJN:	AWSJ:	Hurt By Pound, Japan Car Firms Mull U.K. Plans
DJ	09/03 16:38	DJN:	AWSJ:	U.K.'s Standard Chartered To Buy HK Chase Business
DJ	09/03 16:37	DJN:	AWSJ:	HK's Journal Begins Decimal Quotations In Stock Tabl
DJ	09/03 16:37	DJN:	AWSJ:	Corrections & Amplifications
DJ	09/03 16:37	DJN:	AWSJ:	Hong Kong's Tung Supports Aide In Polling Dispute

I see many rooms that either present false information or hype a stock a lot by the continuous reposting of the same information, trying to drum up interest. The right way to post news in a forum is to post the news once and let the traders decide for themselves on whether or not a trade is viable for the action it receives. Continuous comments or reposting of the news is a key to either get in early or stay away from it and not chase the stock as it is climbing. If you are even 10 seconds late to buy, the chances that you are buying when you should be selling are greater.

4

THE NEW MARKET MOMENTUM

The introduction of new market players in the last few years has changed the face of the stock market forever. The stock market your parents invested in has evolved into a brand new dynamic market with all new players and a whole different type of momentum. Those who are still playing the old style market are playing with old information and are not fully exploiting the current market. This chapter will explore those changes and identify the rudimentary changes and players who have changed it.

THE NEW PLAYERS

Market dynamics is a function of momentum as it relates to upside and downside trends. The dynamics of the market are derived from the actions of mass psychology. Mass psychology of the marketplace stems from the two basic emotions of fear and greed. Greed causes traders to buy stocks in the expectation that the stock will rise in value creating profit. Fear causes traders to sell these stocks. They fear that the stock will cease to climb any longer and reduce any unrealized gains.

However, the opposite side of the trade enables greed and fear to force traders to hold losing positions in equities that are not performing to expectations. This scenario begins to turn small losses into larger losses. The exciting thing about greed and fear is that they produce some incredible market momentum events that ultimately endanger the portfolios of the newer and unknowing active traders. This occurs because they are unaware of the forces behind market momentum and how to react to changes within it. Those who understand the forces of fear and greed can profit from them handsomely.

Before the explosion of the online trading revolution, traders were not given the incredible access to the market information and participation that we have today. Investors were at the mercy of brokerage houses and institutional momentum without any insight into how stocks moved, why they moved, and how to participate within it other than through high-priced brokers. Granted these market professionals had access to the important information and relayed this information to their clients, but it was selective information that was being provided. Although investors have done extremely well during this incredible growth phase of the bull market, they lack the understanding of why they did so well. This is the important aspect of the transition from a passive investor to an active trader that tends to doom many participants as they begin their trading careers.

In 1987, when traders were unable to access the markets in a timely manner to exit positions that they wanted no part of, the SEC decided that more accountability by market participants was needed to fill orders faster. This led to the implementation of SOES and the online explosion began. Visionaries of the time began to expand on this wave of the future. Although direct access to market participants was granted, so was access to market information that was traditionally reserved for the brokerage firms.

This information includes such documents as earnings reports, SEC filings, analyst reviews, and news releases. Although this information was always public domain, it was not as easy to receive it in the speed and efficiency that is available today. This shifts the decision-making power potential from the brokerage firms to the individual traders.

The empowerment of the individual to make his or her own decisions has had some interesting implications in the financial world. The elements of greed and fear are now able to permeate the market at a faster rate of application by active traders. This provides for a whole new market momentum to the trading field. Traders are now able to research, formulate, and then react on a decision faster than they had been able to with traditional brokerage functionality.

Historically, traders would receive a research report or phone call from their broker. They would discuss the issue with their broker and possibly decide to buy or sell a set amount of shares based on their brokers' advice and information. Investors would quickly receive news stories on the television, announcing that the markets were quickly spiraling to new lows or flying to new highs. Upon seeing this information, traders would have to call their brokers to execute a decision. This could take several minutes to a few hours, depending on how well the broker was able to handle his or her client load. The broker would still have to send the order to the market to be executed at the best available price.

This process has traditionally been very slow and stocks are at much different price levels than they were when the investor was first receiving the news. The inefficiency of this method is vastly different from where we are today. Traders can now interact with the market participants in real time without hesitation or barriers to market access. This process bypasses the traditional broker method and adds incredible momentum to the market as a whole. Mass psychology decision-making is now fueling intra-day market momentum at a faster rate.

INSTITUTIONAL MOMENTUM

Institutional participation in the marketplace will always be the primary source of market momentum. Institutions inherently possess large amounts of capital and are able to drive sector rotation at key points of market action. They are able to hold large positions in certain areas of the market as well as dump their shares at any given time. They are able to participate in large buy and sell programs as well as initiate them when the market action triggers such a necessity.

They have been and always will be the smart money of the marketplace. Many newer traders feel they can figure out what institutions are up to in any given stock either by the size of blocks that cross the tape or by a certain research report offered at a given time. I have seen many traders complain that institutions dump their shares into their own initiated upgrades. I have the seen the following comment many times in free rooms and bulletin boards: "There goes big blocks on ABCD. Institutions must know something."

Whether institutions know something or not, it is useless for us to figure out what that something is. We will never know as active traders what institutions are doing while they are doing it. We never know until the momentum is close to reversing its direction. Selective disclosure and other forms of legal knowledge are available to institutional traders that active traders may not be aware of. Think back to how many times a stock has a movement and a spike in volume just prior to big news being released to the general public. Although we may want to complain about this scenario because we do not have general access to it, it has its legality and therefore is utilized to the fullest by those who have the access to it.

Although we see isolated instances of illegal practices, institutions as a whole are not about to engage in a practice that is illegal and that could cost the firm its integrity and image in the financial industry. We may want to blame market action on the unscrupulous wrong doings of institutions, but the reality is that very little of this kind of action occurs when compared to the whole functionality of the marketplace. Furthermore, trying to determine what institutions are about to do in individual stocks is primarily a waste of your time as you will never be able to fully ascertain any answers to this question.

Market dynamics does, however, enable us to derive possible expectations on which sector institutions are participating within. Remember that traders and media sources often discuss sector rotation publicly. The greatest example of this sector participation was the huge Internet stock climbs in the late 1990s. We saw stocks like Rambus, Yahoo, Amazon.com, Lycos, and eBay make incredible gains. These issues richly rewarded many investors. These stocks typically came public with a limited float. The small float size allows for stocks to have incredible moves up and down on any large orders of buying and selling. Thinking back to 1998, I remember Yahoo making a 70-point climb and a 50-point retracement in one day. That is a 120-point swing in one trading day. That is an incredible move in a highly speculative environment.

When CNBC or other financial media sources report on these moves, they are said to be due to daytraders and short-term traders. Although some of the momentum is no doubt provided by these groups of traders, it is ridiculous to say that Yahoo climbs hundreds of points in a few years on daytrading and short-term trading momentum. As we talked about earlier, institutional traders have large amounts of capital. The Internet is clearly the future of our economy. The Industrial Age is over and the Internet economy is in its infancy. When we add up the variables of large institutional money, low float in the majority of the Internet stocks, and an insatiable appetite for Internets, we can expect huge momentum moves in these kinds of stocks.

Media sources report these moves and associate the blame to daytraders. This is far from the truth. The proof that these media sources offer is the share size of the trades that are crossing the tape. I hear reports such as the following:

> "Yes, many are attributing this action in Yahoo to daytraders. We are seeing a lot of 100 and 200 share trades in these stocks crossing the tape. This would indicate a lot of short-term and daytrader participation in these stocks."

This is unreliable proof that daytraders are the sole cause of the moves in these stocks. The underlying truth is provided to us in a simple Level 2 review. When looking at these stocks 3 years ago and even today to some extent, market participants are only required to show a willingness to buy or sell 100 shares at a time. This is their size liability requirement. Once the size liability is filled, the market participant has the right to fill more orders at that price, or he or she must lift off the inside price after 17 seconds. Therefore, because the market participant is required to buy or sell only 100 shares at a time, many 100 and 200 share prints are moving across the tape. The market participant may have 100,000 shares to buy or sell, but he or she may not do it all at one time.

However, on a low-float stock, if a market participant shows this willingness to buy or sell 100,000 shares, it may adversely affect the best price at which the market participant can execute this order. When the Internet stocks were trading the way they were, meaning very fast and at wide price levels, market participants would be less willing to accept a large posted liability by which they could be executed against. Therefore, they show only 100 shares and fill orders beyond that level as they so desire. This is why we see many 100, 200, and 500 share trades. It has less to do with momentum created by active traders than it does with the functionality of how market participants execute their client's orders as well as their own.

To say that a stock momentum is created by active traders with only share size prints going across the tape as proof is not telling the whole story. Although many stocks do move because of active traders, the Internet sector climbs in the past 3 years were more due to institutional-type trading than active trader participation. Later we will discuss the types of stocks that daytraders create momentum within. Market fallacies are abundant. This is just one of them that is now hopefully cleared up to some extent.

As we stated before, the institutions will be primarily referred to as the smart money. This phrase is derived from the notion and assumption that the public is usually the last to know or is just plain wrong. Many will describe events such as failed rallies and market support levels that are responsible for a certain market momentum. Smart money is seen as doing the reverse of what the public is usually doing. A failed rally is simply an event by which institutional money has already been put to work at lower levels of accumulation or consolidation.

Public money then comes rushing in after sensing a market shift in sentiment from bearish to bullish, and the institutions begin to sell their shares to the late public buyers. The selling pressure by institutional exiting of their positions tends to halt any meaningful upside momentum and the market begins to falter. Institutional selling continues and then public buyers get nervous and end up selling their shares when the pain gets too great. As the pain is increasing and the public is selling their shares at a loss, you guessed it, the institutions are once again snapping up shares at value prices again. This is the basic case of bear market rallies and dead cat bounces.

TECHNICAL ANALYSIS MOMENTUM

Much of the market is also weaned on technical analysis. This can include anything from simple chart reading to more complex derivations of stochastics and moving average lines. Although some believe in them and some don't, the point to these analyses is that enough people do buy and sell decisions based on them. Therefore, because of mass psychology, it is important to have a basic understanding of the continued underlying reasons for market momentum.

Simple moving averages such as 50-day and 200-day moving averages can have profound effects on the marketplace psychology as well as individual averages. However, just knowing what these lines are will not help a trader. Anyone can look up the 200-day moving average on a stock. The importance of that line is the key to understanding why stocks move the way they do.

Generally, as a stock or index approaches a 200-day moving average, traders will look to that level for support in a downtrending market. Should that average be broken, technicians will see this as a bearish sign and possibly trigger sell programs that lead to more market downside. Again, just knowing what key levels are will not help you to understand the momentum. Understanding what these levels mean to a trader is what is important.

ONLINE TRADER MOMENTUM

Although institutions have the ability to push and the pull the marketplace, the explosion of the online trading phenomenon has pushed a new market dynamic into reality. When looking at the sector leaders such as Cisco, Microsoft, and Yahoo, these stocks tend to have an incredible amount of Market Maker participation with huge sizes to buy and sell at each price level. The effect of online traders in issues with large floats and enormous market participation is much less than in stocks with lower floats or less market participation at price levels.

Online traders do have the ability to move these kinds of stocks in wider ranges than they would normally trade. Primarily, online traders are attracted to fresh momentum created by one of many forms of interest. Interest can be provided by a press release by the company, a rumor of a takeover, or simple hype by an investment newsletter or stock pickers club. Whatever the reason, Market Maker participants have been increasingly aware of the new dynamic that online traders command.

When looking at firms such as E*TRADE, Ameritrade, or Schwab, their membership numbers continue to grow quarter over quarter. The idea of self-investing and controlling their own money is catching on to more and more of the world. The offering of low commissions versus what brokers were charging them is appealing. Research reports and a wide variety of timely information is now at their fingertips, so they figure, why pay more per trade if they are essentially receiving the same data for free? Informational firms and the distributors of this financial and market information are falling over themselves trying to attract these investors to receive information from their service.

These services provide information for free or possibly for a small fee. They are offering the information over the Internet and thus gain their revenue from advertising by affiliated companies. This keeps information providers' costs to their clients low, while those who advertise on the site can benefit from a larger viewership. When coupling lower commissions and access to the pertinent information in real time, online trading has certainly become a viable force in the trading community.

With the increasing number of online traders, market participants have to now deal with the increasing possibility that interference with normal price action can and will result from timely news releases and simple hype. This is especially frustrating to market participants if they are trying to fill an order at a certain price. If that price is suddenly unattainable due to a spike up or a huge sell-off caused by mass online participation, then the market becomes a bit more complex for them to fill orders at desired prices. They have to evolve their trading techniques to stay ahead of the participation momentum of online traders.

In times of large market speculation and numerous get-rich-quick stories, online trading really gains attention in this environment. Traders tend to throw the underlying fundamentals of companies out the window. Price-to-earnings ratios do not matter to them. Current valuations versus historical valuations do not matter to them. Market sentiment does not matter to them. The only thing that matters to these traders is that their stock moves in a direction that banks them a profit as fast as it can.

Take a look at the valuations and historical charts on stocks like Qualcomm (QCOM), Amazon.com (AMZN), and Yahoo (YHOO) for a few examples from the last 4 years to get the point (see Figures 4-1, 4-2, and 4-3).

This is the new market psychology in times when the economy is hot, inflation is in check, and equity prices are flying. Market participants have to prepare for the fact that traders are not trading companies anymore; they are trading symbols and chasing after momentum stocks. Yesterday's investors saw the tremendous gains being made in these stocks and they wanted a piece of it. They were willing to throw caution to the wind, dump their mutual funds, and chase after it. In short, it turned many investors into true momentum investors. The following is a typical conversation between traders that I hear often.

FIGURE 4-1

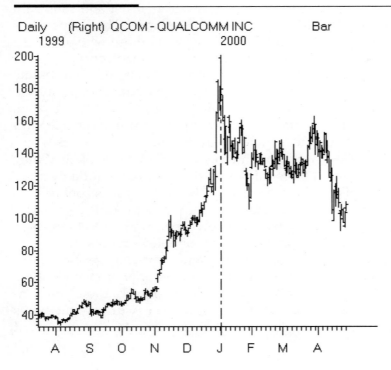

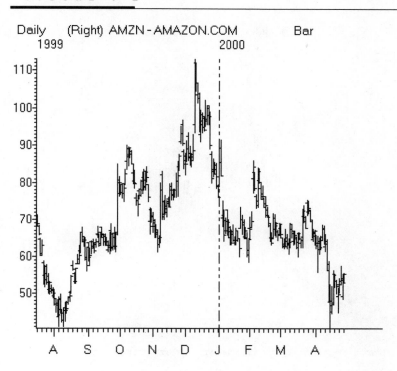

FIGURE 4-2

Daily   (Right) AMZN - AMAZON.COM   Bar

Trader A: "What does ABCD do?"
Trader B: "I don't know, but I just made a nice 2 points on it. That momentum was great."
Trader A: "Why ABCD? They have a market valuation that is way over where it should be. Their P/E is way out of whack with the rest of the sector."
Trader B: "What do I care? I just made 2 points on it. It can go to 0 for all I care. I took what I wanted from the trade and that is all that matters to me."

The new market paradigm is that traders are taking what they can from the market as fast as they can. They are not satisfied anymore with 6-percent a year. They want double-digit portfolio growth and refuse to accept anything less. They believe in the stock market and its sustainability for producing wealth. They want a piece of it. They do not want to be diversified to death by traditional investing methods and they are willing to do it themselves if their brokers are not giving them their desired returns. This type of mentality, while it is reality, provides some

F I G U R E   4 - 3

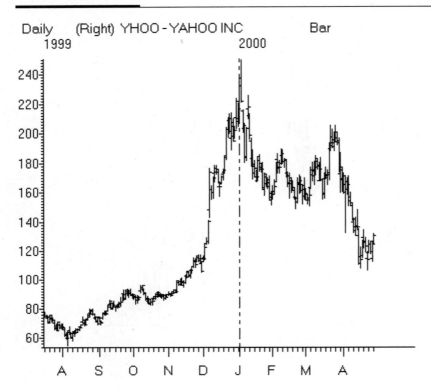

Daily   (Right) YHOO - YAHOO INC   Bar

incredible market shifts as those two basic elements of fear and greed
continue to worm their way through individual investors who are now
making their own decisions.

In times of a strong bull market and expansive growth, such as
we saw in 1999, individual investors could almost do no wrong. They
simply buy a high-growth stock and make a bunch of money. They buy
a high-growth stock, take a nap, wake up, and sell it for a profit. Making
money had never been this easy. Or had it? Each speculative cycle contains a huge market move upward and a severe correction to the downside as many market pundits who missed out on the climb begin to talk
down the market. They cite overvaluations, unsustainability of current
market prices, and high levels of speculation that always end in a bubble that is about to pop. Although we have seen many of these huge
climbs and huge falls in the last 5 years, the underlying point to the story
is that although institutions have a hold of the market, online traders are
figuring out how to ride the wave a bit longer.

SMART MONEY, INFORMED MONEY, AND DUMB MONEY

Each spike of momentum to the upside and crash to the downside provides these online momentum investors with the experience and knowledge of what to look for in times of uncertainty. They begin to understand underlying reasons for market moves and are more apt to participate in them. Smart money is slowly beginning to include online traders. Dumb money is on its way to becoming informed money. They may not be smart enough yet to get in when smart money is getting in, but they are surely learning what to look for as the increased supply and dissemination of information is continuing to educate these traders.

They are not too far behind the learning curve anymore to expect that the public is always wrong. They may still be later than smart money, but we are slowly moving to another tier of traders. We have smart money entering first, informed money entering second, and dumb money entering third. Smart money and informed money will be selling to dumb money. Smart money makes the most in profits. Informed money begins to take a piece of the pie or at least not lose as much as they had been previously. Dumb money continues to get taken to the cleaners. Smart and dumb money will always exist. It will be interesting to see how this middle tier of traders evolves as the increased availability of market knowledge is provided to them.

A perfect example of how smart money profits from dumb money and how this informed money is catching on can be seen in two market catastrophes seen in a 2-year period. In October of 1998, we had a 20-percent decline in the Nasdaq, which caused many online traders a lot of stress as they were not used to this kind of market action (see Figure 4-4). For the previous 3 years, it was simply buy a growth company or Internet stock and profit from it. A newer investor could almost throw a dart and make money because stocks were just continuing to rise. These traders had very little understanding of the economy and how it worked. They didn't understand how the international and global economies interacted with each other to create a foundation for trade and expansion. They were not aware of market internals, the breadth of the market, volume levels, or historical sentiment. They did not understand what was about to happen in October of 1998 and why.

Speculation was high in the early part of 1998. Internet stocks were soaring, growth stocks were growing, and people were getting richer or had friends who were profiting. They felt invincible that the market

F I G U R E   4 - 4

Daily   (Right) $COMPX - NASDAQ COMBINED COMPOSITE INDX
1998

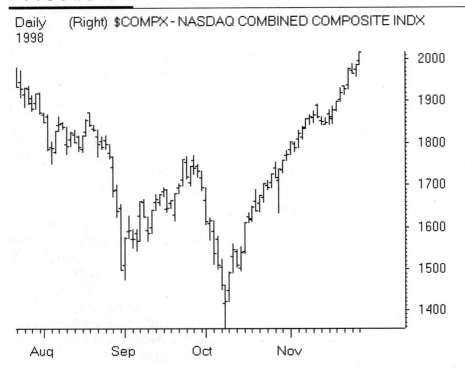

would provide incredible gains for months to come if they could just get in the market at the right time. Outside the market, however, was a serious economic catalyst to problematic global concerns. Primarily, we were seeing a banking crisis in the stronger international economies. Asian financial distress was getting bigger and Russia was devaluing its currency.

Greenspan's comments of irrational exuberance kept getting repeated. Finally, long-term capital was in serious trouble and needed help by Congress for a bailout. The International Monetary Fund was being asked for economic bailout to struggling economies; the world was headed for a global meltdown. Newer traders did not see any of this. All they saw was their growth stock heading higher. Fundamentals of the market or individual stocks were thrown out the window. Everyone just wanted a piece of the action.

As the early October sell-off ensued, many of these traders were wiped out. Panic selling was leading to a capitulation of dumb money selling to smart money. Prior to the event, institutional money was dumping shares ahead of October.

The public money continued to buy shares as institutions were selling all that these newer traders wanted. Eventually, the top in the market was in place. Stocks started to fall, late-to-the-party buyers began selling in panic, and we hit a market bottom. This left the newer traders in disgust as they sold near the bottom; smart money could not count their profits fast enough because the strong market rebound was sharp and decisive.

The Fed began to lower interest rates, the economy was still doing well, and international economies began to benefit a bit from lowering central bank policy. Stocks continued to rise and those who sold near the lows had to buy back in at higher prices. Now we have smart money profiting and dumb money paying for their tuition but now becoming more informed about market events and possible underlying reasons for momentum. Now dumb money continues its cycle to become informed money. The informed money cannot wait to see this event again so they can profit the next time.

For 2 long years the informed money waited. In April of 2000, we saw a very sharp pullback in the marketplace after an incredible rise in the Nasdaq from 1998 lows. We were at near 1,500 in the Nasdaq during that 1998 low. We hit a high over 5,100 in the Nasdaq just 2 years later (see Figure 4-5).

Internet stocks continued to rise, but a new sector began to fly. The bio-tech sector had amazing climbs with some stocks moving from the 40s to over 300. The rises in these stocks were incredible. We slowly topped above 5,100, pulled back a bit, and then failed on that retest of the highs in the Nasdaq. What happened next was clearly ugly as we trended to near the 3,000 level over the next 11 weeks. However, the informed money was begging to see this event about to unfold, while the dumb money was incredibly destroyed as it occurred. This marked, in my opinion, a national personal wealth catastrophe for the newer traders to the market.

In times of market corrections, much of the underlying greed and excess speculation is wiped out as traders' portfolios become more risk-averse. Many of these traders pull away from concept companies with uncertain futures and look to reallocate their risk to more solid growth companies with real earnings or straight dividends. In April of 2000, we saw the majority of Internet and bio-tech companies off some 50- to 80-percent from their highs as continued nervousness hammered these stocks.

F I G U R E   4 - 5

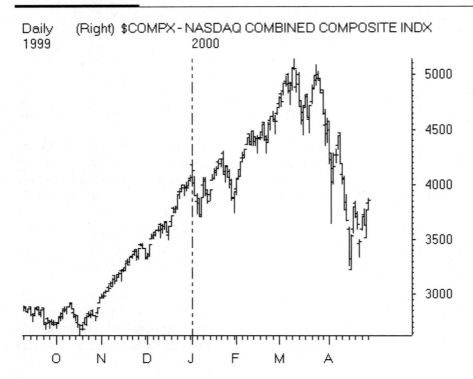

Daily   (Right) $COMPX – NASDAQ COMBINED COMPOSITE INDX
1999   2000

Institutional traders were raising cash and selling stock on any strength. We saw many unsustainable rallies leading to the 3,000 level. A redistribution of stock clearly occurred as active traders were buying stock from the institutions on the way down. Eventually, institutions will be accumulating the shares again from those who can't take the pain of the loss and sell at lower levels. Then markets stabilize and resume their climb.

The two periods were interesting in that the reasons behind the corrections were different. As we noted earlier, in 1998 we had a global crisis with Asia and Russia providing much of the catalyst for the sell-off. The Fed stepped in with interest rate cuts and the IMF was approving bailout funds for struggling economies. Long-term capital received its angel and only a month later, traders were back to buying up shares as interest rates kept falling. As we approached late 1999, we had different fears. Initially, many were looking for a sell-off prior to the New Year on Y2K concerns. We saw very little selling as we approached the New Year, and basically it was a non-event in that nothing major happened to end the world or provide a global computer breakdown.

After the New Year celebration was over, the markets powered to new highs on a very strong market volume, creating excess in the wealth effect that was worrying the Fed as inflation concerns were growing. The Fed had increased interest rates six times in a row and was slowing the economy. The slowing economy and acceleration in inflation was cause for concern as traders who bought in above 4,500 on the Nasdaq, and held, faced a rough road as we neared the 3,000 level on lingering fears of uncertainty as the economic outlook grew larger.

Two totally different reasons for uncertainty and fear lead to the market declines. Those who were unaware of the reasons for the momentum to the downside refused to accept that the trend was lower, and the market itself took care of their closed-mindedness. Those who were aware of the reasons behind the momentum were able to either minimize loss or lock-in surest profits. Again, the paradigm of the smart and informed money was succeeding over the dumb money.

Now that we have explained two of the major forces behind today's new market momentum, it is important to understand that although a shift in portfolios from broker-managed to self-direction is occurring, the old style of money management is still the largest force in the marketplace. Although active traders are able to affect price movements in certain stocks to a varying degree, the action of the market is still controlled by institutional money. This requires that active traders understand and respect their control so as not to negate their effect on their own thinking.

The latest figures of online trading suggest that one of the largest online brokerage firms holds nearly $50 billion in their client's assets. This seems very impressive until we research the traditional style brokerage firms such as Merrill Lynch that manage over $1.5 trillion in assets. Evidence suggests that the old style of investing is still not going anywhere anytime soon. Therefore, we must not fool ourselves into thinking that the online traders are in control of the markets and be aware that institutions are still the big players. They will continue to be big enough to move sectors and stocks on a much grander scale than online traders.

To discuss the new market momentum, a trader has to understand that although institutions still control markets, online traders have become more involved in individual stocks that they deem worth participating within. Market participants cannot simply ignore active online traders but have instead planned ahead to take advantage of the situation. For example, Market Makers are selling order flow and continuing to take profits from the spreads in stocks. They are also learning to mask intentions much better than the professional traders so as not to have any unexpected price spike or sell-off that would worsen the price for their clients on entry or exit. One of the better examples of how online traders can affect a stock price is shown in a stock report newsletter.

Recently, an investment newsletter mentioned the stock Agilent Technologies (A) as a top focus stock (see Figure 4-6). This report had been hailed in previous weeks as something that could move stocks. Basically, traders would receive information about several stocks in this newsletter and one or two stocks would have very positive comments regarding top focus picks. Once the report is released, active traders rush to read the newsletter and find out which stock or stocks are being touted in the newsletter. Once they figure this out, they rush to their order screens and try to get in ahead of the pack. Agilent Technologies was such a stock.

Within 30 minutes of the release of the newsletter, the stock had jumped over $10 a share. In these circumstances, online traders who have access to this information in real time can clearly benefit from the price spikes if they are early enough to get in near the price that it was at as the news came out. If online traders had to call their broker to place a trade, they may very well have been filled at a much higher price after the stock took off on the news, leaving anyone who was late to the news to just watch. Again, although institutions are able to move markets and individual stocks, online traders are continuing to add to the momentum in individual issues.

To be fair, the online trader really needs to be segmented into at least two classes. Some online traders simply do a few trades a year for the decrease in trade costs. These traders do not enter and exit trades within a few minutes, nor do they constantly watch every tick of the market. They are more passive to their trading with a defined short- and long-term plan. The other group, however, is far more interesting as they are more active.

As we discussed earlier in the book, active traders are commonly referred to as daytraders or momentum traders. They tend to use direct access brokers and are in and out of stocks many times a day everyday. Their risk management skills often relate to exiting stocks quickly to avoid sustaining big losses and they rarely hold stocks overnight. They either based their decisions on tape reading, technical analysis, or simple naiveté, depending on where they are in their trading curve. These traders are many times blamed for stock moves to the upside and downside in particular issues. These comments, which you will see on CNBC and other media sources, are only partly correct.

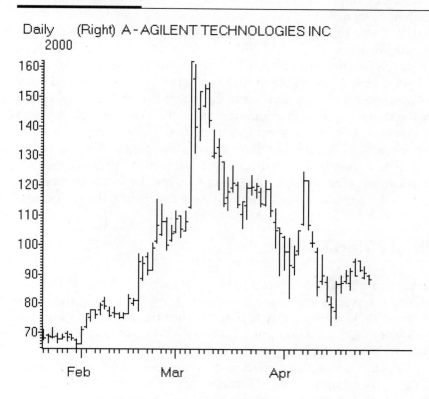

FIGURE 4-6

Daily   (Right) A-AGILENT TECHNOLOGIES INC
2000

We explained that institutions control trillions of dollars of assets and have the ability to move the market more than any online traders do. Certain stocks in the market have an enormous amount of market participation in each stock as well as a large float relative to demand and supply. Sector leaders are characteristically these kinds of stocks. Cisco Systems (CSCO), Dell Computer (DELL), and Intel Corporation (INTC) are examples of stocks with enormous floats and incredible market participation.

Online traders do not have the power to move these stocks out of normal ranges. There simply isn't enough money spread around to these stocks on any given day to make them move abnormally from online traders. When a report is given that daytraders are selling off a certain stock or that active traders are running a stock up and that stock is one with plenty of market participation and a sizable stock float, then those offering that report are misrepresenting the real reason for the move.

Stocks that online traders are able to provide momentum in are stocks that have a relatively low float and some fresh news or hype attached to it. Clear examples of this kind can be seen when one checks the charts on Multiple Zones (MZON), K-Tel (KTEL), Books-a-Million (BAMM), and Xybernaut (XYBR). All of these stocks had released some kind of news that was favorable at that time and the stocks spiked hard on added momentum. More familiar is the quick rise in these stocks followed by the sharp fall back to original levels as those active traders begin to sell shares into strength or short the stock as the stock begins to show signs of weakness. Thousands of these kinds of stocks exhibit this action every year. This is mainly due to the active traders moving into the stock, driving the price up, and then immediately selling the stock as it begins to top or into strength. The stock then makes a reversal to the downside.

THEME MOMENTUM

New market momentum continues to be fueled by the theme of the day as well. Over the past 3 years, we have seen some incredible moves in stocks because they were simply a part of a hot theme at the time. For example, 3 years ago, all a company had to do was announce that they were going to build a Web site and the stock would rise fast as active traders nailed it. Eventually, we moved through themes of Pokemon stocks, China stocks, and Fuel Cell stocks. Active traders watched each theme closely during these times of interest. These traders, for quick profits, jumped on any stock that was tied to the latest theme. However, eventually these themes and newsletter plays will begin to fade as the increased amount of traders entering the same stock tends to destroy the play.

Remember that market momentum includes basically three facets of traders: institutional, online, and daytraders. Institutional traders try to fill clients' orders at specific price levels. When stocks begin to spike up or down unexpectedly, it makes it harder for these traders to fill the orders at those price levels. Let's take the Agilent Technologies (A) in the previous example. Suppose a client of theirs wanted to make a purchase of 100,000 shares at no worse than $85 a share. When the stock receives the newsletter momentum, the client may not get his or her order filled as the stock is now trading over $90 a share and the client becomes upset at the inability to get the price that he or she wanted.

Furthermore, the institutional trader is unhappy that the institution was unable to fill the order. This is because they lose out on the commission of that trade that went unfilled as well as the possible loss of that client if the inability to execute trades consistently occurs over a specific period of time. They are traders the same as we are. If they aren't able to get excellent prices for their clients, their clients may look elsewhere. This is akin to us switching brokers when we are fed up with poor executions and missed trade fills.

Therefore, if institutional traders find it hard to enter and exit trades based on newsletter momentum, then pressure may be on the newsletter writer to release their report at times that will not cause such a momentum run up during the day. For instance, they may release the report before or after the market opens or over the weekend. This way the market can have more time to digest the news before the stock opens for trading and may provide ample opportunity to enter the stock before it jumps. Although this obviously will not cure the whole problem, the point is that these newsletter plays tend to die out as other methods for release are implemented to produce a more orderly trading environment on the stock.

The reason that news alerts and other fast momentum plays tend eventually to fade is due to the increased amount of traders in these plays. The more traders that enter the trade on the way up, the more they are forced to take faster profits. They are selling these stocks much quicker, and are trying to exit before other traders exit. Eventually, the stocks do not react enough that even the small scalpers will enter the trade and the stocks receive no attention. The risk versus reward for these plays becomes greater in risk, and traders leave these plays alone until they begin to show strength again. Usually, they tend to die out as traders look for other areas of momentum.

A great example of this from 1999 is what was called a Dayinvestor alert. Dayinvestor was a site that mentioned breaking or relatively fresh news about stocks on their Web site. The Dayinvestor alert would then be posted to other chat rooms and bulletin boards and active traders would jump on the alert. The stock would climb anywhere from a .50-point to a full point on average and traders would exit within that price range. However, as traders began to notice that the profit potential was only near a .25-point and then .03 of a point and then nothing, they left the Dayinvestor alert alone. It simply wasn't able to provide the same returns as it did previously. This alert potential lasted several months before it died out; it is a great example of how online traders and daytraders can affect stock movements. However, this again shows how these types of stock patterns die out quickly.

Those who understand the new market momentum and how it works will be able to adjust their expectations per trade as they see these tradable patterns come and go in the marketplace. A wise trader learns to recognize and exploit these patterns. Pattern recognition and how to exploit them will be discussed in a later chapter.

5
C H A P T E R

PREDICTABLE MOMENTUM

In this chapter, we will discuss gauging the predictability of momentum and then discuss how other active traders attempt to take advantage of that momentum. Although this is not meant to be an endorsement of those methods, it provides the reader with an understanding of what other active traders are doing and why stocks react the way they do. We do this just as a professional football team studies the tapes of the competition to understand how their actions will affect the game as a whole. Specific methods on how to exploit predictable patterns and momentum will be given in later chapters, fully explaining the Mtrader methods.

PREDICTING MOMENTUM

We discussed in the prior chapter several causes of momentum. We discussed the effect of the vast capital base that institutions have on the markets and on individual stocks. We elaborated on the effect that online brokers and daytraders have on individual stocks but still do not have on the capital base that can move markets or sectors. They can certainly add to the momentum, but it is a following trend rather than a creating trend.

Fortunately, by analyzing momentum in sectors and individual stocks, we can reasonably create expectations for individual trades. Momentum provides predictability in these stocks that traders can rely on with confidence to enter positions. Obviously, predictability utilizes a statistical approach and although no approach to active trading is ever 100-percent effective, predictability does increase the chances of success in individual positions.

Over the years, I have seen many new scientific eurekas to trading. I have seen technical programs based on statistical research with regressions and standard deviations. I have seen the use of stochastics and charting that utilizes moving averages for key entry and exit points. Literally thousands of ways are available to trade the market. The key to these programs is predictability and placing the averages in your favor. Most of these programs should boast a near-70-percent effectiveness in their programs with a strict stop loss discipline if they are to be worth their salt.

I have seen traders with a 50-percent success rate who continue to succeed in the long term simply due to taking larger gains and smaller losses per trade. The main point is putting the odds in your favor. Momentum provides these odds as it pertains to a herd mentality. The herd can consist of institutions, online traders, and active traders together or separately. It is the herd that makes stocks move.

VOLUME AS A FUNCTION OF PREDICTABILITY

The best way to measure predictable momentum is by the volume of the stock. Many programs offer different measurements of volume. Examples are average daily volume, sudden volume increases or decreases, and total daily volume. An important difference must be distinguished early so as not to confuse predictable momentum with the simple rise and fall of a stock.

Many times I will see on bulletin boards and in chat rooms the mention of a stock that is trading higher by a point or two on volume of about 200,000 shares. A lack of volume tends to exacerbate moves both up and down. This means that any sudden rush of buying or selling can move the stock a few points on very few trades. A good example of this action was found in Sonic Foundry (SOFO) (see Figure 5-1).

The stock had come down to about $9.50 a share from a high near $65 a share post-split price. The average daily volume on this stock was under 200,000 shares and its float was about six million shares. After coming down off its highs to the low near 9.50, the stock began to make a reversal taking it as high as 23 in just under two weeks. The volume still never moved much over 350,000 shares a day until a big jump to near 750,000 shares when the stock reached that 23 price level.

The point is that on an average of about 270,000 shares for a week, the stock moved nearly 13 points higher. This type of action is great for those who are long the stock from near the 10 level. However, for active traders, this type of stock is highly dangerous. Lower volume suggests illiquidity in the stock that provides enough buyers and sellers at tight

F I G U R E   5 - 1

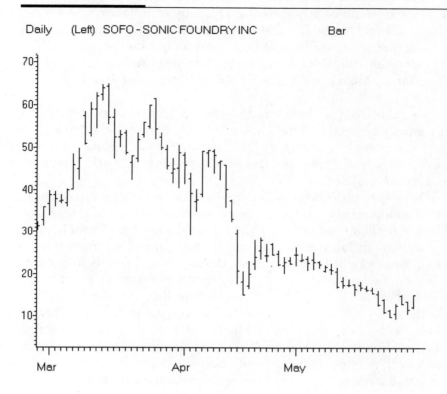

Daily   (Left) SOFO - SONIC FOUNDRY INC   Bar

price levels in which to execute a trade. For every 50,000 shares that can move the stock up 2 points, another 50,000 shares can move the stock down 2 points. Furthermore, the execution of trying to exit 1,000 or 2,000 shares in an illiquid stock becomes more risky. For example, let's look at SOFO on the way down.

On May 10, 2000, SOFO moved down 4 points on 224,000 shares of volume. As the stock was falling, the spread on the stock was very wide, at times a ½ point.

If I were long 1,000 shares at 21 and the best price to sell the stock at is 20.50, then I would be facing a loss of $500 right away without any movement yet. Let's assume the stock received some profit-taking pressure again and 50,000 shares of sell orders came through while I was still holding it long. Those 50,000 shares could easily move the stock down another point to a best exit price of 19.50. Now I'm facing a loss of $1,500 on relatively light volume. If 19.50 is too much pain to take, I decide to take a loss for $1,500.

I enter my exit order and the order is sent to the markets. The Market Maker on the best Bid is only showing a liability of 100 shares and is not a true buyer. Therefore, he fills 100 shares of my order and moves off the best Bid and now the best Bid is 19. Now I'm facing a loss of nearly $2,000 and my exit order still isn't fully executed because I still have 900 shares left. The Market Maker at 19 fills 500 of my exit order and lowers his price too.

On a total of 200,000 shares traded, the stock has dropped 2½ points from my entry price and cost me a loss of anywhere from $2,000 to $3,000. Although these stocks can move higher on lower volume, they can certainly fall just as fast. This is not the type of predictability that momentum traders are looking for.

Predictability must be weighed against the risk of the execution so that when a stop target is hit, one has no trouble in executing that stop price. Trying to fill an exit order on an illiquid stock is considerably more risky as we saw in the previous example. Any strong selling while no buyers are present can move the stock down 2 and 3 points in no time at all. Exiting the stock on a long position into strength is easy because plenty of buyers are willing to buy your shares that you want to sell.

On the other side is the possibility that you are selling to a limited base of buyers and driving the price lower to make it attractive enough that they will finally step in and fill your whole sell order. In an illiquid stock on lower volume, this can easily cost a loss of multi-point potential. For active traders, these kinds of losses must be avoided if the plan calls for a more strict stop loss adherence.

VOLUME AND PACE

Many traders will look at the rise from 9 to 23 and consider this momentum. Although the rise is certainly great to see for those who are holding the stock long, this isn't the momentum that provides predictability. For momentum to provide predictability, we like the volume to move on a pace that is moderate to fast. The pace of a stock is the trades per second or minute. This is usually a visual presentation on a Level 1 screen that is reflecting the time and sales ticker. Using Real Tick software, I am able to see a shading effect for every trade on the stocks that I have listed and I like to think of the pace as those joining a party. The more participants you have in a short period of time, the better the party. Volume indicates interest in the stock and the pace of the trades indicates the current interest in the stock. A fast pace with volume indicates enough momentum by which to trade.

For example, let's assume a company receives pre-market news that they are in a deal with Microsoft in which Microsoft will take a 30-percent stake in them. Yesterday, the stock closed at 20 and today is being bid up in pre-market trading to 23 on total volume near 2,000,000 shares. At first look, we see the volume and easily see that the interest is present because of such huge volume. However, we look a level deeper and see that four 500,000 blocks went off, totaling the two million shares. Although the interest from the volume is certainly present, the momentum is not because the amount of traders interested in the news was no more than four institutional type buys.

Therefore, we need to distinguish volume from pace. Pace is the rate by which trades are happening. We want to know if there are 60 trades per second, 300 trades per second, and so on. Two million shares of volume on 10 thousand trades is much better potential for predictable momentum than four 500,000 trades equaling the same amount.

PRICE ACTION

The next aspect of momentum is price action. A stock that trades two million shares in a day but only has a range from 6¼ to 6½ is not a momentum stock. The volume and interest are present. The pace is great as a lot of trades occurred to form the high volume. However, the stock did not move a bit, providing no profit opportunity. We see this somewhat often in small stocks with large floats or on companies that are bought out at a certain price level. An example of this was Novell Inc. (NOVL) (see Figure 5-2).

Novell Inc. (NOVL) made a great move from 1998 when it was in the single digits to over $40 a share. Recently, the stock has pulled back to single digits and is now looking rather stuck. The volume each day is excellent in the near-5-million-share average area. The price range, however, was no more than a ½-point in the last week of May 2000. The float on this stock was 299 million shares. With so much stock traded each day, the interest is certainly there, but the momentum is weak, providing little opportunity, as explained with the narrow intra-day range.

PREDICTABLE TRADE VOLUME

Therefore, for a stock to have predictable momentum, it must have larger volume. I like the stock to have at least 50,000 shares of volume in pre-market trading. Within the first 10 minutes of the trading day, I like to see the volume at 200,000 to 500,000 shares traded. After the first hour

FIGURE 5-2

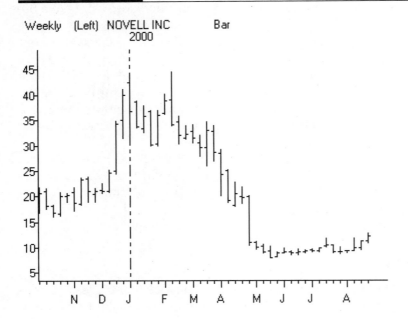

Weekly   (Left) NOVELL INC   Bar
                      2000

of the trading day, I like to see volume nearer 1 million shares traded. I feel this type of volume provides enough predictability for momentum. In addition to the volume, I like to see the pace of the trades at close to 45 to 60 trades per minute. This lets me know that there is enough interest in the stock that is indicative of the volume reading for the day.

Finally, the stock must create a large enough intra-day range that will offer enough potential. This intra-day range is where the unknown of the trade occurs. We develop our expectations reasonably to take profits at key price areas based on how much of a range we expect will be made. Sometimes we expect a range of 10 points to be made, whereas on other trades, we may feel only one point will be available. In each case, we must develop a plan of entry and exit relative to these expectations.

Momentum defined as a rate of change in the pace of trades entails several tradable options throughout a trading day. Momentum accelerates and decelerates within tradable ranges that key us into entry and exit areas. A slow momentum stock can provide the same profit potential as a fast momentum stock. The profit potential is the same, but the time it takes for that profit potential to be realized is different. This is where understanding momentum and setting reasonable expectations in each trade enables a trader to take more profits out of a trade and keep losses small when the trade does not perform to expectations.

Active traders are indifferent to the pace of momentum as long as it offers a reasonable amount of potential for profit. I have seen traders hold a daytrade from 9:30 A.M. EST to 4:00 P.M. EST because the trade offered a nice, slow, consistent climb all day long with very little selling pressure. I have also seen traders hold a stock for no more than 30 seconds because the momentum and price action was such that exiting the stock into strength was the proper exit strategy. Whatever the momentum, as long as the trade is performing to expectations, it can be held. When the momentum shows a conflict in expectations, then it is time to assess how much of the position to exit and at what levels. The following section provides a few examples.

A slow momentum stock will certainly test your patience. Active traders tend to want their profits and want them now. Typically, in this kind of trade, a stock will make a very slow move upward with several market participants selling a lot of shares on the way up to fill client orders while supporting the stock on the opposite side of the trade. The interest in the stock will be a steady flow of volume with a few surges in volume as traders see certain Market Makers adjust their price levels and elect to trade the stock for a quicker scalp type play. The slow momentum stocks offer three different possible trades. The first trade is the buy and hold trade.

The buy and hold trade will entail a trader entering the trade near the absolute top or bottom of the day. Let's assume that we are going long in this situation. As the trading day begins, a trader will look for a bottom at nearly the beginning of the trading day. Typically, he or she will look for any selling pressure to wane, the Bid level to strengthen, and then an up-tick in the price of the stock to confirm the reversal to the upside has occurred.

Often the stock up-ticks right at the open, at which point traders may elect to go long immediately. Once the stock is entered on this bottom, the stop price will be placed at the price that the stock failed to break below. For example, if a stock bottomed off of 20 and up-ticked to 20⅛, then the stock's stop price is no worse than 20. The reason for the trade is that the expectation for 20 will not be broken to the downside. If selling is at 20, then traders will exit the trade with a small loss.

After the trader enters at the first up-tick of the trading day, he or she will begin to monitor stock participants who may be supporting the stock as it rises. Conversely, the trader will be also be looking for market participants who impede the rise of the stock. We call these market participants the *ax* of the stock. They are not allowing the stock to move higher in price at a faster rate. A Market Maker may do this for many reasons and none of which you may find explained in an unmonitored chat room or bulletin board service. Many refer to the axing of a stock as some sort of Market Maker manipulation in which they drive the price up or down to hurt retail and active traders. Although Market Makers clearly have many intentions, focusing on active traders is one of their least priorities. They are filling orders for sizes in the six figures. For the most part, they could care less about my 1,000-share order unless it helps them fill their client's order.

Typically, Market Makers will try to fill orders in a way that is advantageous to their clients so that they receive more orders. They make money on the spread of the stock as well as on commissions by filling client orders in a timely and advantageous fashion; receiving more orders allows for increased revenue. Their priorities lie within their own inventory and executing client orders. Active traders are less important unless they are being used to fill these orders. The comment that Market Makers are driving the price down to buy it back cheaper is one of comical relief for me at times.

This assumes that Market Makers purposely hurt active and retail investors solely for their own amusement. Again, we are last on their list of priorities to see this action as a solid explanation for why stocks move the way they do. Do not blame Market Makers for your profits and losses. They have no idea who you are, nor do they care. They are filling an order for 100,000 shares on which they make commissions and profit on the spread. We will show you a few examples of this later in the book. For now, just realize that Market Makers are more concerned with other things than what active traders are doing.

COMPETITION MENTALITY

The following section describes how many traders actively trade and their logic behind their moves. It is not intended to provide a cookbook of methods that I use, but simply to understand how others can affect the movement of a stock. Specific methodology will be given in later chapters describing the Mtrader method of playing predictable patterns.

Getting back to the buy and hold trade, traders will watch to see what these market participants are doing in the individual stocks to assess if they are true buyers or sellers and whether or not this stock has potential to continue an upward move. Much of this action is relative to the information found in the time and sales ticker. They assess the ratio of buys to sells. They will look for two things. If the stocks have a ratio to the buy side, then they will continue to look for signs that the buy-side pace is weakening.

Should this occur and the stock stops in its tracks, they will look at the sell side pace to see if it picks up. If the selling pace increases, they will next look to see how much of the selling is being absorbed. As a stock climbs and then pauses, many active traders will become impatient sellers, putting pressure on the downside. However, if true buyers are in the stock, the selling will be absorbed and not fall much. If traders see this accumulation of shares on any impatient selling and relative profit-taking, they may want to continue holding the trade.

At each level, they continually monitor this price action and begin to devise an exit strategy based on what they are seeing. One option that most employ is to sell a portion of their trade at a reasonable price level and hold the rest for a possible move upward. This way they lock in their profits and hold the rest for more possible potential. After the first lot is sold, they trail the stop on the rest if it continues to climb. For example, if the stock was bought off 20 for 2,000 shares and made a nice, slow climb to 21, then a trader may elect to sell 1,000 shares for a gain of $1,000 and hold the other 1,000 shares for a possible move to 22 or higher. If the stock moves to 22, then the trader may elect to sell 500 more shares at 22 for a gain of $1,500 and hold the remaining 500 shares. This way a trader can lock in sure and safe profit while letting a bit more of the position climb further. Any signs of negativity that the stock may pull back more sharply and the trader will exit the trade with all shares, profiting from their experience in watching such price action.

The second trade is the pullback trade. As we discussed in the previous example, a stock under heavy accumulation may make a slow climb with a few small pullbacks. Traders will do one of two things on this pullback. If traders entered in near the bottom of the trade, they may want to add to the position on pullbacks as long as the trade is performing to expectations. For example, if a stock bottoms off at 20 and moves higher, traders may buy 1,000 shares at 20.06 or 20.13 and watch the action. If the stock struggles to break 20.50, they may want to sell their position for a small profit. If the stock moves to near 21 on price action that is favorable for a small climb, then they may want to buy another 1,000 shares on a pullback from a move over 21. This way they have averaged up on a stock that is performing nicely and meeting expectations.

I never recommend averaging down on a losing position. I can't see the logic in buying a stock that is not performing to expectations. According to stop loss discipline, a trade is exited as soon as the reason for entering is no longer valid. This is not to say you can't exit the trade and re-enter at the next bottom. A stock selling down past your buy price is a reason for an exit, not a reason to buy more in hopes that your average will provide an easier exit. The other way to play a pullback is for those traders who miss the initial bottom but are looking for an opportune time to enter the trade without having to buy the highs.

Suppose the stock moved from 20 to 21 under nice buying and accumulation and has paused. A trader will look for any selling pressure that may bring the stock back down to near 20.50 or 20.75 in which he or she will enter the trade looking for a break of the high at 21. If the stock breaks 21, he or she will begin to utilize the same strategy as the buy and hold trader that is in from a cheaper price. Otherwise, the trader may just exit the trade under 21 in the expectation that 21 will not be broken to the upside. Basically, a pullback may be used to add to a winning position or to enter the trade with expectations of higher prices after the real bottom has been missed.

The third type of trade from a slow momentum stock is the breakout play. This tends to be a trade more for scalpers in slow momentum stocks relative to active traders. I understand that breakouts can offer incredible returns for short-term traders. However, in relation to daytrading and momentum trading, breakouts are more for smaller, quicker profits. The following section examines two ways a breakout play may occur.

If you remember, we mentioned earlier that many traders watch Market Makers throughout the trade to try and figure out an intention on whether that Market Maker is a true buyer or seller. Once active traders figure out the ax, they will often look for the ax to lift the Ask price higher after filling the client orders. Normally, an ax will lift his or her price after filling a large order. A big block at the Bid price or lower normally crosses the tape at this point, signifying that the order is filled and the ax raises. At this point, traders may elect to enter the trade for a quick .25 to .50 point in expectations as buying comes in once they see the ax is finished selling the stock at that price level.

A breakout play may result from a new intra-day high being made. Using this example, if a stock moves from 20 to 21 and pulls back to 20.50 and pauses again, then a trader may look for buying back to the 21 area. If buying and pace increases at 21, then a trader will elect to buy at 21 or better for the expectation that 21 will be broken. If 21 fails to break, the trader takes a small stop loss. If 21 is penetrated, then expectations for the trade are met and a trader will most likely exit at least half of the position under 21.50 for surest profits.

Normally, breakouts move up a small amount and pull back sharply, forcing traders to be fast to enter and even faster to exit. Some of these breakouts over new highs unfortunately only move higher by .13 of a point, disappointing many traders. However, most scalpers are trading at least 1,000 shares, and .13 of a point profits them $125 for the trade, so they do enjoy breakout plays.

Slow momentum trades aren't sexy and do not provide a lot of excitement. However, if a trader is to be successful for the long term, excitement should not be an emotion that he or she should chase after anyway. Trading is about maximizing profit potential while minimizing loss. It should not provide excitement to profitable trades, nor should it provide anger and frustration to a losing trade. This emotional roller coaster is a big cause for a trader's lack of clarity when analyzing a trade. This lack of clarity impedes a trader's ability to learn and create a database of experience for how stocks move and the price action that they display.

INITIAL PUBLIC OFFERINGS AND FAST STOCKS

Fast momentum stocks are the trades that draw people to trading. Fast momentum inherently provides the battle between good and evil that so many traders experience when beginning to trade. Typically, fast stocks provide great profit potential but offer a greater chance for sizable losses. The clearest example of a fast momentum stock that is dangerous to day-trade is an *Initial Public Offering* (IPO). We all hear how much money traders have made on IPOs. What they fail to tell you is that they were given shares at the offering price rather than at the price where the IPO opened. For example, ONI Systems (ONIS) was priced at $25 a share (see Figure 5-3).

Being able to participate in the stock at the offering price compensates traders who are big clients of institutions and spend a lot of money with them. Recently, online brokerages such as E*TRADE have been able to offer shares to their clients through a screening process to allow great access to IPOs at the offering price. ONIS opened the day near $60 a share and moved as high as $80 a share, which is nearly a 55-point increase in the price of the stock from where the offer was. Traders in chat rooms and bulletin boards will scream about how much money they made on the IPO. The reality is, however, that active traders need to know how tradable IPOs are *after* the stock opens for public trading. This means that we need to know how to profit from the trade as it moves from $60 to $80.

F I G U R E   5 - 3

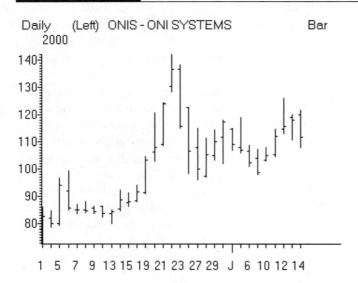

Daily   (Left) ONIS - ONI SYSTEMS   Bar

The reality is that an IPO is not an easily tradable stock once it opens for public trading. As we watch highly regarded IPOs trade, they are fast and furious in the pace of the trade. The stock will trade nearly two million shares in a matter of minutes as institutions and active traders alike are buying and selling the shares of stock. A stock that trades at nearly 300 trades a minute is just too fast to obtain a desirable execution.

I have seen numerous trades in chat rooms where traders place an entry or exit order on the stock only to see their actual execution price many points away from that desired level. We have seen traders lose 10 to 15 points in one of these trades simply because of the poor execution ability in many of these stocks. One would have to use an ECN to trade an IPO after it opens and even then, it is difficult at best to get a great execution price.

Traders can forget reasonable execution prices on SNET and SOES as Market Makers are jumping all over the place on IPOs filling orders. Rarely do they stay on the Bid or Ask price for very long. This lack of execution reliability is what makes trading extremely fast stocks and IPOs after they debut so dangerous. I liken it to gambling because a trader has little readability in the action of the stock due to the jumpiness of price levels. When a trader cannot read the stock and has trouble with the execution of fair prices, then the stock becomes a dangerous trade that is best left to watch for entertainment.

Sure, in some instances, traders can make some profits here and there on IPO's intra-day after they debut. However, over the long term, trading IPOs will cost more in losses than that in profits to your average trader. Do not let those who trade IPOs make you think they are easily tradable at the time they open. They are not. The pace is too fast and the readability of the price action is difficult at best. Much safer momentum trades are available in which to participate.

NEWS ALERTS

One of the active trader's most favorite fast momentum trades is the news alert. News alerts are provided in real time mainly by a news service such as Bloomberg, Dow Jones, Comtex, PR Newswire, or Reuters. Some services such as NewsWare Inc. provide access to most of these at once so that traders can have the news scrolling on their screen while they are trading. Once a bit of news catches their eye, the traders bring that stock on their Level 1 and Level 2 screens, assess the risk and reward scenario, and then execute the decision according to their expectations. This is just one more example of how real-time interactive data can provide active traders with more power over the Internet than they ever had before.

News alerts are generally faster plays as well. Scalp traders look to enter the stock at the price when the news first comes across the wires. After they enter the stock, they look for late-to-the-party momentum players to bid the stock higher. As the stock rises, the scalp trader will exit the trade into strength from usually no more than 1 point in profits. Sometimes the stock will move higher, sometimes not. This is the benefit to exiting into strength. A trader is assured to exit the stock when he wants to, not when he has to.

A typical news alert trade will occur in the following manner. Let's say that at 10:30 A.M. EST, stock XYZ announces a three-year, $1-billion contract to provide Microsoft with software support. This news headline comes across several wires such as Dow Jones and Reuters. Active traders see this information and begin frothing at the mouth. They pull up stock XYZ on their screen and find the stock is trading at $7 a share.

Many traders will quickly assess the risk of the trade by looking at the Bid size in case the stock does not begin to get buying. They want to make sure that any impatient selling won't cost them a fast ½ to 1 point in losses if they are wrong. They will look to make sure the price levels are fairly tight of no more than .15 in spread. They will also look at the chart to see if a price spike has already occurred and whether or not the stock is already up on the day, signifying that the news may not be fresh.

Furthermore, they look at the volume to see if the stock has a substantial volume or not. Remember that volume is important in assessing interest and momentum potential in a stock. If a trader sees a news alert and the stock already has 2 million shares traded but a narrow intra-day range, it may tell them to lower expectations for the potential in the trade as it may take too much buying to really move the stock higher. A common mistake that many traders make also is to assume that when they bring up a news alert stock and the volume is low, that the stock will not move. I tend to think in the fashion that low volume means the news may not be out yet and it may provide a reaction soon. The other side of the coin is that if the news is out and the volume is low, then no one cares and the stock will more than likely not move. This is the importance of being able to assess a stock's potential once the news alert is given. Active traders who have been doing this for a while are able to do this as fast as their software can bring up the information in front of their eyes.

A split second later, they either buy the stock at the Ask or decide to let it go. In most cases, they do not try to enter the stock at the Bid because the chances that someone is selling stock will be much less. Also, they do not chase the stock as it is rising because more often than not, chasing a stock will result in buying near the top of the price spike, lessening the profit potential. If a stock is bought a .50 point higher than the price at which the news was alerted, then they are giving up much of the potential, assuming the highest expectation for the stock to rise is only 1 point. This is what differentiates a trader who is playing high-percentage news trades or low-percentage. I only enter trades that are fresh and only if the stock has not reacted to the news yet.

Once a trader enters this trade, this is where external forces come into play that are quite interesting. First, the headline itself is catching thousands of traders' eyes. Remember that although active traders may not be able to move overall markets, they can certainly have an effect on individual stocks. As thousands of traders see the headline and react, trades begin to occur and the time of sales prints begin scrolling. Volume increases and the pace of the volume quickens. This shows that interest is present and the stock has potential to reach expectations. The hype and comments that follow in some of the free chat rooms is quite comical and it is very easy to spot the amateurs from the professional traders among the hypers. However, the adverse effect of what happens is that newer traders buy into the stock on the excitement generated in the room. This is when they end up buying the stock near the top of the price spike, causing them frustration and losses.

Traders who are currently in their positions will hype the stock incredibly to newer traders. You can often hear comments like this:

"This news is incredible. This stock will go to 50 in no time."

"The long-term chart is great on this stock. There is very little downside and tons of upside."

"This is a buy if I ever saw one."

"This is your last chance to buy at single digits."

"VOLUME alert, this stock has momentum and ain't stopping for no one."

"Ooooooh, baby, this one is going to fly!"

Here are the comments from room leaders:

"Congratulations to those who bought early. We always get them before the market does."

"The market is finally waking up to the news and they like it. Whooo-hooo!!"

"Here comes 8. At least 10 is in the definite future and I would easily expect 20 to be hit in the next few days."

"I'm posting the whole story because this news is great. Just read it and you will understand."

From this scenario, a trader must be aware of a few things in order to not get caught buying at the top of the price spike. Anyone who is consistently hyping these stocks is not a professional trader. They are amateurs or they are room leaders that have enough knowledge to understand that if they continue to hype the stock, enough momentum from the members will allow them a better chance to exit the stock with the surest profits. The rest of the members are entering and getting stuck in at higher levels as the stock is falling.

Professional traders will quietly enter the trade, watch the price action of the stock, and watch the hype that is providing extra momentum that they can exit into on the buying strength. Then they quietly exit the trade and move onto the next trade or wait for a reasonable pullback to enter again. One thing to be looking out for is a stock that is being repeated over and over again by a room leader or a specific trader. They are clearly in the stock at lower levels and are trying to entice more buying from those who follow them in hopes that they can exit to the flock of late buyers.

These subtle forms of hype will only get better and more organized as the online revolution evolves. It is up to us to really challenge ourselves to ask what the underlying reasons are behind these comments. Question them openly if you feel they are doing anything that may misrepresent the true intentions to a stock trade. News alerts are a great form of trader momentum by which a trader can profit. However, traders need to be aware of plenty of instances so they do not get caught buying the stock near the high of the price spike.

Just as in slow momentum stocks, pullbacks on news alerts are also a viable trade in which active traders can participate. For example, let's assume this stock moved on the news from $7 to $10 on the momentum, allowing traders to clearly exit into strength along the way. The first cautionary point to this move would be from those who were caught chasing the stock further away from $7. The $3 move will entice traders to chase the stock the next time they see momentum. More often than not, they will get stuck at a price level that serves as resistance. Therefore, they will couple their frustration of missing the move on this stock from $7 to $10 with the stop loss taken on the next play as they bought the top of the price spike.

It is impossible to tell with 100-percent certainty where stocks will move to on a news alert. Therefore, you must buy nearest to the price at which the stock was alerted and exit into strength as the stock climbs. If you chase the stock higher with the rest of the late-to-the-party buyers or exit when you have to instead of when you want to, then you will find yourself frustrated with less profits than you would have liked to take.

Assuming our stock moved from $7 to $10, then traders will be looking for a pullback on the stock that will offer a scalp trade. Normally on this price range, they will look for a pullback on the stock to near 8¾ to 9 for a scalp trade. This provides them with enough potential to the upside of about a .25 to a .50 point in potential. On 500 to 1,000 shares, in their minds this is more than enough profit potential to risk a trade. If the price action at this area does not look promising and looks to fall further, traders will get more interested.

A move to $8, for example, would bring in traders expecting .50 to .75 of a point in potential based on the momentum. Not all pullback trades offer this potential, but normally, if the momentum from $7 to $10 was strong, then willing buyers should be present to provide another trade off a pullback level. Later when we discuss oscillation plays, we will discuss how to spot pullback bottoms. The final comment I want to make on a news alert pullback play is that once again, you will hear comical conversation in the chat room and on bulletin boards regarding this pullback. For example, we may see these comments:

"This news is weak. This will be back to where it started in no time."

"I do not see why people think this stock is going anywhere. That news was nothing exciting."

Two possible scenarios invite these comments. The trader missed the move altogether and has to explain to him- or herself why he or she was justified in not getting in the trade. The other is that he or she is now short the stock and is trying to panic late-to-the-party buyers into selling the stock and hopefully providing more downward pressure. Those who are stuck in the trade at higher prices are providing comments of why we should buy the stock again. Either way, be careful of comments you see in these chat rooms and on bulletin boards.

Push yourself to think about the underlying reasons why such comments are said. Remember, most professional active traders are the silent majority simply playing the stock based on what they are seeing and not what they are hearing. They do not need to continuously talk about a stock in which they currently own a position. If the trade is to perform to expectations, then their intelligence and trading acumen will prove them right. Hyping the stock will not. If they are wrong, then they take a stop loss immediately. They do not provide commentary that tries to entice buying so that the stock returns to a level that they can exit at again. The more traders talk in the rooms about specific stocks, the more they seem to uncover their true intentions. Realize these intentions and profit from them, rather than become a victim of the trade.

I have discussed in this chapter the ability for momentum to provide predictability. I discussed the potential for slow and faster predictability as it pertains to a few different scenarios. In the next chapter, we will discuss a few niche patterns that I have been tracking, following, and exploiting for years. For now, understand that the pace of the trades relative to volume and price movement defines momentum. Lower volume will lessen the predictability. Traders must be cautious of widespread, low-volume stocks for safety. They tend to cost more in stop losses than profits to both newer traders and experts. More experienced traders are able to possibly profit by splitting the spread and reading the market participant intentions. However, in the beginning, it is best to stick with more liquid stocks that have a reasonable pace and good volume for safety. When assessing a trade, do not be fooled by the hype in chat rooms. This hype is posted for their own benefit, not yours.

6
C H A P T E R

PREDICTABLE PATTERNS

Over the years, I have identified, tracked, and exploited a few niche patterns that tend to repeat themselves over and over. Although these patterns don't always repeat themselves in the same manner, they do a good percentage of the time. The key to high-percentage trading is identifying what will happen a good percentage of the time and exploit it to the fullest. Too many traders simply jump on stocks that are moving without a game plan. A lack of a game plan tends to overwhelm traders due to the large amount of data they are required to absorb in short periods of time. If you know what a certain pattern will do a good percentage of the time, then you increase your winning percentages.

The purpose of this chapter is to point out four predictable patterns and discuss them at the basic level. You will learn how to identify them, track them, and predict their movements. The next two chapters will take an advanced look at all the factors that can influence these patterns at the macro level, which include the indicator method and the overall dynamics of the market. For now, simply follow along and learn to recognize the patterns and understand their predictability.

NICHE PATTERNS

I track and play four niche patterns: gainers, dumpers, end-of-day gaps, and news plays. Gainer patterns are stocks that are up 20-percent or more from the previous day's closing price on good news. An example would be a company that releases a favorable earnings report or is upgraded by an analyst. If reported after the bell, the stock normally gaps up the next day. If the story is very strong, following the gap up, it either sells off a very small amount and then moves upward or simply takes off at the opening bell without a dip. We buy at the first dip or sell off and ride the momentum up.

If the story is weak and the street overreacts as they normally do, we short at the first high and wait for the street to digest and understand the news. Then we exit after the downward momentum slows.

The dumper pattern is a stock that is down 20-percent or more from the previous day's closing price on mediocre bad news such as missing earnings by 1 cent. I play the bounces the following day as the street realizes they have overreacted to the news. I only play mediocre bad news and not devastating news such as huge earnings misses with companies that are dying or are dealing with SEC investigations, fraud, or bankruptcies.

End-of-day gap plays can be either dumpers or gainers. I watch them in the last few minutes of the day, looking for building buying pressure along with several other indicators that will drive the price higher, causing the stock to gap open (open higher than it closed the previous day) the next day. An added risk exposure exists to holding stocks overnight, but, given the proper circumstances, it can be worth the risk.

I touched on news plays earlier in the book, but I scan the news all day long and wait for a good story to hit the wires. An example of a good news story was when ValueJet was cleared to fly again or when Ion Laser Technologies received FDA approval to market their painless dental laser. A real talent is involved in playing news plays and several pitfalls can occur, which will be discussed in the "News Pattern" section.

The momentum that causes these patterns tends to move stocks in a very predictable manner for the next two days, time after time. If you are able to identify these patterns, you can exploit this predictable momentum. They don't always react in the same predictable manner, but they do a good percentage of the time. However, unless key market variables are in place, the patterns will not react predictably. Chapter 7, "Indicators," and Chapter 8, "Market Dynamics," will give you insight as to exactly which variables affect these patterns and how to properly play them. In this chapter, I will explain these patterns without describing the influence of these two variables. So keep in mind that these two chapters go hand in hand with this one. Let's examine the patterns one at a time.

GAINER PATTERN

The first pattern is what I call the gainer pattern. As I said previously, it is a stock that is up 20-percent or more from the previous day's closing price on good news (see Figure 6-1). You can play a gainer that is up less than 20-percent, but the predictability factor decreases. Gainers are divided into two groups: first-day gainers and second-day gainers. First-day gainers receive positive momentum the first day and on the second day after the initial move, they become second-day gainers.

I first identified the gainer pattern when I saw stocks moving on interest by active traders when particular positive news events were released over the news wires. The basic theory behind this has dated back to the beginning of the market itself. Stocks with good news would or should rise. The more interest in the buy side of the stock, the higher it should move.

FIGURE 6 - 1

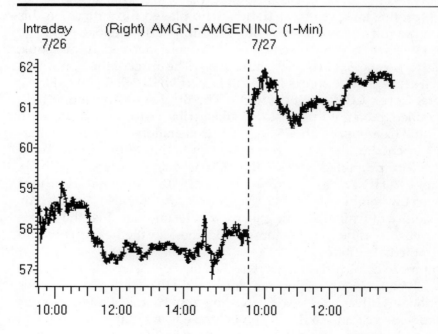

Those traders who bought the stock before or just as the news came out would benefit by the climb that the late buyers would produce. The early buyers would sell to the late buyers for a nice profit. The late buyers would buy the stock normally near the top of the price spike and the prophecy of "the public is usually wrong" continued to hold true. The smart money is in from a lower price, whereas the public is buying shares being distributed to them by the smart money from lower levels.

The type of news that I looked for early was information such as FDA approvals for a new drug, upgrades, or earnings estimates raised by analysts, and the inviting cancer cure. This type of news draws interest from active traders and would normally propel the stock higher. In the past three years, I have seen some incredibly new concepts that propelled stocks to amazing heights. Back in 1997 and 1998, if a company mentioned that they were going to put up a Web site, the stock had an instant reaction. If a stock announced they were involved in deals with the likes of Yahoo Inc. (YHOO), eBay Inc. (EBAY), or Amazon.com (AMZN), the stock would gain immediate interest. I saw incredible climbs in stocks such as Books-a-Million (BAMM) and Multiple Zones (MZON) on this kind of news. Traders who played the pattern on this type of news did very well with a lot of multi-point potential.

In 1999, we saw the likes of news interest derived from Linux, Business-to-Business (B2B), and China plays. The onset of the Linux software market propelled stocks like VA Linux (LNUX), Red Hat (RHAT), and Corel Corp. (CORL) to new highs. The Business-to-Business (B2B) sector gained momentum in stocks like Ariba (ARBA), PurchasePro (PPRO), and CommerceOne (CMRC). The expectations of the China market to be opened to the world through its initiation in the World Trade Organization propelled stocks like Qioa Xing Universal (XING), China.com (CHINA), and China Prosperity International Holdings (CPIH) to new heights. Stocks like Qualcomm (QCOM) also benefited by the possibility of China adopting its CDMA technology. Just the words China, Web site, Linux, or Business-to-Business in the headline would attract immediate interest.

The more comical issues we watched in 1999 were the Pokemon-related stocks. 4 Kids Entertainment (KIDE) and Grand Toys International (GRIN) both made incredible moves in just a few months on announcing relation to the Pokemon craze (see Figures 6-2 and 6-3). Children were trading these Pokemon cards everyday like the nostalgic baseball cards of the past.

F I G U R E   6 - 2

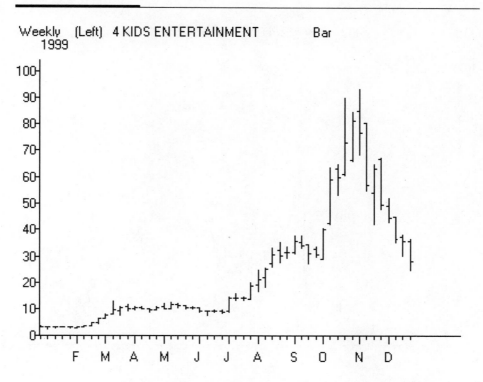

Weekly   (Left)   4 KIDS ENTERTAINMENT   Bar
1999

In the year 2000, we have seen interest in some concepts such as Fuel Cells and Genomics stocks. The Fuel Cell interest fueled runs in stocks such as Ballard Power Systems (BLDP), Electric Fuel Corp. (EFCX), and Fuel Cell Energy (FCEL). Genomics stocks were hot as the mapping of the human gene project was in full swing. Human Genome (HGSI), Genome Therapeutics (GENE), Cell Genesys (CEGE), and Protein Design Labs (PDLI) continued this same sector enthusiasm. It has been an incredible year so far and we continually await the next craze that will create this interest and profit potential.

The evolution of the gainer pattern from simple headlines of positive news such as an upgrade or FDA approval has adapted to the changing market to include hot sector plays such as the examples described previously. It is important for traders to understand when they are hot and when they are not. If traders were still trying to play the Pokemon headline, they would certainly be losing money today as the interest had died in this group.

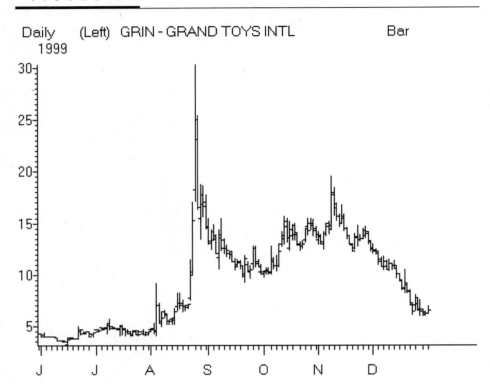

Daily   (Left) GRIN - GRAND TOYS INTL   Bar

THREE BASIC ELEMENTS

The three basic elements to the gainer pattern are positive news, reasonable pre-market volume, and a price gap to the upside. Each morning I gather news from the after-hours headlines from the previous day as well as the current pre-market morning news. If I find stories of interest, I put these stocks on the Level 1 screen and monitor their pre-market action. Specifically, I am looking for trader interest in the stock. The pre-market volume allows me to view this. Normally in pre-market trading, I want the stock to have at least 50,000 shares of pre-market volume on several trades.

If only one block is present for 50,000 shares traded, the volume may be good enough, but the interest is obviously not there. Therefore, we need to look at how many actual trades make up the total number of shares traded in pre-market. I begin this at 8 A.M. EST as this is the time that most of the quote screens begin to update with pre-market information.

After noting the action on stocks with this volume, I then begin to watch this volume to see how much is added as we near the open of the trading day. I have seen many stocks with 100,000 shares traded with about an hour to go in the pre-market trading that end up going into the open with 110,000 shares traded, showing me that the interest in the play may not be worth my time at the open.

Even if 110,000 shares have been traded in 1 hour, it doesn't necessarily imply interest in the stock. I want to be sure that the volume is a steady source of interest throughout the pre-market session and into the open. As the market draws closer to the open of the trading day, I will begin to weed out those stocks with low volume. Certainly anything under 10,000 shares traded is taken off the Level 1 screen. Anything near 25,000 shares I will keep an eye on but not be too interested unless it receives some action as the trading day begins. Anything at 50,000 or higher I will be focusing on intently for trading opportunities.

The next element is the price gap. To understand what a price gap is, we need to define the pre-market quotes in a manner to understand what a gap up is versus a gap down. Let's look at the Level 1 screen for this stock.

This stock closed the previous day at 40. In pre-market trading, the bid shows a price of 52 with the ask showing 50. Because the bid is higher than the ask and higher than the previous close, we would say this stock is gapping up 12 points. This is a gap up and satisfies the criteria for the gainer stock, assuming good volume and positive news has been released. If the stock was showing a bid of 32 and an ask price of 30, then this would signify a gap down as the selling price at the ask is lower than the closing price.

Two big points need to be made on assessing the gainer action. The most commonly asked question by new traders is why a stock is not gapping up on positive news. The answer is simple: no one knows. The label of the "sell the news" effect has been given to this type of action more often than not when traders cannot explain the existence of this scenario. If you remember, I talked about late-to-the-party buyers purchasing shares from the smart money. The smart money buys the stock at lower levels and then awaits an opportunity to unload the shares after the news is released and a price spike occurs. This is what leads to gaps up and then selling right from the open or just plain selling in pre-market trading as traders are exiting the position before the market opens. This gives a distinct advantage to those traders who can trade in both after-hours and in pre-market.

Another reason stocks fall on good news is something called front-running. Front-running a stock refers to buyers purchasing shares in anticipation of an event such as a planned stock split announcement or positive earnings expectations. They begin purchasing shares in advance of this prospect and if the news comes out and produces a price spike, these traders will exit the stock as the expectations for the announcement have been made, so they exit with their profits. This leads to selling pressure.

In the tape reading section of Chapter 11, "Time of Day," we will discuss how to look for accumulation of a stock and possibly benefit from the expectation of news to be released. The important thing to understand about accumulation or front-running is that it is not an illegal manipulation. Stock manipulation does occur in the marketplace; however, blaming stocks that are falling on good news is not manipulation. Understanding the possible reasons behind the stock's counter move from common thought will make you a much better and more indifferent trader. Things happen for a reason.

The second thing to watch on price gaps is where the actual buying is happening. Many times I see a stock gapping up to a level that no real buying is happening at. Using the previous example, if the stock was gapping up at 52 from a closing price of 50, I will see a Market Maker at the bid of 52. However, when I check on the Time of Sales information, the traders are actually looking closer to the 51 area. In pre-market trading, Market Makers are not obligated to fill shares with firm quotes. They can gap the stock up to 100 on a $30 stock if they want to. They aren't required to fill an order at those prices and are usually urged to make the quotes more inline with real demand for the stock as the opening of the trading day draws near. The current trade-or-move rule alleviates this action by forcing Market Makers to unlock or uncross the quotes with 10 minutes to go in the pre-market trading. This way, traders know exactly where the market participants are willing to buy and sell the stock.

In pre-market, Market Makers are trying to get a feel for where buying and selling pressure will happen and adjust quotes accordingly for when the stock opens for trading to the general public. If a Market Maker is showing a 52 bid on a 50 closing priced stock, he or she may be trying to create interest for buying from unknowing traders or willing traders. If he or she sees buying coming in, the Market Maker may actually be a net seller on that stock and although not filling any buy orders at 52, maybe he or she is selling to traders at 51.50 on the other side of the trade. We usually never know until an order is filled.

The best thing to do usually in pre-market trading is figure out at what level the ECNs are trading. This gives a clear picture as to where traders are willing to participate. We can see these prices again on the Time of Sales window. If the Market Maker is sitting at the ask of 52 and trades are happening at 51, we can bet that the Market Maker at 52 is not a real buyer.

Therefore, when watching pre-market action, understand that not all good news attracts interest shown by increasing volume, nor does it guarantee a price gap up. Beware of the fake Market Maker bids and asks on stocks if the prices that trades are happening at are farther from their quoted prices. They are not liable for pre-market orders up until the trade-or-move rule goes into effect. This happens within 10 minutes to go in pre-market trading.

Now let's assume we have a true price gap, positive news, and great volume. This is a stock that I will keep on my Level 1 screen for the open of the trading day. As the pre-market trading moves along, I will be weeding out those stocks that do not fit this criteria and delete them from the quote screen. I do not want to focus on stocks that have little or no predictable momentum, which is usually associated with low volume. The next thing I want to do is bring these stocks up on a Level 2 screen (see Figure 6-4).

The Level 2 screen shows us where the Market Makers and ECNs are at each price level. This also shows us the sizes they are willing to buy and sell. We want to use the Level 2 screen to assess our risk in the trade as it pertains to executions and readability. By this I mean, how easy will it be for me to enter the trade at my desired price? More importantly, if I am wrong, how easy will it be for me to keep a reasonable stop loss in trying to exit? The readability is associated with being able to identify the players of each stock. I want to know if I can identify major buyers or sellers of the stock so that I may try to follow along with their support and resistance.

When first assessing a Level 2 screen, we want to know how many market participants are at each level. The number of participants can work both for and against us depending on how we look at each stock. If we bring up a stock like Cisco Systems (CSCO) or Microsoft (MSFT), we will see a lot of Market Makers and ECNs at each price level.

Although this makes execution risk very low, it provides a tougher time for assessing potential on the stocks in terms of being able to read

F I G U R E   6 - 4

DELL	43 1/16	-9/16	200	Ot	16:
High	43 7/8	Low	42 1/8	Acc. Vol.	283589000
Bid	43 1/16	Ask	43 1/8	Close	43 5/8

	Name	Bid	Time		Name	Ask	Time
L	DKNY	43 1/16	09/01	L	GSCO	43 1/8	09/0
L	GFIN	43 1/16	09/01	L	SLKC	43 1/8	09/0
L	HRZG	43 1/16	09/01	L	ISLD	43 1/8	09/0
L	KCMO	43 1/16	09/01	L	REDI	43 1/8	09/0
L	LEHM	43 1/16	09/01	L	DKNY	43 3/16	09/0
L	MONT	43 1/16	09/01	L	JPMS	43 3/16	09/0
L	PWJC	43 1/16	09/01	L	FBCO	43 1/4	09/0
L	SBSH	43 1/16	09/01	L	FLTT	43 1/4	09/0
L	SHWD	43 1/16	09/01	L	MADF	43 1/4	09/0
L	REDI	43 1/16	09/01	L	MASH	43 1/4	09/0
L	INGC	43	09/01	L	MSCO	43 1/4	09/0

who the major buyers or sellers are. Basically, it will normally take a lot of buying or selling to really move a stock with a lot of market participation at each level, especially if the stock has a large amount of shares in the float. So, although we will have very little trouble executing these kinds of stocks, being able to read them for how much potential to expect is a bit tougher.

Conversely, if we have less market participation at each price level, our execution risk becomes greater. However, if buying really hits the stock and the Market Makers and ECNs aren't true sellers, this stock has the potential to move up quickly for good multi-point potential. If we can couple this with a lower amount of shares available in the float, then this stock has a real potential to run fast.

The problem that newer traders have is that they are drawn to the fast climbers without knowing the risks involved with smaller market participation at each level. Then they try to enter the stock at the desired price. When they are not filled, they chase it higher because it continues to move. By the time they enter the stock, it has reached a peak. Then, as the stock begins to fall, they try to exit fast, but the lack of market participation on the sell side now prevents a reasonable exit. Therefore, they are forced to chase the exit price lower as the stock falls. This buying near the high and selling near the low is a sign of a new trader who needs to learn the basics of stock market trading as it pertains to risk evaluation and price action from a Level 2 screen.

The optimal setup would therefore be a stock that had low to moderate execution risk with a reasonable potential for profits. However, this kind of stock is subjective to the trader. I would never make trades such as those with spreads up to a .50 point with a fast pace. Some traders may feel comfortable doing so. The end result is that you must decide what kind of stock fits your execution ability both for entry and, more importantly, for exit. When beginning to trade stocks, it is best to find an issue with a safer Level 2. This will have about five market participants near the inside price levels so that if you are wrong, it won't cost a wide stop loss.

Make sure the price levels are tight at no wider than .15 of a point, and begin to practice your execution ability from this point. Jumping into the Rambus (RMBS) or Human Genome (HGSI) issues at the start with little understanding of Level 2 risk assessment will lead to more losses than you would care to admit to.

The higher a stock gaps up, the more profit-taking incentive will occur at the open or prior to the open. Many times I will see stocks gapping up, and the Bid and Ask are falling the last five minutes prior to the open. This is a sign of profit-taking and in most cases you will see the stock down-tick from the open. I have a saying: "Selling creates value, value creates buyers, buyers create profits, profits create sellers." This means that a wise trader will know at what value profit-taking occurs, given the circumstances of price, story, and market, which will be discussed in greater detail in the market dynamics section.

TRACKING JOURNALS

After putting together a good gainer list of about five stocks that meet both the gainer criteria and the moderate to low Level 2 risk, it is time to begin to assess the current action of the gainer pattern. In other words, what do you expect today's gainer to do based on what it has historically done in the past? This is done by using a tracking journal. In fact, you should track both your gainer and dumper (explained later in this chapter) patterns: first- and second-day gainers, and first- and second-day dumpers.

Although it is a relatively simple procedure to track these patterns, it is too complicated to throw into the mix while discussing our niche patterns and is better covered as a separate topic by itself. Chapter 9, "Tracking," will walk you through each step in creating a tracking diary for your patterns. For now, what you need to know is what the end product your tracking diary will produce and how it affects the way you play a particular stock. It will tell you how your gainer and dumper patterns have historically reacted:

- How much did they gap up?
- Did they dip at the open and how much did they drop?
- How much did they bounce from the first bottom?
- How many bottoms did they show?
- Did they climb from the open with no dip and how much did they climb?
- How strong was the story behind the momentum?

What we are trying to build with the tracking diary is an expectation of how our patterns will react and give a rough game plan for the upcoming trading day. This is important information to have when trading because it will help you make your buy and sell decisions as the stock opens.

If my tracking diary shows that second-day gainers have been gapping up, but dipping .75 of a point with only one bottom at the open before resuming their climb, should I buy at the open on the first up-tick? No, certainly not. If historically the gainers have been gapping up and dipping .75 of a point before climbing again, it makes more sense to wait for the first bottom to put in and then enter the trade.

If my tracking diary shows that second-day gainers are gapping up a large amount, up-ticking at the opening bell, and climbing 15-percent with no initial dip or sell-off, what does that tell me? It tells me that if all the external forces (explained in the next two chapters) are inline and positive, I should buy at the first up-tick and then look for an exit at about 15-percent. If my tracking diary further shows that after the 15-percent climb they drastically drop, it may tell me to watch for a short at the first high. Conversely, if it climbs up to 15-percent, dips a bit, and then continually stairsteps up to newer highs, this tells me to stay away from shorting gainers and maybe I should ride the momentum a bit longer.

If my tracking diary shows that second-day gainers are currently gapping up and climbing a small amount or none at all before dropping to new lows, this may tell me to do an open short at the bell.

If the tracking diary shows that gainers that gapped up on a weak story have been gapping up, climbing a small amount, and then dropping drastically as they normally do on weak stories, you would have a pretty clear course of action. If, for some reason, even the weaker stories that gapped up climbed another point or two before dropping, it would present a different course of action.

Your tracking diary can also tell you that the gainer pattern is *not* acting predictably over the past few days due to external market influences and you should stay away from them at all costs until they once again start acting predictably.

This is as close as you can get to taking a peek at your opponent's cards. No one can predict with certainty what a stock will do, but the tracking diary can certainly tell you what it has done and might do a good percentage of the time today. Will this always work? Certainly not. Will it work most of the time? That depends on current market conditions and how diligent you are in tracking your patterns. I can tell you it has worked for me for years a good percentage of the time.

TRADING GAINERS

Again, this is only a basic discussion on the gainer pattern. External influences such as indicators and market dynamics will further refine the way you ultimately play these patterns and will be discussed in the next two chapters, but it is easier to take it one concept at a time.

Now that we have our expectations for our gainer group stocks and our Level 2 shows us moderate to low risk, we are ready to act with indifference on the specific price action from the stock. If we want to play the first up-ticks at the open, we simply wait for both the bid and the ask to rise and try to hit the ask price immediately. If we want to wait for pullback bottoms, we will watch the macro-momentum to show us that buying has started to creep in stronger and assess the individual price action of the stocks we are watching to find a relatively safe bottom. If we have been noticing slow weak bounces, we may want to go short instead of off the early tops. The idea is to adapt the strategy to the current action in these stocks and move expectations for each trade along as the stock continues throughout the morning. Eventually, we will be taking profits at reasonable levels with at least half of our shares and be trailing a stop on the rest of the position. The stock will at some point pull back to our stop price and we will fully exit our position on that trade. In case we are wrong, we are hopefully in a trade with relatively easy execution that it will not cost us a wider than desired stop price.

A few points on gainer stocks are important to know. First is the potential for *runner* stocks. I have seen many runner stocks such as Yahoo Inc. (YHOO), K-Tel (KTEL), and Microstrategy (MSTR) over the past few years make incredible moves to the upside. Those who held these stocks from the bottom were richly rewarded. However, those who tried to pick a top to short these huge gains have been badly burned, some even losing their whole portfolios. New traders should never short stocks that are candidates to be runners, and most experienced traders will know to stay away from them. If you absolutely have to short a runner-type stock, expect a wider stop loss and do not trade them if you feel your execution abilities are less than exceptional. It is not worth the trouble in trying to pick the absolute top. It is one of those high-risk trades that can end careers.

Secondly, I have used the 20-percent rule in our gainers over the past few years. Traders were typically reacting to 20-percent price levels, meaning if a stock rose 20-percent in a day, the stock would ultimately top near this price appreciation level for a good reasonable short opportunity. Over the past three years with the rise of Internet stocks and wild speculation, this 20-percent number expectation has been surpassed frequently. Stocks are climbing 40-, 50-, and sometimes 200-percent in one day, offering little predictability for the 20-percent rise rule. I have had to back off shorting strong stocks in this wild speculation market for the sake of safety as stepping in front of these trains has cost many a stop loss.

Just imagine trying to short the top on a stock from a 20-percent increase to a 200-percent increase. The downside potential is obviously incredible, but the loss would be staggering and career-ending. I have seen enough of these over the past three years to keep me sane and clear from stocks that are climbing like this. To identify a runner, mainly you will see a stock that will have a fast pace, have small pullbacks of about a .50 point to 1 point only, and be consistently making new highs all day long. These kinds of stocks are incredible from the long side but a disaster from the short side. Be very careful of shorting runner candidates in markets of strong speculation. This is just one more example of how the gainer pattern has evolved to fit the changing markets.

So far we have been describing the first-day gainers group. The gainer group is divided into subgroups of the first- and second-day. Obviously, first-day gainers are gainers that receive positive momentum on the first day. On the second day after the initial momentum move, they become second-day gainers. In first-day gainers, we primarily look for the first up-ticks and the pullback bottoms to trade.

Experienced traders who can execute efficiently and safely are capable of shorting this group on clear overreactions to the upside. However, new traders need to focus on the trend of the upside momentum when learning to trade this method.

After the initial momentum move on the first day, we move these stocks plus some other gainers that we found throughout the trading day on the second-day gainer quote screen. In understanding that active traders generally have short attention spans, we look for the momentum in the second-day gainers to lessen and provide us with both long and short opportunities. Again, from following our tracking journals, we can ascertain whether to go short early, later, or not at all. In some time periods a trader has to back off the pattern expectations if the current action says to be less aggressive from either the long or short side of the trade.

If the market is clearly strong and the second-day gainers have been strong from the open, it would be better to go long early, take reasonable profits, and short into any runs on stocks that are generally weaker than the market. This again has to be assessed on individual price action relative to how the market is behaving. If the market is staying strong and the second-day gainer group is relatively strong overall, then we would want to back off shorting this group and be more aggressive from the early buying and pullback bottoms side of the trade. All this can be continually read from your tracking journal as you write down thoughts on the market as they pertain to what you have been seeing each day. Patterns change; change with them.

This raises a question: if a gainer stock from the first day does well in the morning and then fails to stay positive and ends negative on the day, will it still be considered for a second-day gainer? By definition, the answer is no. However, I will be putting this stock on my screens for a possible short opportunity on any upside gaps or early runs that may provide such an opportunity, given all other variables are in place.

On the second day, we must do the same thing for risk assessment. The stock must still have good volume to make the stock more predictable from the open. The Level 2 screen must still show a safe execution and readability to risk our trading capital for a trade on this stock on the second day. Level 2 risk can and does change from day to day. Do not fall prey to the assumption that because it was safe on the first day, it is automatically safe on the second day. I have seen Level 2 risk change from safe to dangerous before my eyes, so stay on top of this as you look to trade each stock.

As you move along in your trading, you will begin to develop a sense of which stocks are able to fit your niche criteria for patterns. Some will break the definitional rules but still apply to high-percentage trades. Others will not make the cut. You will be able to decide on which stock is a key player for each day. For a basic review, we look for first-day gainers on the first up-ticks and the pullback plays. We adapt our expectations for each trade based on the tracking and current market conditions relative to its individual price action. On the second-day gainers, we are looking for the momentum to wane enough that we can go short off the tops and possibly play a pullback bottom. Again, we couple the external variables to the trade and relate it to its individual price action.

DUMPER PATTERN

A dumper pattern is a stock that is down 20-percent or more from the previous day's closing price on moderately negative news (see Figures 6-5 and 6-6). Such news can include missing earnings by a penny or two, analyst downgrades, and lost contracts with big name companies. I take advantage of the street's overreaction to this news by finding the turning point and jumping on just as the momentum is turning upward.

One note I want to make about this pattern is that I stay away from devastating bad news that may cause value buyers to not snap up the shares that are perceived as "on sale." News such as SEC investigation into stock manipulation, reviews of accounting methods, fraudulent charges, or bankruptcy proceedings are types of news that I want to stay away from. Mainly I do this to not put myself at risk for the possibility of the stock halting. Halted stocks can close for a few hours or a few months. Either way I do not want to lose that much control with my trading capital for an unspecified period of time.

This pattern moves along in very powerful cycles, which offers opportunities on both sides of the trade. In a strong pattern, going long off the first or second bottom will normally provide a reasonable amount of profit. In a weak pattern, normally shorting after the first run up or going long at the first low will also provide a reasonable profit. But in all cases, dumper patterns must be tracked in your tracking diary just as you do gainer patterns. The tracking diary will give you the same information and a roadmap of what to expect from the current dumper

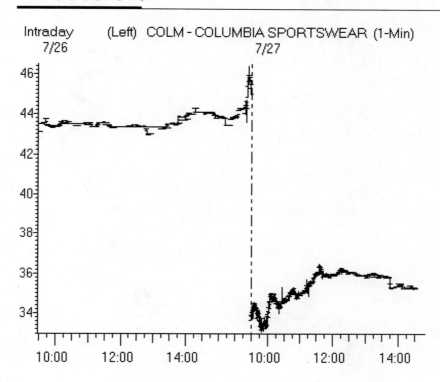

F I G U R E   6 - 5

Intraday   (Left) COLM - COLUMBIA SPORTSWEAR (1-Min)
7/26   7/27

patterns. It can also answer the same type of questions it answered for you on the gainer pattern: when to enter, when to exit, when to go short, when to go long, or when to avoid the pattern all together. But the key is you must track these patterns diligently.

As I said, in a strong pattern, pending all the external factors that will be discussed in the next two chapters, I will basically be buying the first up-tick that I see at the open of the trading day. Of course, this is if the individual stock reacts in a positive manner. What you should not do is blindly follow a set path without letting the action of the stock lead you into action. I will normally have upside expectations for potential based on my tracking of the pattern. From this tracking, I can derive an average of profits to expect. The upside target is an arbitrary target that we can use to gauge how much we are willing to hold through any of the stock's minor pullbacks.

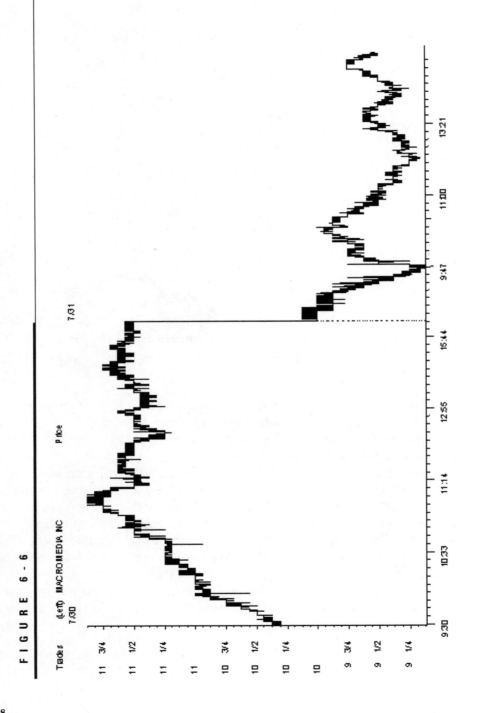

F I G U R E   6 - 6

108

As always, it is important to watch the individual price action of the stock to let yourself know if the momentum will be offering the amount of potential expected. If the momentum is such that the targets can be hit, I will be more willing to hold through pauses and pullbacks. If the momentum is relatively weak, I may be more inclined to take profits below the expectations derived from the tracking. I say this because I do not want to be holding a weak stock that will be forcing me to take a loss just because the pattern is strong. No golden rule says all stocks have to follow the current pattern. Therefore, one must take profits at reasonable levels, depending on how the momentum and price action is behaving at that time.

If the stock makes a good first bottom and offers plenty of upside potential, I will normally be done with the stock the rest of the day as the early expectations were met and anything beyond that may be less predictable. If the stock fails at the first bottom and the pattern is currently strong, I may also be more inclined to buy the second bottom with the same upside potential expectations. The problem that I see many traders face is that they do not stop out at the first bottom with a small loss. They ride the stock down to the second bottom and hope the second bottom produces a reasonable enough bounce that they can exit with the small loss or small profits.

This ultimately leads to large losses. It is better over time to stop out and re-enter if you believe in the pattern and your tracking diary. Normally, if the second bottom fails, I will take my two stop losses or small profits and be done with the stock. Over the years, I was noticing that the fifth bottom on these stocks provided a great opportunity of nearly $2 or more as value buyers came in and swept the shares up. However, over the past year I have not seen a consistency in this any longer. This is just one more example of how to adapt the expectations on the pattern to the current market environment.

As I said, when the pattern is strong, I will be playing the early bottoms on the stock and taking profits based on how the stock is performing relative to my expectations. If my expectations seem to be too high, I will take profits under those expectations. Conversely, if the stock is weak, I will be more apt to short the first run up. In a weak pattern, these stocks can make anywhere from two to six new bottoms providing excellent profit potential when shorting.

The caveat to this strategy is how far to chase the short. As most of you know, the down-tick rule prevents shorting the stock as it is falling, assuming you are unable to short at the ask price at least .10 above the best bid. Normally, if a stock is falling, trying to short the stock at the ask price will be harder. I tend to prevent shorting the stock more than a .25 point past the first top that was made. This would normally keep me from the chasing the stock too far. Again, after this trade is over, I usually back off the stock as the rest of the action may be less predictable. I never trade stocks that are way too hard for me to execute reasonably so I will not need to have live stops as the stock is moving in a certain direction.

These two strategies allow me to take advantage of when the pattern is strong and when the pattern is weak. I tend to not watch the macro-momentum of the market when playing this category as value buyers will normally snap up shares solely on value created in the individual stock. Because this individual stock action is representative of a certain response to the negative news, the overall market will not play much of a factor in the trade.

What does matter, and I have noticed this over the past two years, is that when speculation is dead or when the markets are overly nervous, such as in October 1998, April 1999, and April and May 2000, the dumper pattern is less attractive on the long side. I can reasonably assume this is due to traders wanting to place their money in solid companies with certain futures, not companies that are under-performing their earnings estimates and have clouded futures. The negativity in the market is placing a psychological effect on traders and they are less willing to go bargain shopping. In times of this negativity and uncertainty, I will be shorting this pattern more instead of focusing on the first bottoms.

I follow second-day gainers and play their predictable movements, but I have found the dumper category on the second day over the past two years to be horribly inconsistent. I have backed off trying to trade the second-day dumpers as they were providing me with too much of a headache. Before, traders would come home and see their stock down 40-percent and sell the next day. Therefore, I would be looking to short the stock again at near the open. Lately, however, it has been a guess on whether the stock would climb the next day or continue to fall. I know this because I use a tracking diary. The lessening predictability has made me more cautious and less aggressive on the dumper stocks on the second day of trading. However, patterns tend to repeat themselves in cycles and as with any cycle, this one will be back eventually, so I continue to track second-day dumpers in my diary.

END-OF-DAY GAP PLAYS

Two types of patterns can be held overnight for the gap play: gainers and dumpers. I find them to be a bit more predictable on average, but they still carry an added amount of risk. Normally, unless the patterns are currently active (from my tracking diary) and producing acceptable gains, I will not hold stocks overnight because the potential to gap down or halt is always present.

END-OF-DAY GAINER (FOR THE GAP)

I usually watch the gainers trade the last five minutes of the market to get an idea of which one is likely to gap up the next morning. The concept is fairly simple: watch the stocks in the last half-hour of the market that meet the criteria for a gainer, put them on your screen, and pay particular attention to the action in the last five minutes. We are banking on the momentum that the stock shows just prior to the close to carry through to the next day, causing the stock to gap up (open higher than it closed the day before). This upward momentum is further enhanced if the story behind the momentum is strong and is repeated over and over again after the bell throughout the night.

Many traders make the mistake of identifying and entering gap plays 20 to 30 minutes prior to the closing bell in hopes of squeezing more profit out of the play. I personally enter these trades in the last few minutes or even seconds of the trading day. This ensures that I know the direction of the momentum just before the close. Stocks have a tendency to exhibit tremendous momentum as they reach the day's end but change direction in the last few minutes. This leaves them holding a stock overnight that possesses downward momentum and can actually gap down, leaving you with a loss.

This is what differentiates a high-percentage trader from a low-percentage trader. Sure, you will miss some of the move up, but you will also miss those that turn against you in the last few minutes and in the long term, your winning percentages will be greater. I play gainers for the gap play just as we do dumpers for the gap; only the criteria changes. The criteria are

- The majority of the trades in last 5 minutes should be buys, not sells.
- Stock ends up near the top of the pattern at end of day.

- Gainers have been gapping up, as determined by your tracking system.
- Take into consideration the general market mood and check if any government numbers are due out in the morning possibly shaking the market into a sell-off.
- Consider any news, as I feel many investors come home from work and read the stories on stocks and place overnight orders. The best ones usually will be reported on CNBC and give added buying overnight.

The safe method for exiting an overnight gap play is to exit at or just prior to the opening bell the next day. However, at certain times you may want to hold a bit longer, depending on the external forces acting on the market as a whole, as will be discussed in the next two chapters. Less-experienced traders should always exit at or just prior to the opening bell to avoid the potential for the stock not bouncing after the first initial sell-off. I have seen many traders get stuck in losing trades, which wipes out a large chunk of their portfolio by holding past the opening bell as their stock enters a death spiral and never comes back. Advanced traders can use the advanced methods and techniques in the next two chapters to modify their sell criteria.

END-OF-DAY DUMPER (PLAYING THE GAP)

End-of-day dumper gaps are played in the exact same manner as the gainer gap plays; only the criteria changes. The entry and exits are the same. Two of the biggest differences are that you do not require all or most of the trades at the close to be buys, only a minimum of a 50-50 split between buys and sells in the last five minutes. The second major difference is the pattern does not need to end up near the top of the pattern but actually needs to end up near the bottom of the pattern. The criteria are

- At least 50-percent buying (50-50) in the last 5 minutes
- Stock closing price ending up near the bottom of the pattern at end of day
- You consider news to be not too damaging
- You have determined by your tracking diary that dumpers are currently gapping up a good percentage of the time

As I said previously, holding stocks overnight adds a certain amount of risk. Stocks can and have gapped down after additional news comes out after the closing bell, but if you track your patterns and follow the guidelines, it puts the odds in your favor.

NEWS PATTERNS

The last pattern I would like to discuss is the intra-day news alert. This occurs when a stock receives news of some kind while the market is open for trading. Normally, the news will come across the news wires and active traders will jump on it. News like FDA approvals, stock split announcements, or possible craze headlines like Pokemon stocks that I mentioned earlier in the chapter provide quick profit potential. These news alerts are mostly for the faster traders. At times they will provide small profits, but at other times, extraordinary profits can be made.

I happen to love these plays as I can enter quickly and then sell to the late-to-the-party buyers as they either get caught up in the excitement of seeing the stock moving higher or someone is telling them to buy at higher prices.

Basically, if you can't get into the stock within .15 of a point of the price level the stock was alerted at, it is best to let the trade move away without you. Otherwise, you will be more likely to chase the stock higher and possibly be buying from traders like myself who are more than happy to sell you my shares. Do not get caught chasing news alerts. Either get in fast or leave the trade alone.

Many times I make just as much money waiting for the stock to climb and dip, and then I enter the trade after the first sell-off on a high-momentum stock. If you missed the day's story, do not worry; you can still make money. I buy any high-momentum stock the day after the story hit on the first low of the day, which usually occurs early. This practice is a consistent moneymaker as stocks usually continue with good strength off the low. Anytime you purchase a stock, your target should be at the low of the day. Unless you are quick in reading the news and analyzing it, this is the safest way to trade as most stocks will bounce off their lows.

The news alert has a few key points that need to be discussed. Remember that news is just a catalyst for momentum. Traders actually make the stocks move higher and lower. Therefore, we need to go back to our Level 2 and our risk assessment when this comes up. First, we want to know that if we enter, how easy will it be to exit if the trade fails to move higher. If the bids are thin, I may be less inclined to enter. Secondly, I want to know the volume to see if maybe the news has already come out. The higher the volume, the more likely the news has already come out or people were anticipating the news.

Some use intra-day stock charts on the tick chart to see if a price spike on the day has already occurred. If it has, the freshness may not be there and the stock may offer less potential. Experienced traders will be able to assess the risk within a few seconds. If the risk is low and traders feel comfortable with the trade, they will hit the ask price with their buy orders hopefully no higher than $\frac{1}{8}$ above the best price at the time of the news alert. As the stock begins to climb, they will be exiting into the strength created by the late buyers. Sometimes these produce nice gains near .75 to 1 point in potential. Other times, they only offer a .25 point.

Either way, watching and assessing the individual price action will allow you to know when the right time to exit for you will be. Exiting into strength is normally the best way to go. Waiting for selling pressure to hit may cost a .25 point in slippage, and on a potential for only .50 to 1 point in potential, a .25-point loss in slippage is considerable. On 1,000 shares, that is $250. I'd rather trade with missed profits than lost profits. Exits on news stories can be a complicated process. As I said previously, the safest method is to exit as the upward momentum pauses, but as we will discuss in Chapters 7 and 8, you may want to hold your trades a bit longer, depending on the external influences on the market as a whole.

FINDING NEWS-GENERATED MOMENTUM

The best way to find a big mover is to scan your Dow Jones headlines constantly and wait for a big story. I work toward being there when the big stories break with my capital in hand. I look toward investing in the sure thing. I am waiting for that small bio-tech stock to find the cure to cancer!

I have seen stocks such as BAMM climb from 4.50 to 40 in one day and ENMD going from 12 to 83 in one day. GERON (GERN) is an example of a great news story (see Figure 6-7). Geron Corp announced that they had successfully cloned a gene that could potentially aide the fight against cancer and old age.

I do not enter into any stock until I am sure of the direction of the price. The story moves the stock. The best time to receive stock-moving

F I G U R E   6 - 7

Trades   (Left) GERON CORP   Price
8/15

stories is a few minutes before the stock market opens and a few minutes before the close. You can then react before the market can fully
understand the impact the news will have on the stock. Investors come
home from work, find the story, and buy the stock overnight.

A few years ago I was ready when the news came across my ticker
5 minutes before the market close, declaring that ValueJet had been
cleared to fly again. I made a no-brainer 1.40 when I sold the next morning. It doesn't take many of those types of trades to rack up incredible
profits. I have many times doubled my trade overnight by recognizing
and being ready for a great news story. Needless to say, patience is definitely a virtue in trading.

Another way of finding the big moving stocks is to look on the
leaders board. These are the stocks that have the largest volume and the
highest percentage of gains or losses. Programs are available that will
screen all the stocks on the stock market, such as Powertrader or First
Alert, and give you the big movers. Various other sources to find them
are available such as www.mbtrading.com (movers and shakers).

When I find a big mover with good volume, I put it on my quote
screen and watch it trade. If a large price swing occurs from the high on
a big gainer and I feel potential profits are there, I will buy when I can
identify the low with buying increasing over selling. The temptation will
be to guess, but do not buy unless you can, without a doubt, identify the
bottom.

HOW TO RECOGNIZE A GOOD STORY BY THE HEADLINE

Recognizing a good story by the headline requires patiently educating yourself. While scanning your news headlines, write down the stories you feel will move a stock while placing the symbol of the stock on your quote screen and watch its action. After a while you will get the feel for which ones create momentum and which ones don't.

Generally speaking, a story should have an impact on the immediate future earnings of the company. For example, a $50-million order will have little impact on a stock trading at $90 per share, but it would be a significant order for a stock trading at $3.50 per share. Write the symbol on a piece of paper and then rate the story using a 1 through 10 numbering system, one being the least impact you feel the story will have on the stock and 10 being the greatest. Watch the stock trade and note how much the stock price rises before the sell-off, the first oscillation.

A good story should propel the price at a quick pace over 10-percent, depending on the price. Many good stories will only move the stock .25 of a point before it starts to sell off. That does not leave much room for you to enter and exit, but if you have entered your limit buy at the initial rally price, you should be able to get out of the trade without a loss. Note the time involved that it would take to place a trade before the price goes up. Generally, you will need 20 to 30 seconds after placing your trade for your broker to execute. Note to see if the spread remains relatively constant.

Keeping an accurate log of specific stock movements will soon make you an expert at rating the momentum strength a story will have on a stock. I look for great stories that propel a stock at percentages over 20-percent, but knowing the impact good stories have on a stock will prepare you for the great ones that always come along sooner or later. Many times the impact is also dependent on the sector the stock is in. If it is a hot sector, the impact will be much greater than a sector that is on the outs with the street. Again, this will be fully covered in Chapter 8.

I use a news scanner provided by MB Trading where I can put in keywords to give me a news alert by their news reader. It is extremely helpful to flag potential news stories that might move a stock. The keywords are taken from the following story headlines I constantly look for:

- Unexpected record earnings
- FDA approval
- Patent approval

- New product revealed
- Earnings expectations
- Multi-million-dollar pact
- A large company agreeing to use or sell a smaller company's product
- An agreement of a large company to pay royalties to
- Use a smaller company's patent
- Large notable investors, such as George Soros buying a stock
- Pacts between companies

I have noticed that other news sources do not move a stock like Dow Jones will, but if I get a big story on PR Newswire before Dow Jones picks it up, I can often make more money. The buying on a PR Newswire story will likely move slower but should be bought reasonably well.

I make it a practice to watch CNBC all day long not only to get a feel for stories that affect the market as a whole, but at times you can pick out stories that create incredible momentum.

CHAT ROOM NEWS HYPES

I see anecdotal phrases in the chat rooms and on bulletin boards after news plays are announced. They are mainly the same types that I noted before in previous chapters. If a trader misses a news alert and the stock is moving well, I will read this statement:

"The news isn't really that great. I don't see why people are bidding this stock up so high."

The translation is:

"I didn't enter this trade because I hesitated, so I have to rationalize not entering to myself to make myself feel better." Or "I am short this stock now and I want to scare people into selling their shares."

Or I may read this:

"This stock is going to the moon. This is the last time you will be able to get this stock in the single digits."

This translates to:

"I am in this stock already and I am trying to get you to buy it too so I have someone to sell it to."

As you can see, these comments again are not for your benefit, but for theirs. They are said to serve their originator's motives. Be cautious of comments in the room and trade what is before you. Enter fast or leave it alone. Exit into strength or risk the downside move when selling hits. Either way, news plays are mainly for the faster traders, not the newer traders. Don't let anyone push you into a trade you are not ready for or one in which you cannot assess the risk properly.

PATTERNS TO AVOID

I avoid trading several types of patterns and stocks. I am sure successful methods are available to exploit these types of patterns, but they simply do not work for me. I tend to shy away from bulletin board stocks, or *pink sheets* as they are referred to. These stocks have been de-listed from the Nasdaq Market due to failure to comply with requirements for listing. These stocks have very sporadic movements mainly based on illiquidity and interest. Many of the stock scams on the Internet or on bulletin boards and free chat rooms try to pump and hype bulletin board stocks. Normally, they do this because on some issues, any major buying can move the stock due to its lack of liquidity.

Meanwhile, those who have entered the stock at low levels are again selling to the late buyers who are caught up in the hype. I have read many stories of sharp spikes and fast drops on this kind of stock manipulation either by fake newsletters or bulletin board and chat room leaders.

The main point to take away from this is that bulletin board stocks are de-listed for a reason. If they cannot meet the requirements of eligibility for the Nasdaq Market, then you must think about putting your capital at risk in such a stock. Some opportunities may be legitimate in these stocks, but the majority of the time, it is in your best interest to stay with stocks that have more liquidity in the Nasdaq Market. Obviously, problem stocks are on the Nasdaq board as well, but their requirements are being met and the stock is being monitored closely for illegal actions that may possibly go unnoticed on stocks trading in the pink sheets.

I have mentioned them earlier but will mention them again. *Initial Public Offerings* (IPOs) can be the kiss of death for many new traders for the reasons I described earlier. This also holds true for very fast moving stocks as they are usually one in the same.

Two more unpredictable trades are the earnings trade and the stock split anticipation trade. These two trades are strictly gambling in my opinion as one has no control over the action of the stock both in anticipation and then, if or when the news finally does come out, the reaction. As we discussed before, stocks can gap up on good earnings just as easily as they can gap down on good earnings. The predictability is very small.

Any management team can doctor their books enough to beat the estimates by one penny. I have seen things like investment income included in earnings. If a computer hardware company is selling investments to meet earnings, then I'll have some concerns on their core operations. If others focus on this issue, although the stock met or beat earnings, trades could see this as negative and gap the stock down.

Also, traders may front-run the earnings report and sell the news. Whether the selling hits the stock in pre-market or not is totally unknown and it would be just a guess. First, you'd have to expect earnings to be beaten. Secondly, you'd have to assume everyone loves the earnings report. Lastly, you'd have to hope that the "sell the news" effect doesn't hit the stock in pre-market trading. If you are long this stock, you have three strikes against you. If you are short the stock and traders love the news, you can expect a nice gap up to ruin your morning. In short, it is better to trade the reaction, rather than front-run the expectation.

A stock split is another trade that causes the excitement of the big gains versus the reality of the huge losses. Mainly traders who expect a stock split to occur at the next earnings meeting will buy the stock prior to the expected date. When the news of the split is released, they expect the stock to gap up and offer a nice profit. Stocks like Yahoo, Rambus, Dell, and Amazon.com all saw huge price gaps on announcements of this kind in the last three years. This added fuel to the trade and made some traders great one-time gains.

However, this is another risky trade for two reasons. First, if the stock split is not announced, all those who bought in anticipation will be selling. If on the next day the split is not announced, pre-market trading will normally be lower and harder to exit as everyone is beating down the stock in pre-market trading costing anywhere from 1 to 5 points or more in loss potential. Secondly, if the stock split is announced, the entire front-running of the stock may again fall prey to the "sell the news" effect and the stock will not perform as well as expected or, worse yet, produce a loss.

Furthermore, traders don't have a methodical approach for when to buy the stock. They don't say whether they should buy it one day before the expected announcement, five days, one week, or whenever. What happens if a trader buys one week before the expectations, hoping not to miss out on a run, and the market turns sour and dives? Where is the stop loss regiment on this type of play? There probably isn't a very

safe one. Again, although the rewards may be high, this type of speculation offers big losses over time. Most professional daytraders will not
risk trading 10 anticipation trades to hopefully have one or two work out,
especially if those one or two do not cover the losses on the other eight
or nine failed trades.

To be safe, I will always play the reaction rather than front-run the
expectation. This way I keep control of my capital and control of the
trade. On these types of trades, I am giving my control to the other
traders and the market itself. With the idea that these two forces exist to
take my money from me, I will not be giving them any more control than
I have to.

Another trade to be cautious of is the stock that is moving very fast
on either the buy or sell side, but no news is attached. At times like this,
the stock is a prime candidate for a stock halt so that the stock can be
reviewed for such action. Normally, the stock is usually just moving on
unfettered rumors, but sometimes the action can be explained by such
negative comments as fraud or positive comments such as a takeover
candidate. Either way, if a stock is making a strong move up or down on
no news, be very cautious as these are prime halt candidates. Again,
halted stocks could be halted for a couple hours or a couple weeks. Either
way, losing control of that trading capital is frustrating with no guaran-
teed re-open time. Once the company issues a statement, the stock is usually re-opened, but there is no telling where that stock will open at. It all
depends on the news and the reaction by the traders to that news.

IDENTIFYING SHORT-TERM TOPS AND BOTTOMS

So far we have discussed the core niche patterns that I play. We have
looked at the proper entry and exit points based on what our tracking
has historically shown, but I have not explained how to determine your
exact entry and exit points or how to identify bottoms and tops. In this
section I will show you how I have been able to identify the bottoms and
tops of intra-day swings with great accuracy. I call it my, pause, *inbetweener* buying method.

The bedrock of my trading success has been my unique ability to
call the short-term bottoms and tops of stocks. This is a learned talent
and with some practice you can also learn how to do this with increasing accuracy. Using this simple technique, I have been able to nail the
intra-day tops and bottoms of stocks with great accuracy time after time.

It takes a bit of time to learn, but it is well worth it. It is a simple method, which does not use the Level 2 techniques discussed throughout this book and is a good place for traders to start before moving on to those advanced methods. Advanced methods will be discussed later in this book.

The normal action I would expect from a dumper at the open is a sell down from the open price. I watch the rhythm of the Bid and Ask change and ignore the trades at first:

1. The first indicator of the first bottom on my trade is a pause in the rhythm of the down-ticking Bid and Ask. This can be seen on your Level 1 screen.

2. I now focus on the trades as much as possible, ignoring any out-of-bounds trades (trades that occur at a price below or above the Bid and Ask).

3. After I have noticed a pause, I look for an in-between in the Bid and Ask trade. If a dumper has sold down to a 9.15 bid by a 9.25 ask, I will look for a trade at 9.20, which is the inbetweener (trades between the Bid and Ask are the second indicator to the bottom).

4. Now I will look for buying to pick up in momentum and when it does, I will signal my bottom call. The pace of the buying can be determined by watching your Level 1 screen for an increased number of trades at the ask. In many software packages, you can see this by the total number of blinking green trades (trades at the ask) as opposed to blinking red trades (trades at the bid).

Calling the top is much the same as the bottom, except everything is reversed. Again, it depends on the trade. A simple but very effective technique in spotting momentum shifts. When you combine this with the information in the next two chapters, it forms an unbeatable combination of identifying momentum shifts.

UPSIDE AND DOWNSIDE POTENTIAL

This is a very important concept. If you do not figure out your upside/downside potential (the amount you believe it will bounce or drop), then you have no valid reason in being in any trade. You must determine potential built into the action or you have no reason to believe another new high will occur.

Before we can understand this concept, we must first talk about the law of narrowing oscillations (see Figure 6-8). A stock generally makes its largest movements within the first two hours of the trading day, between 9:30 A.M. and 11:30 A.M. EST. This is normally when the momentum, volatility, and volume are the greatest. As a result, this is where a stock shows the widest intra-day swings.

Not always, but a good percentage of the time, the swing from the first high to the first low is the largest oscillation a stock will show for the day, and the oscillations on average will only get smaller and smaller as the day progresses. This means that the next swing in the oscillation will normally not be as high as the last oscillation, just a bit smaller, like a bouncing ball.

Your upside potential on the first oscillation down is the previous high before the sell-off. The low that was hit on the first sell-off becomes your current downside potential because you have no reason to believe an oscillating stock will make a new low and so on. The next high becomes your upside potential and the next low your downside.

A low is a new low only when it is lower than a previous low and can be only counted as a new low if it climbs in price by at least a .25 point. So if I have a stock that has come off the high by enough percentage where I think the upside potential will support a .75 to 1-point profit, I will buy.

Because of the law of narrowing oscillations, they become smaller and narrowing, so you must keep adjusting the potential based on the most recent low and high if you intend to make money in the middle of the trading day. In fact, the potential on each oscillation must be reduced from that last high or low a small amount because the next oscillation will be a bit less than the last.

The opposite is true if you intend to short sell a stock. The downside potential is calculated by knowing the previous low. If XYZ traded down to $7.50 and then rose to $9, my downside potential would be 1.50. Actually, it will be a bit less if you consider the law of narrowing oscillations. Calculate the downside potential and if it is worth the risk, short it at the top.

Many times you will find stocks that oscillate every day enough for you to make profits. I know traders who follow such stocks and only trade them, knowing their intra-day patterns like the back of their hands. An example of this type of stock is Iomega (IOM). I began watching this stock every day in mid-September of 1996. I noticed it had been sold along with the other technology stocks, but there was still strong inter-

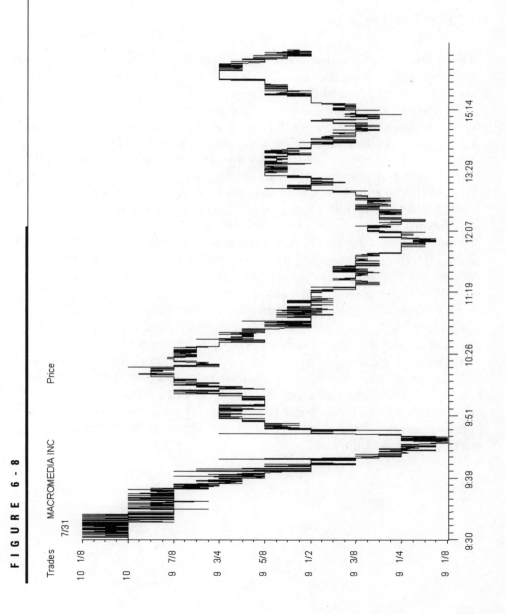

F I G U R E 6 - 8

est in this stock every day. I noticed that it would open up, sell off, and then go up to its high and above almost every day. It could have been bought at the end of each day and almost always opened up the next.

Then the intra-day trading pattern would repeat itself. What a great consistent moneymaker for the wily investor.

CORE METHODS

These are the core trades that usually make up my trading day. I try to stick with the trades that fit my risk criteria and are providing me with enough reasonable and predictable potential based either on my tracking expectations or my ability to read individual stock action and execute the trade accordingly. I have learned to weed out the useless comments I see in trading rooms and trade what is before me based on my knowledge of the patterns and my abilities as an efficient trader.

When one pattern begins to change, I will change with it or cease to profit from it. When a play becomes too difficult to reasonably execute, I will become less aggressive on that trade. Over time, my patterns and trades will be focused on those trades that give me a higher percentage potential for profit. Although I certainly don't trade with 100 percent effectiveness, trading off these patterns creates a high enough potential to be consistent over time.

The explanations of these core methods so far have been fairly basic and a successful trading program has many moving parts. In the next two chapters, I will discuss how to use an advanced look at the overall market as well as some methods that will force you to re-examine the basics described in this chapter and modify your entry and exit decisions. This is where most traders stop their learning process, at the core methods of any trading program. It simply is not enough to compete in this competitive arena. What makes a good trader a great trader is to understand the external forces that are acting on the stock and adapt your decisions based on them.

7 CHAPTER

INDICATORS

In the last chapter, we discussed my core methods and patterns that I track and play. These patterns and methods are good for beginning to intermediate-level traders and have proven to be quite successful. What separates a good trader from the great trader is the ability to see what is happening around them and not just the price action of individual stocks. If a trader does this, he or she is not looking at the whole picture. More forces are acting on a stock than simply the individual momentum of the stock we are watching.

This chapter explains an advanced technique that I use to determine intra-day shifts in the overall market. It is a way of identifying the movement of the macro-momentum. This macro-momentum can and does affect the movement of individual stocks. In the next chapter, I will go further into these forces that pull and tug on individual stocks and give you some insight on how to identify and further modify your trading decisions built on in the core methods discussed in the preceding chapter.

INDICATOR STOCKS

The incredible market climb in 1999 and 2000 lulled traders into a false sense of security. Every downward market dip was met with an upward correction, making new highs everytime. I call this a climbing market, and it rewards anyone who buys for any reason and holds, even ignoring stop losses. This is the tide that floats all boats and many daytraders get sucked into the whirlpool of investment. It is obvious that this method of trading is what wiped out many good traders in the year 2000 and is continuing in 2001. The market is no longer rewarding the investor or anyone who is willing to buy and hold, and it may never be the same again. We are moving up and down to the latest round of news like a yo-yo on a string, and the volatility and unpredictability is causing many sleepless nights for those who make their living at trading stocks.

The foremost thing that denotes the pro from the amateur is that the pro will not trade until he is aware of the percentages of success he can expect, and the amateur continues to trade when the odds are against him. In a volatile market, how does one know when the market has changed and the storm clouds are moving in? I have developed a method for changing with the market in a matter of seconds, and it has enabled me to not only know when to change, but I can even change right along with the market and continue to make money.

The statement has been made that once the market falls, daytraders will lose their money, and some did. Those daytraders who were caught holding stocks played the buy and hold game. Many investors and day-traders made good money as the market continued to climb to record highs during 1999. The professional daytrader played a different game. Let me give you an example. Let's say, for example, that XYZZ had a decent news story in a climbing market and gapped from $20 up to $25. In a strong market, we would expect about $1 of profit-taking at the open, and we would buy at around 24 and expect the first swing up to reward us $5 or $6. We would exit at the top and, providing there was sufficient profit-taking in the day or days preceding, we would go short. We would ride the momentum down for $2 or $3, then reverse again, and go long for another $2 or $3. Theoretically, we have just made $9 to $12 on a $20 stock in one day. We have seen $4 stocks move to $35 in one day, which gives us even more potential, and we continue to do that, pro-viding the stock is still swinging day after day. In six months, you may see the stock at 75 and think, "Gosh, I wish I had held that stock!" Hindsight sucks you into the buy-and-hold investor world, while the true professional has taken a lot more money out of the stock and ended each day in cash. That is the strength of the professional daytrader, and unex-pected market moves will not affect him. We essentially do not care what the market does. All we ask for is movement in either direction.

It is important for a trader to understand the dynamics of news events. The amount of movement for any one event is a tip-off as to how strong or weak the market is on any particular day of trading. In a per-fect daytrading world, we would get the same story on the same stock everyday and watch the pre-market volume and gap to understand just how many buyers and sellers are in the market. The more a stock gaps up, the more incentive there is to take profits and the more selling I would expect to see. A professional trader has a historic idea of just how certain stocks move given certain news events. This is an important platform for trading that enables a peek into the market to form some type of expectation.

For example, if a stock like Ciena Corp. (CIEN) has beat expectations by $0.02 with good forward going next quarter, I might expect a $6 gap up. If the market were not in a buying mood, I might only see a $2 gap up. In a very weak market, the story may not get any gap at all. I will watch on a time and sales screen prior to the open the amount of buying and selling prior to the open to understand the mood of the traders on that day and expect the action to mirror what may occur after the open. If I see heavy pre-market selling on a nice gap up, I will be looking to short the highs because it is obvious sellers are hitting the market more than usual. If I see no selling, then I may assume that the market is strong and the pullbacks at the open may be shallow. A professional trader will keep track of such pre-market activity to set him- or herself up for concentrating on what is higher percentage, buying the bottoms, or shorting the tops. It all comes from knowing what occurs with key news stocks in weak, neutral, and strong markets, and mother market rewards her children who track and know her best.

I will generally expect a trend to continue once the market has established one. For example, if I see $4 of general selling off the top of yesterday's gainers, I will expect the same kind of selling on the next day. Basically, I have good selling in the market, and I will short the highs until I see a change. The same thing applies for buying. I have found the best markets for the daytrader are the nervous ones where I get $4 of buying and $4 of selling, which enables me to buy the bottoms and expect good potential, and I can reverse at the highs, short the tops, and make the same potential on the way down. I watch key stocks to note any changes in the market and always keep a close stop when the buying or selling is not like it has been in subsequent days. The bread and butter for the professional trader is to develop methods to find and play the stocks that are predictable.

Generally, the stock market will give me two types of predictability. One is predictability based on value, which means that my key leaders with the most momentum from the day before will sell down a certain amount. For example, in strong markets, I generally see a .75 to 1-point pullback from the open before the initial climbs and greater pullbacks in weaker markets because of the willingness of traders to take profits from yesterday's momentum. I always look for similarities in the amount of selling and buying with the first few oscillations of the day and keep track from day to day. The other type of predictability that I look for and track is time. Many times, you will see buying and selling come into the market at specific times. A smart trader will always be looking for consistency where profits can be predicted.

When the market is uncertain and moving in unpredictable patterns, the only other method I know of to keep profits in your pocket is the *indicator* method. Indicators are stocks that have the best momentum generally; they move first and they move fast. They are usually popular stocks, such as CSCO, CIEN, and so on. What I have found to be important is to find something in the market that is somewhat the same day after day. An indicator will provide a platform of predictability in which you can play other trades and maintain a relatively safe environment within the eye of the storm called a changing market.

The idea is to find a stock that you can depend on to show you the early action, sufficient to enable you to trade the stocks that follow it. For example, if I have a good news story on a popular stock like CIEN, I can gauge the pre-market buying and selling by the expected action based on good momentum provided by the news. If CIEN is gapping up $2, $4, or $6, I can begin to understand just what kind of buying I have that trading day. I also look at the pre-market selling to get an idea of the willingness to take profits. The trading platform is determined by one stock and it simplifies my approach to trading on the day.

An indicator stock helps me determine the short-term direction of the overall market. This is important because I am not really sure about the direction of the market, and so it is necessary for me to watch and react. I allow the indicator stock to move up or down sufficiently to tell me just how much buying and selling I have as I attempt to play the early oscillations in the market. If the indicator stock moves down at the open more than I am expecting, then I know I have a weaker day, and sellers are in the market, so my attention will turn to shorting the highs. If my indicator moves up more than expected, I will be looking for other likeminded stocks to go long. The beauty of this system is that I need not do anything until my indicator shows the direction of the market to me. If I am in a stock that I purchased because my indicator just climbed and then bottomed and I felt it had enough potential to warrant going long, I will keep a close eye on my indicator to make sure it is still reasonably strong and climbing. If the market shifts negatively, it impacts the action of this stock, and I will see that because my indicator will begin to fall, which will enable me time to get out of my trade with reasonable safety. I will generally let my indicator move at least a point to make sure I am seeing adequate potential in the market, and I am not simply getting small moves up and down that tend to run up stop losses. The more volatile and changing the market is, the more important it is to enable the indicator to move up or down sufficiently to see real buying or selling and not simply little false tops and bottoms.

I use the indicator stock along with my core methods to help me determine how and which stocks to play on a daily basis. I use the core methods to spot and locate a group of potential plays, such as gainers or dumpers. I then use the indicator stock to help me determine which direction the market is going and the amount of potential the market is offering on that particular day. In addition, I use indicator stocks to help me determine and modify my entry and exit points of my core plays.

Simply put, an indicator stock is a stock that I expect to mirror the action of the market as a whole. When the overall market is strong, my indicator stock is normally strong. When the market momentum shifts, the indicator stock normally shifts. The beauty about it is the indicator stock normally shifts direction prior to the overall market and the overall market follows suit. The indicator stock not only leads the overall market, but also the other stocks that I call follower stocks chase after it. Sometimes, this lead-time is a few minutes and other times only a few seconds.

If I am in a stock that followed the indicator stock at the bottom and my stock started to show signs of pausing or weakened momentum, and if my indicator stock is still showing upward momentum, I may choose to hold that particular stock a bit longer and play with my profits. A good percentage of the time, if I have picked a proper indicator and the overall market is showing good momentum shifts, the stock I am in will pause or dip a small amount, then continue its upward climb, and finally top out after the indicator stock tops. This may tell me to hold a bit longer to see if the pause is actually a reversal or just a pause.

This is about as close to knowing what a stock is about to do as you can get. No method is 100-percent all the time, but I have found that this indicator method is fairly reliable in markets that are showing high volatility. However, it is less effective in sideways markets as well as low-momentum markets. During these periods of reduced momentum, it tends to reduce the amount of lead-time the indicator stock will give you, and they can at times be so quick, the followers and the leaders change direction at the same time.

Yes, sometimes the indicator stock does not follow suit, and stocks travel not in packs, but in many different directions at once, rendering it a useless technique. This is the importance of logging and tracking the effectiveness of it on a daily basis. When it is not working, don't use it. When it works, exploit it to the fullest. Markets change; change with it. However, you will never know unless you track its effectiveness, when it is working and when it is not.

PICKING AN INDICATOR STOCK

I gather all the news I can in the pre-market to locate an indicator stock. It is normally the most popular stock that has the highest pre-market volume and has the greatest amount of momentum. I look for stocks that are gapping up a good percentage, have great stories attached to them, and are being mentioned on CNBC and in the free chat rooms. This is where the value of chat rooms can come in handy. If there is tremendous talk and interest in a particular stock in the chat rooms and on television, it will most likely be a good indicator stock. It is important to note that we are looking not just for a high-momentum stock with a good story, we are looking for the best one, because it will be the leader and lead the market. This is also where constant mention on CNBC comes in handy. If analysts are constantly talking about it, and the pre-market gap and volume are good, it should become a candidate for your indicator stock. It is normally one of your higher priced stocks.

This is a way to help identify the indicator stock before the market opens, but a possibility exists that you may have picked the wrong stock initially. You may have picked a strong follower stock and missed the real indicator stock. This is where monitoring your stronger stocks that are gapping up in a single group on your quote screen becomes important. If you see the stock you picked as the indicator stock bottom out and the rest of the stocks following it shortly thereafter, then you picked the right stock. If you see another stock on your screen bottom or top out and the remaining stocks on your screen follow it instead, then you have picked the wrong stock. This still gives you plenty of time to re-think your decision. As you see one stock bottom out first, be watchful for the others to bottom out and start picking entry points on the remaining stocks.

As we are watching the indicator stock change momentum and climb, we want to ensure that this momentum shift will be sustained before we start buying the follower stocks. A good rule of thumb is to wait until the indicator stock climbs a full point from its bottom to ensure that the momentum will carry through and not falter. If the indicator stock climbs a full point, then it is time to start looking for entries into the follower stocks. Remember, the follower stocks are all leaders; they are gapping up also, but they are also identified on your quote screen because they meet the criteria for the core plays described in the previous chapter. Mostly gainers, but this can also work on stocks you identify as dumpers. If one of your gainers or dumpers bottom shortly after the indicator stock, it becomes a follower stock and tends to follow the indicator stock through its oscillations.

This method tends to work better early on in the trading day and becomes a bit more clouded as the day gets long into the afternoons. The best times to use this are in the first two hours after the market opens, but I have found it to be even more accurate in the first 30 minutes. Although it still works later on in the day, it is harder to read and follow. The first 90 minutes is when most of the high value targets can be found anyway. After that, you are simply playing oscillations and news.

I have found that it is a good idea to open up a one-minute chart after the trading day, beginning with the indicator, and note the time it climbed, topped, and sold. I will note the times of all the major oscillations. I will then look for the same repeated action with other similar stocks to see which ones lagged behind sufficiently to enable me time to enter not only the long positions, but also the shorts. You will find a basket of stocks this way that will consistently give you plenty of potential, but also, more importantly, time to enter and exit the trades in relative safety as your indicator moves up and down with the momentum in the market. I have found that stocks such as CSCO, MSFT, QCOM, and a few others move slowly but still offer potential and follow my indicators very well.

TRENDS

If you combine the core patterns, tops and bottoms calls, upside potential calculations, and the indicator method with overall trends, you are starting to build a very successful trading program. By trends, I mean recurring market momentum. For example, for periods of days to many weeks, the market can exhibit the same type of buying or selling pressure at certain times of the day. In the summer months of 2000, there was a trend that lasted for almost two months. It was a considerable amount of buying for the first 20 minutes following the opening bell.

I used this knowledge to add to my core patterns and indicator method to help me determine what to expect during that time frame. I would see stocks dip a very small amount; the indicator would bottom and then quickly climb. Due to this amount of constant buying pressure, the time lag between the indicator stock and the follower stocks bottoming and reversing course was reduced. This gave me less time to pick out my follower stocks for entries and I reduced the 1-point rule that the indicator must climb before buying the follower stocks.

What else this did for me was to take a very close look at the indicator stock as it paused. This overall increased buying pressure would cause indicator stocks to pause for a few seconds, and instead of changing direction, they would continue their upward climb. It enabled me the insight to sit out the first pause and ride the momentum a bit more.

As I said, when we are in markets with less momentum or periods where the market as a whole is consolidating or basing and moving sideways, this method does not work as well, unless the intra-day swings are still wide. Even so, during these periods, it does decrease your lag time between the indicator and the follower stocks. You increase your risk when you do not allow the indicator stock to climb one point and prove to you that the momentum can be sustained, and you can increase the number of times you get stopped out of stocks due to early reversals.

But these periods of consolidation can be sustained and last for long periods, forcing you to adapt to current market conditions. I have always been of the belief that it is better to sit out market conditions that are not optimal and to not chase after trades with a low percentage chance of being successful. Each trader must decide for himself the risks he or she is willing to accept. This is not to say that if the indicator method is not currently working that you cannot fall back to the core methods of playing individual stock movements, but it is nice to have the confirmation of the indicator stock tipping you off to the direction of the overall market swings.

You can see from the progression of this book that one chapter builds upon the next. We have discussed the causes of momentum; the core patterns and core methods for calculating tops, bottoms, and upside potential; and now the indicator stock method. Each one compliments the other. The next chapter will take a look at the overall market and the forces that tug and pull on individual stocks. As I said, there are a lot of moving parts to building a successful trading program. Take the time to learn the topic discussed in the next chapter, and you will not be sorry.

8
CHAPTER

MARKET DYNAMICS

In this chapter, I will discuss the larger forces that have a direct impact on individual stocks. The majority of traders only understand specific core methods as they apply to individual stocks and do not fully understand the macro forces that tug and pull on each stock as they move through their normal momentum swings. Market dynamics involves many moving parts and it is recommended that the reader not move onto these concepts until the core methods are fully understood and successfully practiced. This chapter will give you a look at the hidden forces that are commonly overlooked by less-experienced traders.

MARKET DYNAMICS

Before we begin our discussion on market dynamics, we need to know that we only apply market dynamics to our gainer groups. Dumper stocks live within a world of their own and are not necessarily subject to the sector and overall market tone. Therefore, when applying market dynamics to our trading expectations, we must remember that our first- and second-day gainers are the only groups that we have to shift our thinking on. This makes it easier and also harder.

It is easier because we do not have to think too much about adjusting our expectations on our dumper stocks. It makes it harder because market dynamics in our gainer stocks can make our patterns change and deviate from our expectations in the blink of an eye. We must understand market dynamics in full to validate our expectations. Expectations are not of any use to us if they are based on the wrong assumptions in how we expect the market, in sectors and as a whole, to react.

Market dynamics is a compilation of all the pressures you are faced with on a daily basis. It is what causes stocks to climb up to tremendous highs or lows that sometimes make no sense unless you are aware of all the pressures and how they are interrelated. The importance of accurately understanding the pressures within the market is the fact that most of the market potential occurs very early. The forces that make up our market dynamics are the overall market, sectors, individual stocks, and traders.

TWO PHASES

When a trader begins to consider market dynamics, he or she must approach it in two phases. Phase one involves tracking the movements of groups of stocks with *like-mindedness*, or the tracking results (the springboard for consistent profits) will be too confusing to be able to find any predictability. A trader must know what skews the percentages and eliminate them to find the diamonds in the rough. Like-mindedness means that given a certain set of circumstances, a particular type of momentum will produce similar movements over a short period of time. These predictable movements are what I call *historical evidence*, which is the percentages of behavior predictability over time.

For example, we are interested in the movements of all good news stocks that climb over 10-percent at the open over the last few days, weeks, and months. We are particularly interested in information on pre-market gaps, pre-market volume, the amount of selling or lack of selling at the open, the amount of climb off the first bottom, and the potential off the next highs and lows as the stock oscillates during the day. To understand the predictability and potential, you must become familiar with those movements in a dynamic market. This means that you should become a student of news momentum and how it applies to a negative, neutral, and positive market. You also have the challenge of interpreting news events and developing reasonable expectations as stocks move under the umbrella of our dynamic market.

For example, anything unexpected in our market will cause excellent momentum, both positive and negative. If a stock misses earnings expectations by 10 cents, I will look for a gap down of around 20-percent and expect value players to buy off the first or second bottom. When the pattern is in favor, I will simply buy the first up-tick and set a stop loss at about a .25 point below the buy price. I expect returns in line with the average gain for the last week minus .25 or .50 a point as I always try to leave room for error. I track these dumpers and as you will find with all patterns, they will come and go in cycles that repeat. When they are in favor, they can lead to predictable and dramatic profits for the wise student of stock movements.

Phase two involves watching the day's behavior at the open to confirm what you expect. When the market has been consistently selling gainers at the open to the tune of about $1 (depending on the price) and then running up $2 or $3, the expectations become easier and profits more reliable. But on the day that it changes, you must recognize the small nuances in the market and get out with a small loss. Foolishly holding onto a cycle that has been established because it has been your bread and butter can be devastating and you should realize that "all good things come to an end" in our stock market. You must essentially "trade on your toes" the more volatile and changing the stock market is. I have learned to change so fast that I take few losses and quickly pick up on the next profitable pattern. A good boxer will follow movements so fast that a bob and weave will be met with a solid right hand to the jaw of the unwary opponent.

I like to place my hottest stocks together and allow them to lead me during the day. If they move up well, I will have a nest of stragglers to pick from should I miss the movements of the leaders. If the leaders don't move as expected, then I will back off trading until they show me the more reliable potentials both at the bottoms and the tops. Remember, a trader needs room for error, and a trade must justify a stop or two. The market may be bobbing and weaving and whacking you on the chin, but if you pay attention, you can anticipate the next move and land a few of your own.

The winds of change that have blown across our market in the last 10 years would be comparable to the move from the Model T to a 747 Jetliner. Ten years ago, a single swing of $4 on an $8 stock was the great potential of the day. Most recently, we have seen $6 stocks move to $54 in a single day, which typifies the difference between now and then, as the market moves more toward momentum trading, holding stocks for a long period of time is diminishing.

The potential for quick profits is bringing in a vast amount of traders who have no idea how to play momentum, causing wild swings on a daily basis on the latest hot stocks. TV advertisements for self-execution trading is looking more and more like Lotto commercials hinting at instant wealth and gains far beyond what your traditional mutual fund broker has been able to attain for the vast majority of investors. Wherever instant wealth is promised, you will find the enticement to bring in the gambler instinct within individuals to our stock market.

As traders treat the business of momentum-investing as gambling, we will see wild swings in stocks and the stock market growing wider, providing more opportunity for those who are true professionals and know how to ride the swinging pendulum of opportunity. Traders who are able to establish discipline and rules are cleaning up in this environment and are finding the wild bronco exciting and wild, but also extremely profitable.

THE PLAYERS

To understand the basics of stock movements at the macro level, it is necessary to know who is behind the scenes pushing the buy and sell buttons. Although we discussed this topic earlier in the book, it warrants a closer look when moving into the macro discussion of market dynamics. The purpose of this knowledge is to gain an understanding of the time frame of each trade so a trader can place time horizons on the exit and take normal profits. The bread and butter of a professional momentum player are consistency and a thorough knowledge of the amount of profit he or she can normally expect given the circumstances and the various influences propelling the trade.

Institutions and hedge funds typically move in and out of stocks slower than the average momentum player, and can be identified by large block trades. Another way to identify the large players moving into a high-momentum stock is to listen to CNBC or read popular publications to spot a consistent interest in particular sectors with money managers and analysts. When such sector momentum is spotted, it puts a longer time horizon on many trades and you can play the swinging momentum for days or weeks.

Some momentum players will move into hot sectors for the long term, but it is generally more profitable to time the daily swings with the hottest stocks in the sector. It is a good idea to look for undiscovered cheaper stocks when sector momentum first begins. Many times daytraders will begin to move into cheaper stocks looking for a sympathy move and try to get on the train before it leaves the station. A professional momentum trader can make some very dramatic profits in a short period of time. I group sector stocks together and watch them daily as long as the momentum is present and they regularly glean profits from the action provided by a consistent pattern of similar movements.

Daytraders are an important source of momentum and they usually hang out in chats on the Internet. Chats are an important source of information and a gauge of how strong the daytrading community is. Like everything else in the market, the momentum they provide runs in cycles. To gauge the momentum of daytraders, one must watch news plays during the day and the resulting momentum. Most of the time it will be an exercise in patience as many daytrading chats will throw out one stock after another in a machine gun style that would require you to buy 20 stocks just to get three good ones. But with some patience and careful observation, it will become apparent when the stocks mentioned by many chats begin to get action at the same time, and the momentum can be incredible.

Generally, I will gauge the daytrading community's momentum by watching stocks under $10 and seeing how far they run after a news story comes out, but you must also be aware of the strength of the story. Many times when the daytrading community is extremely active, an FDA approval on a new flavor of toothpaste can send a small company up double in 20 minutes. At other times, the reactions are less than stellar. The market has changed dramatically over the last few years in that we are seeing large cap stocks moving like the small daytrading stocks. They swing large percentages on a daily basis, but I believe these moves are the responsibility of our third group of movers and shakers: *online traders*.

In late 1999, I began getting calls from Dow Jones News asking me if we were playing the Internets. I told them that we were not and I did not know of many daytraders who were. Daytraders at the time did not play large-priced stocks because most of the 20-percent runs in a few hours were happening with the cheaper stocks. It is true that the techs in the past have provided action up, until they climbed to a price of over $40 and then they would run out of gas, providing small potential with a few exceptions.

Most of the time a daytrader would look for a $2 run on a $4 stock in which he or she could buy 5,000 shares and make a handsome profit of $10K. Making $10K on a $40 stock would require an exceptional move and more capital invested, which has always been somewhat of a deterrent for the majority of daytraders. Internets have probably changed that forever and the reason is, in my opinion, the growth of our online amateurs who enter the market and buy stocks ignoring fundamentals used by the professional investors for years.

I believe they are buying with the intention of riding the wave of the future for many years and putting their own retirement portfolios on the line as they play with their new toy, online trading. They are another source of momentum that have caused moves of $40 stocks up to $400 in a matter of weeks. The exceptional moves have given credence to any hype coming down the pipe, and the daytrading community is involved so that the potential created has had a snowball effect. When all the trading powers line up at the same time, the resulting moves are nothing short of amazing. Gauging the strength of this group has been more difficult because their actions are becoming much like the daytrading community, but generally they invest small shares in larger stocks. They have been holding these stocks for less time than they originally intended, I believe, because they see incredible profits in a short period of time that they simply cannot ignore.

I believe we now have online traders who are teaching themselves to move more into the daytraders' arena, which has caused a great increase in momentum potential. I believe the best way to gauge this group is to watch sector moves after the initial news with the latest technology. They seem to be a technology-oriented group causing bio-techs, business-to-business, China-related stocks, fuel cell technology stocks, and Internet-related stocks. They are looking down the road intending to invest, but are jumping from one hyped stock after another, living in a world somewhere between the daytrader and the investor.

When you get all three groups jumping on the same stock or sector, you can have huge potential gains that began with the Internets and have subsequently moved into China-related stocks, Linux, business-to-business, and bio-techs. If a trader suspects he or she is seeing abnormal action in any one group, the upward potential can last for days, weeks, and even months. I have seen $5 stocks rise to over $50 in one day; QCOM moved up almost $100 in one day. It all begins with news and unusually strong movements. When this occurs, I like to go looking for sympathy trades where stocks might get attention because they are in the same industry and have not been discovered yet. News is the honey that draws the flies, and you must be aware of what types of stories will draw the three groups together.

THE MOVING PARTS

There are many moving parts to market dynamics. Let's look at them one at a time.

THE MARKET

The market is the giver and taker of profits, making up the potential to each day's profits or lack thereof. You cannot fight the flow of the market and expect to last very long, and the flow is determined by understanding the two parts, which make up the whole.

I like to separate the market into two distinctive areas of movement. One is the day's action, and the second is the preceding day and days of action that I call the undercurrent. Each of the two parts will apply upward or downward pressure on each trade. The strongest influence is today's market. I will call it the *NOW market*. As a professional daytrader, you must know what type of influence you have at the open, during the early trading, in the afternoon, and at the end, or you will be left out in the cold. The undercurrent is the *WAS market*. It is made up of the market dynamics from the previous day or days of trading and can seriously impact your trades. The WAS market is what alerts you to potential changes during the day and puts you on guard or in a defensive posture as you actively play the NOW market.

The WAS market provides a subtle influence of opportunity each day because the WAS market usually repeats itself in the following day of trading. For example, if the momentum trades, under positive momentum, have been going up off the bottoms for the last four days on average of $5 per trade, then I will consider the NOW market able to provide at least $4 of continuing momentum. So if my NOW market looked much like my WAS market of the preceding days, I would expect profits to be potentially around $5 on average until I see something that would indicate a change is in the air.

When markets climb, they will build selling pressure, and I will look for signs of that occurring as stocks sell down off the tops. For example, if the momentum trades have been selling down off the tops on average of only $1, I will expect the day's selling to be $1 on average if the market is going to remain consistent. But when I see the selling greater than the preceding days, I will go on alert for a possible change and try to find stocks that are at the highs to consider shorting.

Everyday of trading provides opportunity at the bottoms and the tops. The market tends to set up the opportunity by moving stocks into profit-taking territory (the highs) or value-buying territory (the lows). We have to understand what the market is providing on our plate of trades or we will miss the opportunities of a consistent market or lose severely in a yo-yoing market. Each day of trading provides a trader with the opportunity to gather statistics such that each day of trading can be analyzed. Profits can be calculated by what is expected and what in fact is occurring in real time as the stock quotes flow in your quote window. So the NOW market will reflect the undercurrent of the WAS market until indications prove otherwise and the market takes a turn.

I have become very adept at spotting those changes, which enables me to take fast profits and ride the changing momentum. As you follow along and begin to understand these forces, you will be able to change and adapt quickly also.

If the market that WAS has been selling is down consistently for a few days, the selling pressure should be rode as you short the highs. The reverse is also true as a climbing WAS market would be providing good profits by going long on the bottoms. The WAS market really determines your aggression as each day brings the same indications and enables you to increase share size and ride the flow of consistency. When the market begins to change dramatically, traders become defensive, backing away from trading, and we see less potential in our trades. When traders become confused, the market will begin to get less volume, and fewer swings will occur with the momentum stocks.

The basic truth of market dynamics is that with sufficient movement, you will see increased selling pressure as stocks and markets climb, and as stocks and markets fall, buying pressure will increase. Daytraders feed on the movements that are sufficient to create potential between the highs and lows as stocks trade each day. No movement means no trading for pros.

THE WAS MARKET

Markets are estimated by watching news event stocks and their trading prior to the open, after the open, at late morning, in the afternoon, and at end. Your high-momentum gainers (stocks that have positive news events on very good volume) will be watched for 2 days and each day is estimated by watching how the gainers swing during the day. On a normal day I would expect a typical gainer to receive pre-market volume over 50K and gap up.

The higher the volume pre-market, the more traders are interested, and the more apt they are to continue the buying after the open. The gap will produce a very short period of profit-taking, depending on the percentage it is gapping in relationship to yesterday's closing price. When I see an overly optimistic gap on a mediocre story, I will consider a short prior to the open. Normally, profit-taking will occur at the open and the gainers will drop to some value and then climb to some high, depending on the momentum. They will then settle into a range of oscillations between the high and low most of the day. The amount of drop will give me a peek into the day's profit-taking demeanor and the potential for shorting off the tops. This is because I feel that if traders are willing to take profits early, they will usually take profits off the tops during the day's trading.

The amount of selling and buying will be generally considered strong, neutral, or weak. If stocks swing up, and get little selling, I will consider the market very strong. If stocks swing up, but sell down off the tops fairly well, I will consider the market becoming weak. If stocks swing up and sell down to end near the lows, I will consider the market weak going into the next day of trading. You can also look at the Nasdaq numbers and consider generalities about the preceding days of trading, but sometimes the general numbers can be misleading. It is better to understand the market by looking at the strongest members.

Remember a general rule of movement: most of the time stocks that are strong will begin to weaken during subsequent days of trading and will produce drops in volume and price. Strong stocks are always in a state of dwindling momentum with a few exceptions. Most of the time exceptions are within sector momentum where traders are rotating into a hot sector, and as our three groups of traders turn their attention to an area of trading, the gains can last much longer than my typical 2 days. I will keep playing momentum stocks until the swings become too narrow to extract sufficient profits or the volume drops dramatically.

If the market has been ending near the highs with little selling off the tops of our gainers, the market is strong and climbing. As the market continues to climb, you should begin to be aware of gainers retreating off the highs to indicate a weakening market. The longer a market climbs, the more selling pressure I would expect as we trade each subsequent day. Daytraders make the most money when the swings are big and the market is consistent. We trade on percentages and when the market consistently behaves the same day after day, it enables our aggression to grow as we see the same patterns. We only need movement and we do not care if it is down or up.

When a market goes into patterns of up one day and down the next, it puts traders in a defensive posture. You really need to understand the components of momentum to change adequately to take advantage of the changes. So, the real point of the WAS market is to play consistency, but understand that as a market climbs or drops, the likelihood of a change is growing greater and greater. A trader should be on his or her toes to look for the signs of change and go with the flow.

The daytrader's job each day is to buy the bottoms and short the tops while understanding the potential of each. When the market is changing and volatile, the bottoms become more difficult to ascertain, and so will the tops. A daytrader attempts to ride the tide of the trading, entering, and exiting just before the tide changes. Going against the tidal flow of the market is a losing proposition over time, so a daytrader needs some leverage before he or she commits his or her dollars to the prospective trades.

THE NOW MARKET

Understanding the NOW market begins by reading the news and watching the pre-market gapping and volume. This is a reflection of the impact of the news event. Your first peek into the future is to have a working knowledge of how news events will affect a stock in a positive, neutral, and negative market. You must have a springboard for trading by watching for the same things over and over until the movements of stocks become second-nature supports to your foundation of trading.

The NOW market is defined by the pre-market action; the first drops when stocks move down at the open, if they do, and the first climbs as traders buy the hot trades and the oscillations during the day. It finishes with the end of the day's trading that moves you into the aftermarket.

Preparing properly for the open will enable you to take advantage early, and is usually the best opportunity after the market opens. Many traders cannot trade early because they are not prepared properly and will take the small profits during the narrowing part of the trading day. I like to trade the big gainers as they climb off those first bottoms and move up dramatically, providing the daytrader the best returns; however, if you are ill prepared, it can be most volatile and costly as the trades are moving very fast and quotes can be delayed. What looks like buying can actually be selling and vice versa. Once a stock begins to move against you, it takes experience to anticipate the trade and move ahead of the stock and execute properly. I will usually preset exit targets if the bid and ask move against me and I will accept a larger loss, but sometimes the risk/reward justifies the early trade.

If you tend to be a greedy person, you will have a tendency to set unrealistic exits and miss your executions when the trade is under your control and you are able to take reasonable losses. Some traders are penny-wise but dollar-foolish and try for that perfect execution to keep from losing another few dollars when the prudent action is to take a wider loss and get out of the trade safely. Living on the trading edge will guarantee a big fall one day, and big falls cause mental and monetary damage that many traders never recover from.

Normally, when I enter a long position, I will immediately set an exit price; my hand will be on the mouse ready to execute if I see the stock is moving against me. If the stock is very volatile, I will set a wider stop loss and accept a bigger loss to make sure I can get out adequately and in a timely manner. Many traders will adjust the price as the stock climbs to have a moving stop to protect profits in the event of a direction reversal, but I usually have a predetermined idea of the amount of profits I can expect given all the factors of the trade. I simply focus on the stop loss and the sell price as I usually take smaller profits than the full potential of the trade. This ensures I put the profits where they belong, in my pocket.

If I feel I have a trade that can exceed the normal profit potential, I will take ½ shares off the table at the normal sell price and let the others ride. I like to focus solely on the bid, ask at the open, and watch their movements to give me a hint of the stock's general direction. Focusing on the individual trades at the open is a waste of time. I will also watch the positive gaps very closely in the last half-hour prior to the open to see if they are climbing (which would indicate a buying and strengthening market) or if they begin to dwindle down (which would indicate a weakening or profit-taking market). I have found that the last 5 minutes prior to the open is the most important, and many times the open direction will be an exact copy of the last 5 minutes of buying or selling.

I remember a dramatic example of watching the gaps disappear one day in late 1999 when I was watching YHOO (see Figure 8-1). It had been on a screaming upward trend for days. I was expecting some serious profit-taking any day and about 10 minutes before the open, the gap really began to disappear fast. I told my traders that I would be shorting YHOO at the open due to the indication of change and the growing selling pressure as the stock had been climbing straight up for days. I told them to short at or just prior to the open and if YHOO only dropped $5 or less and began to climb, it would signal that the stock could go up again. But if it dropped more than $5 at the open, the stock would be very weak and they should hold the short. To our enjoyment, YHOO dropped $100 after the open, paused, and began to get some buying where I suggested we go long. We sat back in more amazement as it climbed 50 bucks!

Trading profitably and consistently means you must put all the pieces of the trading puzzle together each day and you will find that each morning the market will present you with a new disassembled puzzle that you must contend with. I find it challenging and exciting. A real professional knows when to trade aggressively, when to back off trading altogether, and when to allow the money market percentages to work for him or her as he or she sits in cash.

F I G U R E   8 - 1

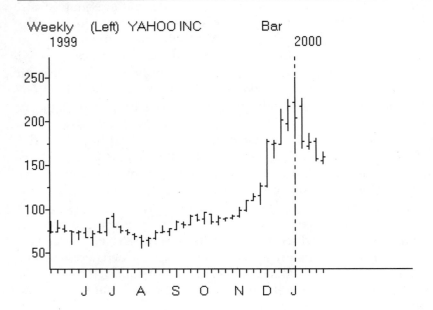

Weekly   (Left) YAHOO INC   Bar
   1999   2000

I remember a student of mine who was once a young aggressive trader who would pounce on any trade like a new puppy pounces on a ball, all four feet at maximum energy. During the market climbs, he would do extremely well and the word "back off" was not in his vocabulary. He was continually asking for the next trade. I warned him that once the market changed, and it always does, he would need to exercise some patience and wait for the next cycle of opportunity with long positions. The market did indeed change and I began to short the opens, which in his book was a retreat in the face of the enemy, and he kept going long come hell or high water. I wound up shorting almost exclusively for about 2 months; the poor guy saw his great profits disappear and he eventually headed back into the work force.

During one buying frenzy market, I saw a news event that was a wonder to behold. Anything with a .com at the end of the story was fodder for the fire. KTEL hit the wires regarding its intention to sell '70s music on the Internet; it was a cheap stock so I knew daytraders would be interested. I did not think much of most of the '70s music scene, so I was not too excited about the story, but my opinion did not matter as daytraders and others jumped on the bandwagon. KTEL was one of those NASA rockets launching into the stratosphere. The amazing thing about KTEL is it climbed and held its price for much longer than normal (see Figure 8-2).

That is really what gave me my first clue to the fact that a new dynamic was entering the market: the online investor. KTEL ended careers as shorters blew stop losses, expecting KTEL to fall big. I too was on the shorters bandwagon, but thankfully I stopped out and protected my money. Remember to always control the trade and never let it control you.

To understand what the market is telling me, I will watch the market in different phases of the day's trading. I watch the pre-market, the open, the mid-morning, and the afternoon trading, as well as the end and the post-market. I try to break up the trading demeanor in relationship to time because quite often you will see waves of buying and selling occurring during specific times of the day. I have seen early buying, late buying, early selling, and late selling because the market tends to run in

F I G U R E   8 - 2

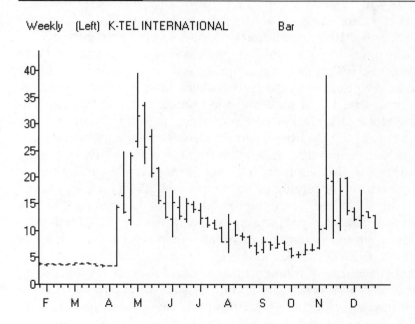

cycles. I will look for repeating patterns of time-related activity. When I see a change during one of the phases of the market, I will take careful note because it can be the first whisper of the winds of change.

TRADING THE MARKET

As we consider market dynamics, we quickly understand that many variables are in the stock market, and successful trading depends on how one assesses all the factors that are moving the trade. It takes experience to gain a working knowledge of how one dynamic reflects upon another. Basically, I would like to begin our discussion of trading by making some generalizations before we attempt to get more in-depth.

I like to think of the market in terms of negative, neutral, and positive, even though there are shades of gray between a negative and neutral, and a neutral and positive market.

I have taught using a numbering system that we can use to clarify the market behavior. A value of −10 will represent a very negative market and be seen at an open by most stocks gapping down very big. A negative market where gaps are generally down with the first-day gainers gapping up moderately will be represented by −5. A neutral market where gainers will be slightly gapping up and down will be represented by 0. A market where the gainers are gapping fairly well will be represented by +5, and +10 will be a market that is gapping up very big.

Generally speaking, the first-day gainers will be gapping up more than the second-day gainers, so gapping and momentum would be expected to be dropping with the second-day gainer group. It is usually from this group that I will pick my open shorts. I try to find a nonparticipating stock in a market where gapping is good. I will look for stocks that are gapping slightly down or even. Remember, any big gaps down will bring in value-traders, and buying can occur early, especially in a −10 market. I find it helpful to look at a 20-day chart to find out how much selling pressure or buying pressure will be built into the stock. For example, if a stock has been climbing for 3 days straight beginning at $10, has climbed to $25, and is gapping up on good news to $35, I will consider the selling pressure to be much greater than with a stock that has dwindled down from $50 to $25 and is gapping up to $35.

Remember the rule of momentum: time and movement. The faster a stock moves in one direction, the more pressure it will have to reverse and go in the opposite direction. The rule applies to days, hours, and minutes. The slower a stock moves, the less pressure it will have to reverse.

So the gaps can have added selling pressure due to the historical move-ment of the stock. It is much like a moving pendulum.

Let's look at the market as a swinging pendulum where the farthest left side is the -10 very negative market and the farthest right side is the $+10$ very positive market. I would also like to apply the same calibra-tion measure to stocks. The farthest left position is a very negative stock move, and the farthest right is a very positive stock move. The news event begins the movement of our pendulum and we have momentum that should be predictable about 90-percent of the time. The more con-sistent the market has been behaving, the more consistent the news event reactions. So our best trading occurs when the WAS market is doing the same thing day after day.

We have bad news reactions and good news reactions, and we make our living on the overreactions to the upside and downside. During earn-ings season, we get a lot of overreactions as stocks can move dramati-cally up or down, and pre-earnings season brings earnings warnings, which is great for downside action. Anything unexpected will cause a knee-jerk reaction by the market, and daytraders should be ready to play the overactive pendulum. CNBC has always been a huge force of momentum since the days of Dan Dorfman and now Joe Kernen, and it pays to listen with both ears whenever stocks are talked about in detail. I normally listen for the spin of the story, and go with the spin before I see any buying or selling action because once the CNBC train leaves the station, it is really tough to execute.

I have found that the amount of force a story has on a trade can be gauged by the first move before profit-taking begins. On cheaper stocks trading under $5, a basic rule of thumb is about .50 point. In other words, I will look for selling to begin when cheap stocks go up .50 point. However, sometimes we get daytrader buying frenzies where cheap stocks will double or triple. It pays to track the reactions of news to dif-ferently priced stocks because it also runs in cycles. Normally, if I see a cheap stock make an unusually dramatic move to the upside, I will then be on daytrader-buying-frenzy alert as daytraders will be looking for the next candidate to make them unusual profits.

Generally, I have an average expected rise, based on the news event stored in my trading memory, and I can quickly note any significant sur-prises. So, if I get a story on a $30 stock that I expect to rise about $2, and the first selling doesn't occur until it has risen $5, I know that I have more traders interested in the story than normal. When the first rise is much more than my mental average, I will classify the trade as a *potential runner*. If I have executed a long position right after the news event, I will take my profits on ½ shares at the $5 rise when I see the stock is topping, but I am ready to exit at the normal $2 expected rise.

If I have not entered the trade, I will expect the runner to fall about .50 point after the initial $5 climb and at that price I will make my decision to give it a chance or not. Generally, runners will only go down off the first climb by about .50 to .75 of a point, and then begin to climb again. No real exit price is set when a runner makes unusual moves because by definition they are the exception and not the rule. One rule that should be fixed in your brain is, "Don't go short unless you are very good at stops." This is because exceptional runners can advance for days and go up hundreds of points, wiping the stop blower out of a career. The eventual tops take a lot of experience to accurately judge and I have become quite adept at doing it, but it takes an accurate read on the players involved, the market, and the news event to even come close.

The pace of trading can also judge the beginning of a momentum move. The pace is defined by the amount of small trades per second showing up on your Level 1 quote screen. Generally speaking, a news event will trigger a few buys in the beginning, and it is at that juncture in the trade that a daytrader must commit to buying after a quick read of the headline because the trading can get faster and faster and you can easily miss the train pulling out of the station. You will generally have a maximum of 10 seconds to enter the trade in the beginning of a very big story as the news gets published from one daytrading chat to another until it gets to CNBC potentially. Many times, early bio-tech stories can get repeated on CNBC and the momentum can increase dramatically. Buying early is essential to riding the big wave, and many traders regularly buy bio-tech news and they hold, hoping for a repeat of the story by CNBC.

MID-RANGE RULE

Normally, I will expect the trading range to be established by the leaders in the first 2 hours of trading, and I go into watching mode for any quick moves up or down or fresh news. I will also keep an eye on my gainers to see how their prices relate to the lows and highs made early. If the prices are drifting under the middle of the price range, I will look for an opportunity to go long because in normally climbing markets, the gainers will end the day above the mid-range, and any dips under will bring in buyers. If my gainers move down to form a new low, I will buy the bottoms, but I will place a weaker value to the market and expect my gainers to end nearer to the lower end of the day's trading range.

In normal inclining markets, I will always expect the gainers to move off the highs and dip toward the middle of the day's trading range and end just above that target. The moves below mid-range mean we are increasing profit-taking, and anytime the gainers hold near the highs, I increase the day's momentum going into the close and expect tomorrow to be an up open. On many strong days, you will see the gainers gap up $5 and then retreat $3 and end there. The market will still be strong because of the gaps, but the ending numbers can be misleading. When the gainers are ending at the day's lows, it can signal a weak market going into the next day, and I will be on alert for more selling at the open.

Once in a while, you will encounter stocks that have $50 swings in the early hours. If a market has been exhibiting normal profit-taking, I will play the mid-range rule by shorting near the high and waiting for the ending above the mid-range price. The only problem is that some stocks can run unusually high, and you must set reasonable stop losses. I have found that it is best to simply stop out and try another short at the next high. I will accept three stops of about .50 point each because if a stock has run up by $50, it should potentially fall at least $20. So the risk-reward is 1.50 in stops and $20 in gains.

The nice thing about the mid-range rule is when high flyers begin to lose momentum and you are short the stock, you can ride the downward momentum for a few days. If my high flyer has ended the day under the middle of the price range, I consider that stock to be weakening and I will hold subsequent days until I see it gap up, at which time I will cover the short at the first up-tick. Many times high flyers will come down over $100. If I have shorted the high flyer and it does not retreat as expected but ends near my short price well above the mid-range price, I will cover and look for another short on the next day. I will keep doing this mid-range trading until the swings are too narrow to give me adequate profits or I get acceptable profits. High flyers can run anytime and controlling the trade is of the utmost importance; you control a trade by taking small losses.

Over the years, the worst conversations I had in my chat room went something like this:

Trader: Hey, Ken.

KenWolff: Hey, Bob. What's up?

Trader: I did something dumb.

KenWolff: Uh-oh, what did you do??

Trader: Remember that short the other day, XYZZ?

KenWolff: Yeah, I remember. We took two stop losses on it before we found the top and only made 1.50 because it never

weakened as much as we normally see. Barely worth the
effort.

Trader: Well, Ken, I never stopped out and I am down big thinking
it would go down sooner or later. What do you think it will do
today?

Sometimes this scenario will indeed take a trader out of the game
as he or she can get a margin call that terminates the trader's career. This
is very sad for me because it can happen to the best of traders and it
serves as a way of stressing a big point that is probably the biggest reason for eliminating a trader's career: stop losses. This topic will be covered completely in Chapter 12, "Rules of a Trader."

MID-MORNING AND AFTERNOON

The normal action during an average day of trading in the early going
will be faster action. As you progress into the mid-morning and afternoon trading, you will see the trading slow down. I call the trading action
pace of trading. I usually watch the stocks buy and sell on a Level 1 screen.
I like to use RealTick 3 because it has a shadowing feature that enables
me to see each trade on each stock by highlighting the symbol, trade size,
Bid, and Ask. This shadowing feature is great to get a visual presentation on a number of stocks on my quote screen. When I watch the slower
part of the day, I can easily see when one stock may be getting some extra
momentum by the shadow quickening as trades begin to appear faster
than what I had been seeing.

This pace of trading is good to watch for individual stocks as well
as the whole market. Many times you can spot unusual momentum by
paying attention to quickened pace as it can signal waves of fresh buying or selling. Unless I see abnormal quick action in the slower parts of
the day, I will not consider trades to have much potential. Again, the market tends to run in cycles and I have seen markets provide adequate
potential all day long. Most of the time I am simply watching the news
and my gainers to see how they relate to the lows and highs.

THE END

I will focus on the market intently for the last half-hour of trading. I watch
the news closely and look for the buying or selling pace to quicken. I am

narrowing down the end of the market to the last 10 minutes where I will begin to consider gappers. I want my potential gapper candidates to begin to get quickened buying 10 minutes before the end. The last 5 minutes will be more crucial as I watch for gapper candidates to have mostly buying. I have found over the years that the more selling you see with gainers in the last 5 minutes, the more apt they are to not gap very well. I will also consider the gaps of the previous days and go according to the historical flow of the WAS market.

Sometimes the market will gap up for days on end, defying the law of gravity, and the biggest profits can be in the gaps. I have found that my percentages for picking winners lie within the confines of the last 5 minutes when I spot stocks making new highs on very fast-paced buying. Gapper candidates should also be nearer the high to indicate trader buying interest.

If any important government numbers are due out the next trading day, the risk for playing gappers will increase. The overnight risk will also increase if the market has been very volatile and changing. I normally encourage traders who have good profits after the market close to take profits and thereby decrease the increased risk of holding longer. I will normally only play gappers when I feel the market is stable and very likely to open up the next day.

THE SPECIFICS

So far we have talked about market dynamics in general terms. Now it is time to narrow it down into more practical terms: how the trader can identify, classify, and use this information.

A daytrader who plays the same game over and over again, over time, will get slaughtered when the market changes. What worked yesterday and the day before may not necessarily work today. A good trader can change with the changing market. This has been one of the main reasons for my success as a daytrader. When the market changes, I recognize that it has changed, hold back on my trading until I understand how it has changed, and then change my tactics to adapt to the new market dynamics.

In the Mtrader.com chat room, I hear comments all the time such as "how did Ken know XYZ would run from the open?" or "how did he know the stock would drop after a short climb?" I have even heard some of my students claim that I must have my own special crystal ball to be able to determine a large percentage of the time what a stock is expected to do. It is nothing of the sort. It is a simple understanding of these forces and how they affect a stock's movement. If you can master these concepts, you too can have your own crystal ball. There is nothing magical about it.

This concept has many separate components, so I have broken them down into five basic sections: sector strength, historical market strength, market strength (macro-momentum), daytrader strength, and micro-momentum strength. Again, remember this only applies to our gainers and not our dumper patterns.

SECTOR STRENGTH

To determine sector strength, I monitor 5 to 10 stocks in the sector I am watching with the highest volume (from the previous day). You can find this on the leaders board, *Investor's Business Daily*, CNBC, or any scanning program. Once they are on my Level 1 screen, I simply watch them to determine general trends. Are they all running or dumping? Are they all up? Did they all gap up or down? I then give the sector a strength score, from −10 to +10, with zero being neutral. If a sector has gapped up, and the stocks are all running like wildfire, I score it as a +10. If they are all aggressively dumping and have gapped down, I give it a score of −10. Generally, they will be somewhere in between these two extremes and are scored accordingly. Once a sector is hot for a period of 2 to 3 days in a row, the momentum catches on and any positive news will greatly affect a stock.

If a sector is hot, I will not short at the high as the dips will be small, if any occur at all, and I may consider holding a bit longer as the upside potential is larger. I normally consider a stock that has price swings of 20-percent or greater to be appropriate potential, but if a sector is hot, I will consider swings of 10-percent or so as long as the sector has good momentum.

If the sector leaders end near the high end of the price range for the day, they are excellent candidates for position plays that I will hold for longer periods. Once a stock or stocks in a sector end below the mid-range on the day, I exit the long-term trade. Many times you can have a fairly neutral market in which nothing much is happening, but one sector will be hot and moving, such as the Internets. They can be at +10 when all other indicators are neutral and your only window of opportunity is with that sector. When this occurs, I will take smaller, short-term profits because of the uncertainty with the other indicators. I write down the sector strength number and then move onto figuring out the market strength score.

MARKET STRENGTH

Market strength is the strength of the general market that day. We determine market strength in two ways:

1. Watching first-day gainers gapping and volume prior to the open
2. Watching second-day gainers for follow-through buying volume and gapping

Note that the gapping and volume will normally be a bit weaker on second-day gainers than first-day gainers. A market strength of +10 would be first-day gainers gapping up a large percentage with huge volume just prior to the open and second-day gainers following through, gapping up on large volume. A market strength of −10 would be the exact opposite. Note that market strength as we use it is not a normal indicator. In other words, you cannot listen to CNBC for comments such as "a strong market is expected today"; this is not the same type of indicator.

If I see big gapping on first-day gainers but second-day gainers are not participating with gapping and volume (or even gapping minimally), I will consider open shorts to be very good. If everything is gapping up from the open a large amount, I will consider the possibility of a strong run-up from the open and will not short anything. I may also consider buying the first up-tick instead of waiting for the first bottom. If I see gapping fade near the open, this will be a tip-off to early profit-taking and I will short. This fading trend is very important to understanding how the open selling will go. If first-day gainers are trending down before the open, it will indicate selling pressure. The same is true for first-day gainers; if the gapping is trending up or climbing near the open, I will expect buying and a possible run-up. Once I determine and give the market strength a score, I write it down and move onto the historical market.

THE HISTORICAL MARKET

Although the historical market has the least effect of all the indicators, it has an effect nonetheless and needs to be factored in. It is determined by the combination of two indicators. The first is simply watching what score you gave the first- and second-day gainers over the last 3 days. The second is watching the Nasdaq numbers and how they are affecting the psychology of a trader's mentality. For example, if the Nasdaq is up 90 points one day, we will see more selling as it continues to climb the following days on profit-taking.

So selling pressure climbs as the market climbs and buying pressure climbs as the market dives. Those are my general rules. Each bottom or weakness will bring in buyers to some degree and each top or market strength will bring in sellers. For historical market implications, you do a bit of both in that you track the gainers for selling pressure as a market climbs and track for buying as the market retreats. You must take the historical market strength into consideration. If the historical market strength trend has been up, the daily market strength is up, and the sector strength is up, you have a powerful combination and you must play it accordingly. Once I give the historical market strength a score between +10 and −10, I move onto the daytraders indicator.

DAYTRADER STRENGTH

To determine daytrader strength, I watch the small stocks ($5 to $10) and look for unusual runs. On my Level 1 screen, I put up the hottest 10 small stocks. I look for the following things:

- The initial runs to see how far up they go (what percentage)
- The bounces at the bottoms to see how much they bounce
- Where the stock ends up at the end of the day (that is, near the high, middle, or low)

I also watch to see if stocks peter out or run strong on the initial runs. If they peter out, that indicates that a lot of daytraders are losing money on residual bounces and are not playing them anymore. If stocks are running up big on their initial runs, bouncing big at the bottom, and ending up near the high of the day, I would consider the daytrader strength score to be high. Daytrader strength is also measured by the reaction of stocks to news, especially on CNBC or in chat rooms. The initial climbs and the selling are good measures of how active they are. At times, good news will not move stocks very much, indicating they are a group of losers. Other times a CEO burping can cause a 20-percent move in the stock. When daytraders are very active, you can get days in which the gainers will oscillate with very good potential most of the day. You can learn to evaluate this indicator by tracking stories and watching how they react to that news.

On a side note, the amateur online investor is a new factor that has a similar effect. Remember, they are not looking at typical valuations such as price to earnings; they seem to be buying what they feel will be good investments in the next several years and are trading on much the same mentality as the daytrader: hype. I consider this force to be much the same as the daytrader strength, but it can cause huge runs that can last much longer. The only way to play them is to watch for sector strength like the Internet explosion. Once I give the daytrader strength a score between +10 and −10, I move onto the micro-momentum.

MICRO-MOMENTUM

This is *the* most important indicator, but it must be taken into context with all the other indicators. This is the force affecting the individual stock and the daily swings a stock will make. This is what causes a stock's momentum, what gets the stock rolling. A number of causes, such as analysts' opinions or estimates, publication stories, news releases, hype in chat rooms, splits, or even a simple mention of the stock on CNBC or other news programs, can cause this momentum. The number one cause for this momentum is news. Although we touched on the news pattern earlier, it warrants a closer look when discussing market dynamics. Remember, as I stated earlier, the street *always* overreacts to news. We need to learn to rate the value of news and how it affects the momentum of a stock.

All news must be evaluated according to how it will affect the bottom line: earnings. News has many different categories, but let's go over what some of these are and how they are interpreted.

- **Mergers and acquisitions:** It is very difficult to evaluate who will benefit from these. The terms are often complicated and the trades are generally unpredictable. We do not play these for this reason. The only exceptions are for those stocks that are under very obvious momentum. If we get any good pullbacks off the highs, we play them like any other oscillating stock under strong momentum. Keep in mind that the pace, volume, and upside potential must be good.
- **Pacts and deals:** Two factors must be taken into account: time frame and amount. For example, $100M over 1 year for a stock worth $5 is a big deal, but $500M over 25 years on an expensive stock will not affect the stock's momentum much at all. The news must affect short-term earnings to entice traders. No one cares about 10 years from now, so most of the time the potential is short lived.
- **Inventions and services:** We must consider marketability, cost, and competitors. A new digital television that costs $30K may be the best TV in the world, but who is going to buy it? Remember, it is the short-term potential that is the key.

- **FDA news/bio-tech news:** News that breaks concerning a cure for cancer always has more value over a breakthrough for some obscure disease. Generally, daytraders overreact to this type of news and the stock drops as fast as it rises. Ask yourself the following questions when evaluating this news: What phase trial is it in (I, II, III)? How expensive is the testing? How marketable is it? For example, a pill to cure some rare disease will not be as profitable as a pill to eliminate lung tumors. Again, remember, it is the short-term potential you need to evaluate.
- **Earnings:** Earnings are tricky. If a company announces earnings of 25 cents per share compared to 2 cents last year same quarter, it will get little reaction if this is exactly what everyone was expecting, but a company that is expected to release earnings of 8 cents a share but announces 35 cents a share will have a much greater impact on the stock's movement. Earnings must be evaluated not only according to how well they did in comparison to last year's same quarter, but also to as what the street was expecting.

Another factor is how the stock looks pre-market. Is it gapping up or down? How much volume does it have? The stronger it gaps, the better score it gets. The gap will determine selling. If a stock gaps up from $5 to $9 a share, you will get some profit-taking; however, if the story is a great story, it may only dip a small amount and then take off again. If a stock with a mediocre story gaps up from $10 to $12, it will most likely fall and never reach its high again.

For second-day gainers, you must also look at where the stock ended up on the previous day: near the high, middle, or low of the day. If you have a stock that ended up near the high the previous day, was up due to an absolutely great story with huge short-term earnings potential, and was gapping up big on good volume, we would give this a very high score. The volume and pace also play an important role. A low-volume stock will not score as well as a high-volume stock. The price swing must be taken into account also.

A stock that has too high a pace should be noted as being volatile. We are mostly interested in finding a stock that has a good pace, but not such that the trades become unreadable and therefore the direction becomes unreadable. A very high-paced stock is scored high, but a trader must wait for the volatility to end, or the risk is just as high as the low-volume stock. With overly volatile stocks, I will generally look for the action to settle down and play any pullbacks if they occur. From all this, I give the stock a score from +10 to −10.

PUTTING IT ALL TOGETHER

Do not concentrate on any one part of this five-part equation alone. For example, a great story, a huge short-term earnings potential, a huge gap up on good volume, and an end up near the high of the day yesterday sound great. But if the sector strength, historical market strength, market strength, and daytraders strength are all weak, you may not get the follow-through you expected. You must look at all five indicators. The very definition of *dynamics* implies change. As a result, these values need to be assessed all day long. A good trader must keep track of first-day gainers and second-day gainers to reevaluate the values on an ongoing basis.

The worst environment to trade in is one in which the indicators are all pretty much neutral. Panic buying or selling is always the best for us. This rule of movement and extremes is why our best and most predictable trades are those that have moved at least 20-percent.

EXAMPLE SCENARIOS

Let's look at a few scenarios. Use the following format for each example.

SS = Sector Strength
MS = Market Strength
HM = Historical Market
DS = Daytrader Strength
MM = Micro-Momentum

SCENARIO #1

1. SS (+9) Mostly running up and gapping.
2. MS (+10) First-day gainers are gapping high on big volume pre-market, an dsecond-day gainers are gapping on large volume.
3. HM (+8) Fairly strong last 3 days, up 90 points total.
4. DS (+9) Small stocks are running up, with large bounces at bottoms, mostly ending near the top of the pattern.
5. MM Good story; pre-market looks good with gapping and volume, and ended up at high of day yesterday.

Well, it doesn't get much better than this. This scenario will determine how much selling you can expect at the open and when you buy. All the indicators are working in our favor. I would either buy at first up-tick or pre-market with indicators like this.

If the Nasdaq was up for 3 days but only a total of 20 points instead of 90, then, yes, it can continue up and selling could be minimal. But if the Nasdaq was up 90 points for 3 days straight, then I would expect selling to hit anytime. I would still buy the first up-tick, but at the first high I would take short-term profits and be more cautious.

But if you change one or two of the indicators to a lower number, you must change the way you play it. For instance, let's change the SS to a negative and the MM to a 6. How would this affect the way you play this stock? Here is a good story in a strong market that daytraders like, but the sector is negative. It depends on how good the story is, but the sector will dampen the momentum on this stock. We may still want to play this stock but certainly not buy it at pre-market or first up-tick. You may want to play the first bottom instead of right at the open as the DS is high, but play it with caution as the MM is now a 6. I would expect the high to be a good short also. The greater the run-up, the more selling would occur at the top from the negative pull from the sector. This is what brings some of the high flyers down. So this would be an excellent candidate to go both ways on the trade, long and short.

Now change the MS to a 4. How would this change the way you play this stock? You have a good story in a strong sector, but second-day gainers are not following through, not gapping, and volume is down. Many different scenarios and combinations of each of these indicators can play out.

SCENARIO #2

1. HM (−10) The historical market is down for several days.
2. SS (−5) Most sectors will be selling off, but they will be those that have been hot recently and have gone up.
3. DS (−8) Most of the time when the market is under a big downtrend, daytraders will be losing money as they almost always attempt to go long. Unless we have a good climbing market, daytraders would be selling, and small stocks would not be really active. When a steady decline happens, this number can go up as daytraders will find smaller stocks to buy.
4. MS (−5) The market is gapping down.
5. MM Under these conditions, I am looking for big gaps down at the open. I expect the highs on any unusual gaps up or any climbs to facilitate shorting the highs. The historical market is such that it will take over the pulse of all trading and we will be primarily shorting, expecting the early highs to be sold

down dramatically on the day. So any micro-momentum will be short-lived and shorting anything at the highs would be our action. We would be doing quite a bit of open shorting, and it may be the only thing we would be doing. So any gaps even or up will be candidates for open shorts.

Under this down market, we are looking in our micro-environment for the gainers and sectors to begin to hit bottom and for buying to increase. When that occurs, we can still nail the highs and do open shorts, but we are on alert. Remember that as the market dives, more value is presented to the traders in cheap prices. But until we actually see signs of stocks climbing, we are expecting stair-stepping down on the day.

SCENARIO #3

1. HM (0) Begins to move from −10 to 0 or even a bit positive.
2. SS (+5) We should begin to see some leadership in the last hot sectors or we can even see new leadership with hot earnings in bio-techs, chip makers, computer makers, and Internets. Anything can catch fire and bring us out of a negative market. So this sector action should also be watched to see if we have a sector that is leading us out of a negative market, such as if the sector is a +5 after being a −5.
3. DS (0) Daytraders will be a bit slow to react to a correcting market, but they should be getting active after a big downtrend that seems to be reversing, which is the intent of the previous example.
4. MS (+5) Gapping is looking good and we have the second-day gainers doing OK. Gaps seem to be holding.
5. MM I am expecting a pretty good run on this stock because the market has been under a big downtrend and our market is now correcting to the upside. The selling at the open will begin to decrease as traders smell a market correction. I would be getting more aggressive with bottom buys, but to be sure the nervousness is behind us I will still be watching for an indicator. So the stair-step should be up from the first low.

SCENARIO #4

1. HM (+5)
2. SS (+10)

3. MS (+5)

4. DS (+5)

5. MM Under these conditions, I am expecting to catch the bottoms on the sector stocks that are hot, especially if I have a good story. If the daytraders are +5 and above, I will probably be looking at any small stock from $1 to $6. They will probably climb from the open with very little selling. I like to target whole prices for support and resistance on small stocks. In this market, I will be actively looking for news on small stocks.

SCENARIO #5

1. HM (+5)

2. SS (+10)

3. MS (+5)

4. DS (−5)

5. MM I will not be playing many small stocks unless the story is exceptional because even though everything is looking good in the general market, small stocks are primarily the target of daytraders. If they are not active, even good news stories will not move a stock. I will not be apt to be playing news plays on small stocks.

SCENARIO #6

1. HM (+10)

2. SS (+5)

3. MS (+10)

4. DS (+5)

5. MM I am on extreme caution for selling due to the climbing market and it should be topping and making a short-term reversal. I will still not be shorting, but I will need an indicator before going shopping off the bottoms. Daytraders are still active, so I will be jumping on small stocks still. Stocks running from the open will be highly unlikely, and selling should be increasing. Any extreme in the historical market such as big 3- or 4-day drops or 3- or 4-day extreme climbs are primed to reverse.

SCENARIO #7

1. HM (+5)
2. SS (+5)
3. MS (+5)
4. DS (0)
5. MM I am looking for a very nicely climbing stable market that has been on a steady climb, which would probably be Nasdaq numbers climbing about +15 to +20 per day and the Dow up about +35 per day. I will anticipate a stair-stepping up on any first- and second-day gainers and I would expect fairly consistent pullbacks about $.75 or so with climbs about $1 to $2. Daytraders are not active, so I am not hot on news or smaller stocks. Sectors are good, so they would be in play. Looking for about $.75 to $1 sell-offs and $1 to $2 runs.

SCENARIO #8

1. HM (0)
2. SS (+1)
3. MS (0)
4. DS (−5)
5. MM I am looking for very little opportunity and we would need the cure to cancer on a day like today to make over a ½ point. Forget any news on small stocks. This is one of the worst types of markets we play. Swings will be very narrow and we will have to be very picky and only play the very best stocks. Time to sit it out.

These examples and the concept of market dynamics have a lot of moving parts. Don't feel discouraged if you don't fully understand it all yet. It takes time, and the only way to truly understand and use these concepts in daytrading is to keep a meticulous diary and track all indicators, one at a time at first.

When you combine the concepts in market dynamics with the core methods and the indicator method, you have a fuller understanding of all the forces that act on individual stocks and are more apt to predict their expected movements and exploit them to their fullest.

9
CHAPTER

TRACKING

In Chapter 6, "Predictable Patterns," we briefly discussed tracking and its importance to the professional trader. We said it was paramount that traders track their patterns to determine their expectations. Without it, they are trading blindly and only guessing what will happen. In this chapter, we will show you how to build your own tracking diary. Follow along with the chart at the end of this chapter as we discuss it.

BUILDING A TRACKING DIARY

When developing a tracking diary, we basically want to derive a general action from the stocks as a whole. The tracking diary will answer many important questions such as

- Did gainers or dumpers sell down from the open or did they get immediate buying?
- Were the first up-ticks in the gainers worth enough potential to go long immediately? Should I be more patient and wait for pull-back bottoms?
- Should I short the tops? Does the risk not warrant it?

Overall, we want to know how the gainers behaved. By keeping a tracking diary, you can act according to your expectations instead of just a feeling. The purpose of tracking stocks is to develop patterns within the stock groups that we focus our methods on and then to develop expectations for the next day of trading based on those patterns. It will enhance your confidence in developing a plan for the next day of trading.

Learning how to track stocks is something everyone can do. It is simple enough that you may do it manually in a notebook or as I recommend, using a Microsoft Excel or a Lotus spreadsheet template. It takes a bit longer to enter the data using a spreadsheet program , but the program enables you to analyze the information with statistical tools later on if you so desire.

The point is that tracking stocks is not hard to do. The hard part is developing patterns and expectations from what you track. Being able to develop patterns and expectations becomes harder when you add market dynamics to the mix. Therefore, you must enhance your skills in market dynamics and then be able to associate those skills with your tracking sheets in order to develop a clear tracking summary.

It can be a hard process for many, but when it finally clicks, it can really improve trading percentages. It builds your confidence in the trades that you enter. More importantly, it keys you in to trades that you should not enter. Daytrading is about minimizing losses and riding gains. Tracking can better aid you in doing that as it provides an inside look to which groups are providing the most potential for high-percentage trades.

Take a look at the tracking chart in Figure 9-1 at the end of the chapter. Now that we have our tracking sheet set up and ready to go, we can begin to enter data into the tracking sheet to make it come alive. We must know what to put into the tracking sheet that will help us determine which stocks to watch, track, and develop our patterns and expectations from. Let us assume that this is your first tracking sheet.

We look for stocks to put into one of our four categories. Again, momentum causes our stocks to move and momentum is created by news. We need to look for news that we feel will create momentum. We can do this by watching television commentary like CNBC, scanning news services, and watching the chat rooms for news postings. We can also scan stock screens to alert us to stocks that are trading higher and lower and then try to find news associated with that stock. We begin to make a list on our screen of the stocks that have news attached to them, positive and negative. Then we attach the criteria to each stock. We look for the volume parameters and the price appreciation or depreciation parameters. If both of those are being met, we can begin to enter the symbols of those stocks into the appropriate group in our tracking sheet.

At 9:15 A.M. EST, we look to see where our futures closed and we place that number in our tracking sheet under the futures heading. By 9:20 A.M. EST, you should have a tracking sheet that includes the date, the symbols for each stock group, and the fair value and futures figures. You are now done with the tracking sheet until the end of the trading day.

Now it's 4:00 P.M. EST and the market has closed. The first thing you do is check to see what the ending figures were for the three indices: Dow, S&P 500, and Nasdaq. Under each heading, you need to enter the data. Take note to wait about 5 minutes after the market closes to copy down the indices figures as settlement orders fluctuate the ending index figures a couple minutes after the close of the trading day. What we are about to do with the rest of the tracking sheet is the most important part of your day: entering in the data for each stock symbol. It is from this information that we gauge our stock's behavior and develop our patterns. Therefore, you must be as accurate as you can about the information that you place in this part of the tracking sheet.

The first thing we need to do is determine the gap of the stock, the opening price, and the closing price of the stock. We can do this by simply looking at the Level 1 stock screen. To determine the gap of the stock, you need to subtract yesterday's closing price with today's opening price. So if a stock closed yesterday at 40 and opened today at 40½ , then we enter +½ into our Gap column next the corresponding stock. If the stock closed yesterday at 40 and opened today at 39½, then we enter ½ in the Gap column next to the corresponding stock. We must do this with all of our stock symbols. We can also determine the open and the closing price of the stock from the Level 1 stock screen. Simply look under the heading in your stock screen that says Open and Close, and copy those figures into the tracking sheet corresponding to the stock symbol those prices are associated with.

Finally, we have to enter in the data for the half-hour intervals and then note the stock action. To retrieve the data for the half-hour intervals, I suggest you use a 1-minute bar chart, which should be provided to you by your broker. If you do not have access to a one-minute bar chart, then you can use the following URL to retrieve a line chart for the corresponding stock: **http://quote.yahoo.com**. I recommend that you find a service that gives you access to a one-minute interval chart for the future. It will help you determine prices at specific intervals better than a line chart will.

Now you need to simply connect the time intervals with the price levels on the one-minute bar chart and find out at which price level those two data inputs meet on the chart. Record those figures in your tracking sheet for each half-hour interval until you reach the closing price.

After you complete entering in the data in each half-hour interval, you need to complete the last phase of entering data, noting the stock action. When you begin to assess the stock's action for the day, the most important information that you want to bring from the stock chart is from the open to near 12:00 P.M. EST. This time period is where most of our momentum occurs. Therefore, this time period is where our highest percentage trades are found. Afternoon trading has weakening momentum and less percentage trading. Although we note the price of each interval in the afternoon, we are more interested in tracking the first two and a half hours of the market.

When we begin to note our stock's behavior in writing, we need to be looking for the following things that may have occurred. In our first-day gainers, we need to determine how much potential our first up-ticks were worth. We need to know if that stock sold down from the open and if so, by how much. We need to determine how many bottoms the gainer had and how much each bottom was worth in upside potential. Finally, we need to note if the gainer was strong, weak, or flat into the closing of the trading day.

For second-day gainers, we need to note if the stocks were safe to open short or not. If so, how much did the stock sell down and how strong was the resulting bounce? Also, we need to know if the bottom occurred within the first 5 to 10 minutes or not as we want to note fast bottoms if they occurred. If the stock ran from the open, how many points did it run before selling down and was the resulting bounce off that first sell-off enough to regain or take over the previous high? If it wasn't, then how much lower did the stock sell off? Finally, we want to note the action of the stock into the closing of the day. Was it strong, weak, or flat?

For first-day dumpers, we need to determine if the stock sold off from the open and if so, by how much. Then we need to note how many bottoms the dumpers made during the day and how much each bottom was worth. If the stock ran from the open, then we need to note how many points until its first top and if it ever regained that high for the rest of the day. Again, we need to note the ending action of the stock.

Complete this process for each resulting stock until you move through the four groups and are completely finished entering all the data for each data field. It's important that when you are entering the data into the fields, you are using information from stocks that have traded at least 1,000,000 shares on the day. If you pick a stock that has lower volume than that, then the data is skewed and may be unreliable. Also, try not to write down each oscillation that occurs as it will cloud the tracking sheet with more information than you need. Remember that we need to make this as clear and readable as possible, so noting the point potential for tops and bottoms is what is important.

After you are finished entering the data, you can then begin to enter data into the next day's tracking sheet. Your first-day gainers from today can be entered into the tracking sheet's second-day gainer group for tomorrow. The same can be done for today's first-day dumper group. They will be tomorrow's second-day dumper group. When you are finished with all of this, it is time to begin analyzing the data you entered into the tracking sheet. From this, you can begin developing patterns in our stock groups.

ANALYZING THE DATA

As we begin to analyze the data that we have entered into our tracking sheets, we need to understand what we are looking for. Remember that we already have expectations of each group, such as buying the first up-ticks in first-day gainers and weakness at the open in second-day gainers. Now we would like to compare our tracking data to those expectations to see if the pattern still holds true. More importantly, we need to assess how much potential each expectation has given us to assess whether or not that pattern is worth trading.

For instance, if our first-day up-tick play was worth .15 of a point on the upside before selling off near 2 points, then we would not consider that enough potential to say that the action followed our patterns of expectations.

To illustrate this point, let us take a look at the tracking chart again. We have tracked five first-day gainers. The symbols are QLGC, REGI, THDO, AMTD, and EGRP. To analyze our data, we move to our column heading Stock's Action and see what happened. It says that QLGC went up from the open near 14 points before making its first top. On QLGC, our first up-tick occurred at the open and it would have given us near 14 points in potential if we had played the first up-tick. REGI sold off from the open ⅝ points. Then the resulting up-tick off that bottom was worth a ¾-point climb.

THDO went up ⅝ points from the open and then never made a nice bounce the rest of the day off its first top. So the first up-tick occurred at the open and it went up ⅝ points from the open price. AMTD went up 5 points from the open, so the first up-tick also occurred at the open. EGRP sold down off ¾ points from the open price and then went up 4 points from the resulting first up-tick. So each first up-tick on our first-day gainers held true to the pattern that our first up-ticks would give us good potential.

Next, we look at the second moves on our first-day gainers to assess if we can play a pullback on the stock that can warrant another trade. The reason we do this is because if a stock moves up from the open, we have no expectations on how far the stock can go up. The result of this is that traders may wait for a pullback on the stock so that they have a better gauge of its strength as it is more readable on a pullback than it is from the open.

We notice that QLGC sold down 7 points from its high before bouncing 5 points. THDO never gave a reasonable bounce as it was weak the rest of the day. AMTD sold down 11 points from its top with a near 7½ point potential upside. We note that our bounces were great for two of the three stocks. However, we can't expect to always get the bottom on the first try. This is where our stops come in handy. We would probably have taken one or two stops trying to find the bottom on QLGC and AMTD. Suppose each stop was ½ at the most. We would have lost 1 point potentially in stops with a near 7 points in potential off that last bottom.

This is where we assess the risk of stops in relation to their potential. The risk is well worth the stops and therefore we would expect to search for bottoms in this group. THDO was simply not a participator in the group; therefore, if you played it, you would have stopped out once or twice, but the stops would have been small and you most likely would have lost money on it. You must not let one stock in a group dictate your expectations. You must assess the group as a whole. Based on the action as a whole, we have a pattern of buying the first up-ticks and pullbacks, giving us potential that is worth the stops.

In our second-day gainer group, we tracked three stocks: QWST, SNRZ, and PCLN. The first move that we look for is which stocks sold down from the open and by how much. It is also important to see how fast because sometimes a fast jumpy bottom will be just as dangerous to play. For instance, QWST and SNRZ both down-ticked merely ⅟₁₆ of a point before bouncing 2 and 1¼ points respectively. PCLN, however, sold down 13 points from the open. Therefore, unless we played PCLN, we would have stopped out on our open shorts. The next move we look for is the resulting bounce from PCLN's bottom. It gave us 11 points on potential. QWST, after running 2 points, sold down 4 points with a 1¾ bounce and then down another 3 with strength into the close. SNRZ rose 1¼ points with a 1-point sell-off from that top. Therefore, we note that our second-day gainer pattern of open shorts had mixed action and we need to be very careful on doing open shorts on the next day. The bottoms on these stocks were worth looking for as the upside potential should have been enough to cover at least one if not two stops on them.

Our first-day dumper was FEET. Note that your tracking sheet will have more stocks to get a better feel of the overall group. Remember that we need value buyers in this group to create momentum on the upside. We will know how strong the value buying is by how many bottoms our dumpers make. FEET had one bottom (showing strength in value buying) going down merely ⅜ points and went up 2⅜ points off that bottom. Therefore, our pattern shows us that one bottom is good enough to ride gains on. With this rise of 2⅜ points, we can expect our dumpers to give us 1½ to 2 points in potential, depending on how long you want to risk holding the stock. Also, it is well worth the risk of taking a stop or two on. We also notice that FEET was flat into the close of the trading day, not making it a high-percentage gap candidate as we like to see buying strength into the close.

Our second-day dumper was RSTO. Remember that we expect some weakness from the open and then we need to see if the resulting bottom was worth the risk of taking a stop. RSTO went down 1/16 points from the open and then made a nice climb, giving ⅞ points potential before selling down ⅜ points and then becoming flat into the close. Therefore, we need to be careful of expecting weakness in this group from the open while looking for a bottom that won't cost us more than one stop.

We've just compared our stock's action to the current patterns that we have. Let's recap what we have. On first-day gainers, the first up-ticks were worth the potential of playing. The pullbacks on these stocks were also worth the play if you wanted to wait for a pullback. THDO was our exception of the group. Second-day gainers were not safe open shorts, as we had two of three make small downticks from the open with strong runs. However, the resulting bottoms on the stocks were worth the stops. The first-day dumpers show us strong value buying is present as our stock only made one bottom and rose 2⅜ points off that bottom. Our second-day dumper shows us to be careful on the weakness at the open and the upside potential off a bottom is worth looking for.

FORMING EXPECTATIONS

Now that we have analyzed our patterns and compared today's stock action to our current patterns, we can begin to form expectations for tomorrow's trading. These expectations will be the beginning of your game plan for the next day. This game plan will be a great aid in developing confidence in your trading. Once you become familiar with recognizing patterns and what potential each pattern is currently offering, then you are ready to form expectations. We should only enter a trade that we have expectations on. We should not simply enter a trade blindly or follow someone else's call. We must have a firm grasp of how that stock can react, the potential it can have, and what to do if it begins to trade against us—this is called an expectation.

When we trade on expectations, we begin to gain a higher percentage of trading. Gaining a higher percentage of trading requires that you enter trades that you feel will have enough potential for profits even if you are required to take one or two stops. It will also keep you out of stocks that you either cannot read or see, or, worse, cannot enter and exit expeditiously. By trading on expectations, you inherently miss hundreds of trades a week. You miss thousands of trades a year. However, you catch the four, five, or six trades a day that have a greater potential to attain your expectations. Therefore, you have a better chance to attain profits on the stocks you do trade.

Another benefit of trading on expectations is that you can tell whether or not you are in sync with the market and what the market is telling you. If you simply guess that a stock will go up and it does, you are lucky. If you guess that the stock will go up and it goes down, then you are simply wrong. You cannot enhance guessing skills because guessing is simply a flip of the coin and gambling. If you have done your tracking, analyzed your patterns, developed an expectation of the trade, and expect the stock will go up and it does, then you have done the right thing for the right reasons. It wasn't simply a guess. If the stock goes down after all that preparation, then you stop out and simply look for a re-entry point or tell yourself you are out of sync with that trade and leave it alone. Those who guess have no idea how far it can go down or back up. Those who guess have less percentage of a chance of making money in this market than those who have a solid understanding of the market and prepare for it every day.

Do not let a bull market lead you to believe that trading stocks is as easy as throwing darts to find stock picks. When and if this market turns bearish or sharply corrects, those who are guessing can really be hurt. Each day we see wild swings in stocks, sometimes 25 points or more. Those who have expectations will be more likely to exit the trade and save capital for the next play.

Let us form expectations for tomorrow based again on our tracking sheet. We've determined that on first-day gainers, the first up-ticks were safe to play. So we begin to divide our stocks into price range levels. The three stock levels that we play are

- Under $10
- $10 to $100
- $100+

As we can see, the stocks that were priced under $10 were REGI and THDO. REGI offered ¾ points off its first up-tick. THDO offered ⅝ points on its first up-tick. Therefore, tomorrow we can reasonably expect a stock that is trading under $10 to not give us more than 1 point in potential off its first up-tick. Now playing a stock with under a point in potential requires excellent timing and execution. Traders like to play more shares on trades like this so that they can take profits conservatively as it climbs or sell half lots as it reaches the first target on our expectations. Selling half lots means that if I bought 1,000 shares at 10 and I expect 10¾ to be the high on it, I can sell 500 of my shares at 10½ and sell the remaining 500 at 10¾ if it gets there. Notice how expectations on our stocks let us determine exit points. If the stock starts to sell below 10, we can immediately stop out and look for a re-entry if we still believe 10¾ to be our target.

QLGC was a stock in the $10 to $100 price range. Now we need to look at this stock with a bit more skepticism. I would not expect most stocks in this price range to run 14 points from the open, so we need to scale our expectations back to be a bit more conservative. However, we can set a conservative target and if it hits it, we can again sell a half lot and save the other half to see if it rises more.

AMTD and EGRP are in our $100+ group. AMTD offered us 5 points from the first up-tick and EGRP offered 4 points. Therefore, we can expect 5 points or less in this group off the first up-tick. We set a conservative target of maybe 2 to 2½ points, sell a half lot there, and see if the stock rises more. Notice again our expectations are helping to develop exit points. We have just developed expectations for the next day of trading in first-day gainers.

We have two second-day gainers, QWST and SNRZ, in the $10 to $100 range. Both stocks sold down only ¹⁄₁₆ points before rising 2 and 1¼ points respectively. Therefore, we have to be careful of open shorts in this dollar range. However, we can short the first top, which gave us 4 points potential on QWST and 1 point in potential in SNRZ. You may try to play a bottom off that first high. However, note that because our bounce was only 1¾ on QWST and only about ½ point on SNRZ, we need to be very conservative on taking profits if we choose to play a bounce in this group. We may even consider not playing the bottoms as the upside may not be worth the stops trying to find them.

PCLN was in our $100+ group. It sold down 13 points from the open with an 11-point bounce. Then it ended near the low. We can expect better weakness in this group so we can hold our shorts a bit longer and we can also be more aggressive in this group when looking for the bottom as the 11-point potential is well worth one or two stops and possibly even three.

Our first-day dumper, FEET, was in the $10 to $100 range. FEET gave us 2⅜ points off its first bottom. So off the first bottom we can expect at least 1½ to 2 points in potential. We expect this potential to be worth two stops at the most. We also sell as it reaches that 1½ to 2 target, either whole lot or half lot if you want to hold it closer to 2.

Our second-day dumper, RSTO, was also in the $10 to $100 range and it went down ¹⁄₁₆ from the open with a ⅞-point rise. We need to be a bit more cautious of this group as the volume tends to be lighter. We would be weary of jumpy price levels and would be selling the whole lot as fast as we could as it rises over ½ point.

Now we have expectations on our stocks for tomorrow. This is now our trading plan for tomorrow. Again, by developing these expectations, we leave a lot on the table; however, we play the highest percentage trades. We get out with the surest of profits. We stop out with the least amount of loss as possible (according to our execution abilities). I do not know too many traders who go broke taking profits. You need to understand that not every trade will be a home run. Those 14-point climbs do not happen every day, nor can you always catch them. Because we trade on expectations, we rarely take the full 14 points as it climbs anyway. However, we are taking the best stock that we can based on our expectations. Again, by trading on those expectations, we take out the hoping and guessing. It is from that discipline that we stay in this business. The last piece of the tracking puzzle is applying market dynamics to our expectations.

RELATING MARKET DYNAMICS WITH TRACKING

You'll remember that on our tracking sheets, we entered in the data for each of our three indices: Dow, S&P 500, and Nasdaq. We also entered in the figures for our futures in relation to fair value. This is our first indication of the overall market tone every morning when we awake. We compare the indices figures from yesterday to the day before, to the month before, and so on. We assess what market we are currently in. We want to know if our market is inclining, declining, or short-term correcting. We look for fair value and assess our futures number in relation to that figure to gauge positive, stable, or negative tone in the market. This is the most basic and unreliable look into the strength and weakness of the market because index figures are based on a macro view of the overall market. We need to become more focused on the next micro level below the overall market. This next level is sector momentum.

We can group our sector momentum by using four or five stocks in each sector to provide a better look into the micro-dynamics of the market. For example, for our Internets, we can use such stocks as YHOO, AMZN, EBAY, PCLN, and so on. For the Tech sector, we can use AMAT, INTC, TLAB, DELL, SUNW, and so on. For brokerages, we can use NITE, EGRP, AMTD, and so on. The point is that we can find four or five stocks to place in each sector. We use sector as an indicator because we need to find a leader to show us strength and weakness. If our Internets are reaching new highs, we can expect the others to follow. We need leadership to show us the way. Now that we can see how our sectors are doing as a whole, we can begin to focus on individual stock in that sector.

We need to be more aware of the market mood before the market opens. We cannot simply use the futures numbers as they are based on the macro view and can be easily skewed. The way we begin to assess the market strength at the open is by the gapping in the stocks in our sectors. If we are gapping up, then we are seeing positive tones in the market. If we are seeing little if any gaps up, then we are seeing a nervous market with unpredictable direction. If we are seeing gaps down, then we are seeing a negative bias at the open. Next, we assess the gaps in our other sectors and find out how strong or weak each sector is. We are gaining a more micro view of the open as we get closer to it. The only piece missing now is our traders and how they are going to react.

Our traders will either take a stock from 4 to 40, from 40 to 4, or make a stock sit at 20 all day long. It is their willingness to buy and sell stocks that gives us the best micro view of the market. If you see a stock go from 4 to 40, then we can see a crazy buying market. If we see a stock go from 40 to 4, then we are seeing a panic in the market. If we see a stock make nice easy climbs or profit-taking on stocks from 20 to 24 or from 24 to 20, then we have more stability in the market where overwhelming buying or profit-taking do not occur either way. It is in this aspect of market dynamics that we can begin to make true assumptions of the market and base our expectations upon them.

Again, let us use the tracking sheet to fully assess the next day of trading. This time we can apply our market dynamics. So we have first-day gainers. We've already made our expectations. We expect a good pattern of buying off the first up-ticks to be worth some good point potential. For tomorrow, we need to be aware of the market open. If we see the stocks in our sectors stable in their gaps, we can reasonably expect our first up-ticks to behave like our patterns have shown us. If we see many of our stocks gapping down at the open, we have to be more cautious about going long aggressively. Negativity will make the buyers more cautious in the market and that negativity can affect the upside potential in our gainer groups. Note how the market dynamics can shift our thinking on our expectations.

If we saw gapping down in our stocks, we would begin to think more conservatively on the upside. We can now elect to stay out of first-day gainers ifwe feel the negativity would not offer enough potential on the upside or we could lower our expectations from 5 points on $100+ stocks to nearer 2 to 3 points. Then we can take more conservative profits at nearer 1 to 2 points or sell half lots at that price and hold the other half for more.

On our second-day gainers, if we see some weakness or gaps down, we expect more weakness at the open and for our open shorts to be high-percentage plays. We would also be more inclined to not go long off the bottoms as the negativity can affect our upside potential. If we see many of our stocks gapping up, we can still note open shorts at the open. However, this is very dangerous as the bottoms can be fast and the upside potential can easily regain and overtake new highs on the day. We would also be more inclined to play the bottoms on these stocks as the upside potential would be more reasonable when expecting an up morning. As we understand how our market dynamics function, we can adjust our expectations accordingly. We also understand now that market dynamics will be the determining factor in changing our patterns.

Patterns will change—they always do. When they do change, we will be making less money on our trades. In some cases, we will lose money. This is where our stops become the most crucial. If we have excellent expectations based on our patterns and our understanding of market dynamics and the stock still goes against us, then we have the preparation to stop out immediately. We can reassess the market, the potential of the stock, and our ability to re-enter the trade if we feel the upside potential is still present. Never fight a stock—it will always find a way to win.

TRACKING SUMMARY

By now, we should have learned to develop patterns, analyze our patterns to develop expectations, and apply our expectations to market dynamics. Once we master this process, we can begin to write a tracking summary. A tracking summary is simply a collection of all your thoughts, put on paper, to prepare you clearly for the next day. A tracking summary must include how the stocks in each group acted. You can simply transfer the information in the Stock's Action column of your tracking sheet to the tracking summary. Then you can note your expectations that include each scenario.

For example, if our stocks are gapping down this morning, I will have certain expectations about our first-day and second-day gainers. If our stocks are stable to up in the morning, I will have a different set of expectations about our first- and second-day gainers. I will be expecting our first-day dumpers to be good off the first bottoms and 1½ to 2 points from that bottom. I would look for more volume on our second-day dumpers if we want to play that first bottom and expect to take profits at anything over ½ point.

Please follow along with the tracking sheet to gain a sense of how to write a summary that best fits your style. Remember that you are the only one who will be reading this summary and trading from it. Therefore, it must be accurate, true, and readable for the next day of trading. If your tracking summary includes those three characteristics, then you are ready to trade from your tracking summary.

WRAP-UP

The more time you invest in tracking, the better you will begin to understand, develop, and refine your tracking abilities. When you do this, you can begin to add groups to your tracking sheets. You simply need to track

F I G U R E   9 - 1

May 7, 1999	Fair Value	Futures	DOW	S & P 500	NASDAQ
	-4.5	+1.7	11,031.59	1,345.00	2,503.62
			+84.77	+12.95	+31.34

	Gap	Open	10:00	10:30	11:00	11:30	12:00	12:30	1:00	1:30	2:00	3:00	3:30	Close	
First Day Gainers																
QLGC	+3/8	81 3/4	93 5/8	90 1/2	93	95	92 1/8	91 3/4	91 3/4	89 7/8	92 3/8	91 1/8	88	90 1/16	Went up from the open –14 points. Then down near 7, up near 5.
REGI	+1/2	7 3/4	8 1/8	8	7 3/4	7 3/4	7 5/8	7 1/8	7	7	6 7/8	7	7 1/8	7 1/6	Went down 5/8 from the open. 3/4 bounce. Weak rest of day.
THDO	+5/8	7 1/2	7 5/8	7 5/8	7 3/8	7 1/4	7 1/16	7	6 15/16	7	7	7 1/8	7	7	Went up 5/8 from the open, then down the rest of the day.
AMTD	+4 3/8	112 7/8	118	113 1/2	108	112 1/2	114 1/2	115 1/2	113 1/2	116	115 1/8	113 1/2	113	114 3/4	Up 5 from the open. Down 11 from the high, then up 7 1/2 and strong into the close.
EGRP	+5 3/16	110 1/4	113 1/4	110 1/4	106 1/8	111	111 3/8	111 3/4	110 1/4	110 5/8	109 1/2	109 1/8	110	110 3/8	Fast bottom, down 3/4 points. Up 4 from the bottom, then down 7 and up 5 3/4. Buying into the close.
Second Day Gainers																
QWST	+13/16	89 1/2	90 9/16	88 1/8	89 1/8	86 7/8	88 5/8	90 1/8	88 5/8	90 1/8	88 5/8	90	88 7/8	90 1/16	Small downtick from open. Up 2 then down 4 points. Bounced 1 3/4, then down 3 and strong into the close.
SNRZ	+1/16	36 1/16	36	36 1/2	37 1/4	36 3/4	36 1/2	36 3/8	36 3/8	36 1/4	36 5/16	36 1/4	36 1/2	36 1/2	Down only 1/16 from the open. Rose 1 1/4 points from the bottom. Then down 1 from that high.
PCLN	+4 13/16	144 1/4	142 3/4	133 1/2	138 1/8	134 3/4	138	142 3/4	136 5/8	141 1/4	135 3/4	133 1/2	132 5/8	130 21/32	Down near 13 points from the open with 11 point bounce. Ended the day near the low.
First Day Dumpers																
FEET*	-4 3/8	13	12 5/8	14 1/2	15	14 1/4	13 7/8	14	14	13 7/8	13 3/4	13 7/8	14	14	Up 2 3/8 off the first bottom. Flat into the close.
Second Day Dumpers																
RSTO	+3/16	13 1/16	13 7/8	13 1/2	13 7/16	13 1/2	13 1/2	13 9/16	13 3/8	13 1/2	13 3/8	13 9/16	13 1/2	13 1/2	Down 1/16 from the open, then ran 7/8 points and then falling near 3/8 points flat into the close.

*"FEET" wasn't really a dumper on this day and is for informational purposes only.

these the same as you would any other stock. This is how new patterns are found. You may be able to find other patterns that I have not discussed in this book. If you do, contact me, I would love to see what you have discovered.

As you begin to enhance your tracking sheets, you need to be looking for interesting movements in the stock's action. For instance, see if you can spot a general time of day the stocks sell down at or move up. See if you can use the groups to signal a pattern change or a possible short-term reversal in the market mood. To do this, simply assess the ending prices of the stocks using the mid-range rule. The mid-range of a stock is simply the difference between the high of the day and the low of the day divided by two. So, if the high is 42 and the low is 40, then $42 - 40 = 2$ divided by $2 = 1$. $40 + 1 = 41$, so 41 is our mid-range.

If the stocks in your group have been ending at or above the mid-range and the market indices look positive, then we can reasonably expect our stocks to move up tomorrow too. If we see our stocks ending below the mid-range, then we can expect more selling pressure in our stocks on the next day. If we have been experiencing several days where the stocks have been ending below their mid-range, then we get a day where our stocks end above the mid-range and we can spot a possible short-term reversal. If the next day our stocks do the same, we have confirmed it and we expect our gainers to do well again off their bottoms and first up-ticks. We look to our tracking to develop our expectations of how those gainers might do. As you finally refine your skills in tracking, taking into account every piece of the puzzle and applying this data to market dynamics, your winning percentages will increase.

The ultimate goal of tracking is to take this intra-day information and begin to apply it in a general sense. This way we aren't spending countless hours on the tracking sheets but rather getting an overview of the action so we know what to expect. Remember, although we can derive many expectations for our stocks, it is the individual price action at that given point in time that we have to assess. We should only use our expectations as a guide. The more familiar you become with the stock market, the less specific tracking you will have to do on individual stocks. This will slowly wean you off the spreadsheet-tracking diary and into more of a notebook-type journal where you can record your thoughts and expectations on what happened to the groups on that day.

10 CHAPTER

TIME OF DAY

As I discussed in previous chapters, momentum provides predictability. Momentum can be defined as slow in stocks that are being accumulated by institutional traders, or they can be defined as fast, as active traders in numbers take a position in the stock when interest is created by news or a related event. Slow-momentum stocks are best traded by individuals that are able to identify key buyers and sellers in the stock. I will discuss a tape reading of this nature in the next chapter, which should shed some light on this issue.

Fast-momentum stocks tend to be traded by those active traders looking for the faster and smaller profits. They tend to be harder to execute and therefore smart traders will take profits into the strength of the direction that the stock is moving. Beginning traders tend to buy these stocks with much added risk. The first added risk relates to execution ability. Because the stocks are harder to execute, traders tend to buy at prices that are farther away from the best price that was available when the position should have been entered.

For example, if a stock makes a bottom off 40, the trader may buy the stock as high as 40.50 or sometimes a full point higher near 41. In our realm of trading, this is referred to as "chasing the stock." Buying the stock farther away from the real bottom or shorting it farther away from the real top is chasing. Chasing a stock normally leads to a trader entering a position near the end of its momentum move. If a trader were to enter the stock at 40.50 and the stock moves to 40.75 and pauses, the trader will have to try to exit as it climbs to 40.75. However, remember that the stock is hard to execute due to its fast momentum. This makes exiting near 40.75 relatively tough. The trader will more likely take a loss on this type of trade.

The trader that bought the stock near 40.25 or lower would be able to take the profit as the stock clears 40.50 into the strength as it moves closer to 40.75. In this example, the trader that chased took out 75-percent of the profit potential. The trader that bought nearer to 40 offered themselves near a .50 point in potential and kept the risk relatively lower. The main point is that on fast stocks, a trader needs to understand his or her execution abilities. If the stocks bottoms off 40 and you can't enter efficiently nearest to 40, then leave the stock alone. If you are unable to enter efficiently, there is no reason why you should expect to exit efficiently.

The other risk that beginners tend to make on fast stocks is turning a profit into a loss. This occurs mainly when the stock makes a climb of 1 to 1.50 points and the trader expects more in potential, so they hold it longer. Just as fast as the stock moved higher, the stock can move down with the same velocity. The old saying of "exit when you want to, not when you have to" applies here. Many times a trader will see the stock that climbs 10 points off an intra-day bottom. He will then associate that stock's climb with the stock that he currently owns a position in. His thinking is that he does not want to miss that kind of momentum move if it happens in his position. Remember that the majority of the stocks are mutually exclusive. Just because XYZ moved 10 points does not guarantee that any other stocks will perform in the same fashion.

A trader must watch the price action on each individual stock, and if it suggests that selling is about to hit, take the profits. Once the validity of the trade is no longer present, the exit strategy must be in place with the understanding that on fast selling, the exit strategy may have to include prices that are not at inside levels. On fast momentum issues, reading such price action is much harder. Market Makers and ECNs are constantly jumping on and off inside levels, not giving a clear picture as to their true intentions on being buyers or sellers. Without this knowledge, you are relying solely on momentum.

If momentum is up and you are long, great. If you are long and momentum is down, look out below. So if the stock begins to weaken and fast selling comes in again, you may turn a 1- to 1.50-point gain into a flat to .50-point gain stock. Worse yet, you may freeze with indecision and disbelief that the stock is not climbing 10 points and turn that 1- to 1.50-point gain into a loss on the trade. Under no circumstances should a profit of .50 point or more turn into a loss on the trade. If it does, you either are trading a stock that is out of your execution ability or you are not executing your decisions well enough. Remember, exit when you want to, not when you have to.

Momentum in a stock can happen at any time. News alerts or chat-room alerts can be a catalyst for such a move. With respect to momentum during the normal trading day, traders need to be aware of distinct momentum periods in order to enhance their trading plans. Over the years, I have found that nearly 90-percent of my trading potential to be found in the first 2 hours and the last hour of the trading day. Generally, the lunchtime period of about 11:30 A.M. to 2:30 P.M. is relatively boring as market momentum slows.

The first 2 hours of the trading day are generally when the traders are both entering and exiting positions from overnight holds and for new positions for the trading day ahead. The last hour of the trading day is when most traders are taking profits or losses from the early morning's trading and are entering or exiting positions ahead of the overnight trading session and into the next day's pre-market period. Traders that do not feel comfortable with trading right at the open are waiting for resulting moves from the initial opening direction. A flurry of decisions are made in the first 2 hours as traders position themselves for expected momentum in a certain direction. Buy, sell, short or cover, traders are participating actively in the first 2 hours and the last hour of the day. These are the time periods that I am most interested in.

DELAYED QUOTES

At the open of the trading day, many active traders are plagued by the bottleneck of delayed quotes provided by the Nasdaq. This is a bottleneck that can't be solved by our ISPs or faster computers. It is simply a problem that the Nasdaq is continuing to work on when literally hundreds of thousands of trades and more are being sent to the price servers of many different data feeds. That amount of transactions runs into the problem of being filtered out efficiently and timely. Therefore, many traders will see their Level 1 and Time of Sales information delayed at times. We call this the *funnel effect* of the market open. This is important to know because traders that are looking for buying and selling at the open have a tough time gauging the strength and weakness of the stock relative to the tape and what it's showing.

Beginning traders don't even notice this delay and are simply confused why their orders did not fill. Most of the time, my quotes are cleared up within 10 minutes and I'm okay. However, on occasion, there are times when it is longer, and I cannot rely much on my quote system to be accurate. If I sense a delay, I will more likely let the trades go until the system from the Nasdaq end, as well as my own end, is no longer bogged down with an overwhelming number of trades at once.

There are several ways to sense if you are delayed. First, on the Level 1 screen, if you see that the Bid and Ask prices are not near the same price as the Last Price column, you can bet that the Time of Sales information is delayed. Secondly, if the majority of the Bid and Ask are at prices that are out of bounds from the high and low of the day, then the Bid/Ask prices may not be true as well. To combat this issue, I have found my Level 2 screen to be the most accurate for me. When my Time of Sales and Level 1 screen is off, I can usually tell by comparing the prevailing inside prices on my Level 2 screen to those on the Level 1 screen. If the Level 1 screen is behind the Level 2, then obviously my quotes are delayed, and I have to be more cautious on trading. There is a way to know if the Level 2 screen is delayed as well.

On my execution software, if I want to enter a position at the inside prices, I will normally use a SNET PREF or ECN order to match against those at the prices that I want. If I were to enter in a SNET PREF order to a Market Maker or ECN and the order is rejected by the software immediately, I know that my Level 2 is delayed. I know this because the SNET PREF order is being sent to market participants that aren't there. If no participants accept the PREF order, the software rejects me immediately. This is the same with selling. I remember a while back I was trading a stock and put in an order to buy at 4.56 and was filled with no trouble at all. The stock failed to break my breakout point of 4.63 and I wanted to exit at 4.50 based on what I was seeing on my Level 2.

So I entered my sell order with a SNET PREF to the ECN REDI (Redibook) and my order was immediately rejected. However, REDI sat there at the bid of 4.50 with sizes of 2,000 shares. My order should have been accepted as auto execution against an ECN. However, because my order was being rejected, I quickly asked in the MTrader chat room what the price of this stock was and it was said to be at 4.38 × 4.44. I was clearly delayed and because I was blind with no quotes, I simply used an ISLD order at 4.25 and was taken out, giving me a larger than desired loss on the trade. However, because I was not getting my desired price and was immediately rejected, it was a hint that I was delayed.

The same goes for an entry. If you enter an order to buy at a price of 10 at inside levels and you are executed at 9.50, then you should be checking your quotes against someone else's system to make sure you aren't delayed. If you buy at 9.50, and stock is selling hard, then you may be taking a bigger loss than desired on the exit. This makes trading safer stocks all the more better. If you are finding yourself delayed and need to exit, there is usually enough ECN participation that you can match an SNET or ECN order against at reasonable price levels. If you try to trade a stock that is offering .50-points spreads and the volatility of an intra-day range near 10 points, exiting and entering if the quotes are delayed is nearly impossible. You would have to enter in a price and hope. This is not safe trading.

As the first 2 hours of the trading day go by, the funnel effect is usually cleared up within 10 to 15 minutes, and most stocks have made their intra-day highs and lows. Obviously, there are exceptions to this action, as some stocks continue to make new highs and lows into the afternoon, but for the purposes of my methods, I am interested in the highs and lows of the first two hours. Moves from the high to the low and vice versa, I refer to as an *intra-day oscillation*. Again, the momentum in the early part of the day is generally the best and provides for nice intra-day oscillations between the high- and low-point range of the morning. As we discussed in Chapter 6, "Predictable Patterns," in the section, "The Law of Narrowing Oscillations," as the day moves along, these oscillations tend to narrow and provide less point potential per trade.

As the morning trading opens, I will look for the first high or low to be made. Then I will look to see how much buying and selling happens from those points. I discussed earlier in Chapter 8, "Market Dynamics," the mid-range rule, but I would like to discuss it again in context with the time of day. The wider the intra-day range initially, the more profit potential I feel the initial oscillations will provide. I base this on the mid-range rule. This is basically the rule stating that stocks generally do not end the day at the highs or lows of the day, but somewhere in between. Therefore, if stocks have a mid-range, I will use this as a gauge to know where to look for reasonable exit and entry points.

For example, if a stock moves from 40 to 45 early on in the trading day, I will look for a pullback initially near 43 to 43.50 from the high of 45 to go long off, if the market looks strong. If the stock makes a pullback bottom somewhere near this level, I will look for a move back over 44 to near 44.25. I don't expect a new high to be made, and I want reasonable potential and safety. Therefore, if I see a good move up off near 43.50 and it clears 44, I will more than likely exit near 44.25 when I want to, not when I have to. If the stock bottoms off 43.50 and fails to clear 44, I have a decision to make at this point. I will most likely take the smaller profits at nearer .25 point to .35 point if the trade is easier to execute.

If the stock is harder to execute, I will definitely take the profits under 44. If the stock pulls back off the 45 high and moves under a mid-range of 42.50 and buying is still relatively stable in the market, I will expect an ending on this stock over 42.50 and look for buying under that level to go long and take profits back over the mid-range levels. This all assumes that the market is reasonably stable and that the stock itself isn't unsafe to trade, nor is it showing weak pullback bottoms that will cost me too many stops in finding the bottom. I have no reason to overtrade a stock's bottoms in the hopes of finding the real bottom. I'd much rather wait for a clear bottom based on safe and readable price action than go fishing for the bottom and take too many stops in finding it.

NUMBERS

I see a lot of traders ask how they can take bigger profits on stocks. Two very good options let you keep conservative profits while letting the stock run a bit if you are right and have a good bottom or top. The one we want to talk about in depth involves using whole number theory and fractional theory. First off, we have stock on the Nasdaq that can trade in fractions as small as .001. However, most trades do not trade below .01 and even those are few relative to the rest of the trades that trade in multiples of .05.

Prior to the transition from fractions to decimals, some traders have a horrible time learning fractions and knowing, "Is $^{13}\!/_{16}$ bigger or smaller than $^5\!/_8$?" and so forth.

Let us assume a stock is trading at 8.50 (Bid) $\times$ 8.60 (Ask). You will hear people in the chat rooms say a stock "is about to up-tick" or "it is about to down-tick." When we look for an up-tick, what we have to see is the stock price move up one level, meaning we would need to see this stock move from 8.50 (Bid) $\times$ 8.60 (Ask) to 8.60 (Bid) $\times$ 8.70 (Ask).

UP-TICKS/DOWN-TICKS

Notice how the previous Ask of 8.60 became the new Bid of 8.60 and the Ask rose .10 to 8.70. That is an up-tick. A downtick is just the opposite. The stock will move from 8.50 (Bid) $\times$ 8.60 (Ask) to 8.40 (Bid) $\times$ 8.50 (Ask). Notice how the stock's Ask replaces the previous Bid at 8.50 and the new Bid moves down .10 to 8.40. Those are up-ticks and down-ticks. Again, that is important to know when we move into learning our trading methods.

WHOLE NUMBER AND FRACTIONAL THEORY

When we trade stocks, we try to gauge predictability on how the masses will react to a certain price. Although we trade stocks, we must actually trade traders because they are the momentum behind the stocks. We must think like the masses and stay one step ahead of them, being ready to get in and out of a stock before they do, and we can use fractional theory to do this.

A difference exists between fractional theory and whole theory and it will be explained in a bit. Whole number theory deals with what fractions people are most familiar with. When we watch a basketball game, the game is divided into four quarters. The fraction for that is .25. When we watch a soccer game, the game is divided into two halves or .50.

When you go to a restaurant and someone asks, "Do you want a refill on that Coke?," you might say, "Fill it up half-way, please." We would not ask to have it filled $^{13}/_{16}$ or .81. We tend to think in whole points first (1, 2, 3, 4); then we think in half-points (1.50 points, 2, 2.50, and so on). Then less often, we can use .25 points, but not as much as half-points and whole points. As we begin to assess the action in stocks, we will look for bottoms and tops on those stocks using whole number theory, but we will determine exit points using fractional theory, which is setting prices one level above or below the whole number.

This is the difference between whole number and fractional theory. Using the whole number theory, if we see stock XYZ selling down from 42 and it is currently at 40.86, we will look for buying above 40.50. If it sells through 40.50 and then 40.25, we will look for buying above 40 and so on. Now, suppose it bottoms at 40 and climbs off 40; we will look for its first resistance point at 40.50. If it goes above that, we will look for resistance at 41. Because we know the masses are doing what we are doing, we can sometimes get out a little earlier than they do. They may be waiting for 41, but we will take profits at 40.75 if we think 41 will be a big resistance point. Always take sure profits; never get greedy.

Waiting for that extra .25 point may sometimes cost you another .25 point if it turns downward again. As we begin to get better in developing our expectations of our trading, trading on fractional theory will become automatic, and you can begin to shift your style to what fits you best. We use whole number theory to determine our resistance and support points, and we use our fractional theory to let stocks run that we are on the right side of. The following example will illustrate what we mean.

We will get a good bottom on a stock at 50 using whole number theory, and it begins to climb. We immediately keep our stop at 49.95, one level below the whole number. Then it rises above 50.50 and is on its way to 51. This is not to say we abandon our core methods of tops and bottoms and throw out the indicator or market dynamics; it is intended to be used in conjunction with everything else. If we feel the expectation of the trade is that it should rise to 52, we will raise our exit price to 50.45, one level below the 50.50 whole number.

Let's say it meets resistance at 51 and starts to sell down. Normally, we would exit or set our stop at 50.50 because of whole number theory, but we raised it to only .45 because we are expecting it to climb again off 50.50, and remember we expect 52 on it. If it sells through 50.50, then we know the stock is weak and we would sell at .45, making .45 on the trade. We just took conservative profits. If it climbs off 50.50 and goes up to 51 and possibly over, then we can adjust the exit price upward to 50.70.

What we are doing is assuring conservative profits while we continue to let it run up a bit more. If it gets to 51.50, we would begin to take profits at 51.50 or raise the exit price to near 51.20 and see if it can get over 51.50. If it doesn't go over 51.50, we exit, take 1 point profit, and we are happy. If it gets over 51.50, we set the exit price at 51.45 and as it approaches 52, we can begin to sell it. It may go to 60, but our expectation is 52, and we will get out as close to that target as we can. We never get greedy. We trade on our expectations using fractional theory to let the winners run or exit out with conservative profits. We are willing to risk an extra .05, hoping for another .50 to 2.0 point potential in gains.

AFTER-HOURS AND PRE-MARKET TRADING

The majority of these rules and observations occur in the time period from 9:30 A.M. to 4:00 P.M. EST each day in the market. There is enough liquidity, plenty of firm quotes by Market Makers and ECNs to trade against, and readable momentum. Much lately has been in the media about extended hours trading and its benefits for individual investors. For online and other trading companies to offer this type of trading without explaining the risks involved has been irresponsible to say the least. I have seen traders become confused on how to buy and sell stocks numerous times in after-hours and in pre-market trading. Let's discuss pre-market trading first.

In pre-market trading, although Instinet is basically open 24 hours day, most other routes do not offer trading until about 8 A.M. EST. Normally, the ECNs, such as ISLD, are open at this time period, but SNET is not offered for another half-hour, and SOES is not available at all in pre-market trading. SOES is not available for a major reason. The quotes that are being displayed by Market Makers are not firm and do not require a fill if the size shown is available. Remember that SOES makes a Market Maker obligated to fill the order if they are showing size when the SOES order comes up and they have not filled their liability issues. Because pre-market trading has no liability issues, there is no use for SOES and therefore does not get turned on until 9:30 A.M. ECN and SNET routes are therefore the only way to trade.

Although ECN participation is fairly active in pre-market in active stocks, using SNET to match against these orders or offer a BROD order at or near prices may have some luck. However, let's look at the liquidity issue. If a Market Maker is not obligated to fill any pre-market orders, then no "real" market is being made, other than by ECN traders. With spreads getting wider due to lack of liquidity, this makes trading in the pre-market much more difficult and adds risk. Many times, we will see a stock gapping up with the Market Maker showing a price higher than where ECNs are trading, hoping to entice buying. More often than not, if you SNET PREF this Market Maker for an order, it will go unfilled, as he or she is not a true buyer of the stock. The Market Maker is most likely trying to entice buying so he or she can exit the stock with his or her inventory or clients' order.

Many pre-market games are played as Market Makers try to get an idea of "perceived" value for the stock at the open of the trading day. Relatively little is readable and safe to trade and should be avoided by anyone that is not familiar with pre-market trading. The only times I will trade in pre-market is to exit a gap play or to enter a stock that I think has reasonable potential to climb from the open. If this is not the case, I will not buy or short the stock in pre-market, as stocks can move up or down pretty fast in an illiquid market. The same is true with after-hours trading.

Very little market marker participation exists, and mainly day-trading ECN users are trading. Big stocks like AAPL or MSFT that may be trading in after-hours on the news may have some institutional interest, but again, the dangers of wide spreads, the lack of liquidity because no quotes from Market Makers are firm, and obligatory and no readability being present make these trading periods dangerous. The only time I will trade in after-hours trading is when I want to exit a gap play. I never buy stocks after-hours, as it is akin to the purest form of gambling.

One day, I saw Rambus announce good news in after-hours trading and they moved up nearly 50 points. I saw traders shorting the stock from the low 100s. This stock hit near 150 in after-hours on relatively good volume, but the liquidity and ECN participation made the stock stronger than it was. The next day, the stock traded in the 110's, down near 40 points from the after-hours high. This explains the dangers of trading in after-hours: being short near 100 and having it move to 150 or buying near 140 to 150 and having it trade lower near 110 the next day. There is no reason to accept such risks, and individual investors need to understand the issue of liquidity before becoming interested in such trading time periods.

Some day, we may have 24-hour trading, but for right now, obligatory issues by market participants present an unsafe and highly dangerous environment by which to trade. Newer traders should avoid pre- and after-market trading altogether and stick to stocks with predictable momentum and readability, using the defined methods previously stated in this book and in this chapter.

11
C H A P T E R

IDENTIFYING TRADING OPPORTUNITIES

Each day the market offers thousands of trading opportunities with each up-tick and down-tick of individual stocks. The traders' main goal is to capitalize on the expected future of those up-ticks and down-ticks, knowing when to enter and, more importantly, when to exit. There have been thousands of systems by which one tries to trade these expectations, and I have described a few of my methods in previous chapters that I use to capitalize on these price moves. However, the simple mechanical approach to trading this system will more than likely result in failure if you are unable to understand how to apply external variables, such as the execution risk, the ability to see the trade correctly, and, most importantly, to automate the decision-making process to overcome hesitation. Anyone can trade in theory because no real money is involved in trading opportunities of this nature. Application of the theory and automation of this to live trading is the true test of one's ability to effectively trade over time.

As we discussed in Chapter 10, "Time of Day," the oscillations of a trading day occur mainly in the first couple hours of the day, and being able to identify these oscillations is key to the momentum methods of my gainer and dumper trades. Recognizing and understanding waning buying and selling pressure and then analyzing a point in time that should provide a reversal is the next step of the process of identification of trading opportunities. Finally, understanding how to execute and automate that decision so that hesitation is not a part of the trading plan for both entry and exit is the final step. However, to really understand what is happening in these stocks as they make tops and bottoms should be added to your trading knowledge, and I'd like to discuss this information in this chapter. It is assumed that the reader is already familiar with and has a working knowledge of the Level 2 screen. If you are not, it is recommended you study the basic information on Level 2 found in many books and on Internet sites.

TAPE READING

Many amateurs refer to tape reading in the basic sense that has been derived from the old days of a simple ticker tape that ran prices of stocks across a tape reading machine, much like we see on CNBC screens or on some Web pages. Today, this tape is referred to as the Time and Sales window, or ticker, which is offered by most online and direct access brokerages. This notion of tape reading loses most of the meaning behind what tape reading is really supposed to be telling us. Tape reading is not just assessing a ratio of buys and sells in a particular issue. Tape reading is not just about watching the prices of stocks at a certain interval in time.

Tape reading is beneficial in the sense that we can apply knowledge about what specific Market Makers are doing or at least gain an idea of an intention that they may have. Market Makers can mask these intentions in numerous ways, and also show us something that we see to be true, when in fact the exact opposite is about to occur. Tape reading is neither an exact science nor a 100-percent trading tool. It is simply a benefit to traders that are interested in key market players of a particular issue and are interested in what they may be doing in order to find a reason to enter, exit, or hold a trade.

Tape reading can be applied in both the micro sense of a stock as well as what the overall market index is doing. Understanding the forces of accumulation and distribution, both in the overall market as well as in specific stocks, will help to know why stocks move higher in advance of news and why they sell down in the face of no news. Understanding these market forces on a deeper level will take much of the mystery out of the market and provide you with a much more sober approach to your trading plan. This will alleviate the conspiracy theories that claim Market Makers are out to intentionally hurt daytraders, that institutions' specific plans include the demise of individual trading portfolios, and that there is some kind of "they" that is always out to personally separate you from your money.

Let's be truthful. Traders don't trade to lose money and although institutions and Market Makers do have specific intentions each day in the stocks they are responsible for, they are just traders like you and me, both making money for their firms as well as for their clients. None of these intentions has anything to do with you as a daytrader. If they happen to fill their order or their clients' order because you lost money, then that is your fault, not their intention. They don't know who you are, nor do they care. Their responsibility is to fill their orders and their clients' orders.

THE MACRO VIEW

Let's talk about a few main ideas of tape reading. From the macro view, many traders in the face of a market correction talk about capitulation or panic selling. It is interesting that when I ask traders what their idea of capitulation is, they fully know what it is. It is when traders just give up on the stocks they own and just say, "Get me out as fast as I can," and sell at any price. However, what's interesting is that they don't know what leads to this kind of action. Let's take the most recent correction as traders were moving the Nasdaq market over the 5,000 level on amazing volume, only to see it crash 40-percent to near the 3,000 level in less than 7 weeks (see Figure 11-1).

F I G U R E   1 1 - 1

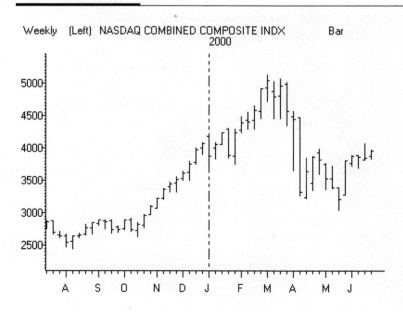

Remember that institutions drive the markets up and down. Although online traders and daytraders can affect individual stocks to some degree, we do not have the capital base to provide moves of a great magnitude for any length of time.

The cause of the move from 1,500 to 5,000 in the Nasdaq in 2 years was caused by an influx of monies from both domestic and foreign economies as faith in the Technology sector was evident, and the U.S. economy and companies were utilizing it. Traders didn't care what it was. If it was Tech or Internet, they wanted in. 401(k) monies, mutual funds, hedge funds, insurance companies, and major brokerage houses were all investing heavily in the stock market. Margin debt was at its highest levels and an inflow of billions a week was coming into U.S. financial markets, providing such a push. However, all this speculation and increase in monies to the markets was setting us up for something ominous, the 40-percent correction.

In October 1998, when we were facing the Asian crisis, Russian devaluation, and a long-term capital crisis, the world felt like it was going into a global meltdown. However, the lowering of interest rates and a bail-out by the IMF provided a nice boost to the outlook for the domestic economy, as well as the future of the global economic community. What happened in October of 1998 was a clear market capitulation that was brought on by global nervousness. These institutions were frothing at the mouth just waiting to buy up their favorite companies shares at lower prices. They began to buy these stocks on sale, accumulating over time and reallocating their positions based on both market variables and analyst reviews of the companies they were interested in.

For purposes of this discussion on the macro view, let's just focus on sector leaders like INTC and MSFT. Suppose in latter 1998, the big boys began to buy up shares of these stocks on sale. Over the course of the next year and a half, they were accumulating and distributing at prices that were advantageous to their inventory as well as to their client's inventories. Their accumulation of these issues over specific periods of time will lead to eventual distribution, as either these stocks hit certain price levels or personal exit strategy points. Defining these price levels and exit strategies is what makes the market work.

Traders enter and exit stocks based on a belief in both the stock's action as well as the overall market and how it may affect that stock. As long as the belief is that the stock will continue in a direction that is beneficial to them, they will hold this issue. As soon as this belief changes, the trade is exited. Beliefs about a stock's value changes for everyone at each up-tick and down-tick of this market. The thought of whether or not this stock will continue in the same direction or not is thought about by traders as the stock continues its momentum and pause.

Everyone's beliefs are different at each level or else you wouldn't have trades going off at inside prices. Furthermore, if everyone were to have the same belief, this is what normally leads to end of the move. So, based on this fact that if everyone believes the same thing or at some point in a market moves up or down, this is when smart money begins to get contrary. Applying this to our most recent market correction is now easier to explain. In 1998, when investors were selling their shares in panic and foreign money was repatriating funds back to their home country, stocks went on sale. Capitulation set in, panic selling led to bargain prices, and shares of stocks like MSFT and INTC were heavily invested.

The next few days saw huge amounts of price spikes off those lows, creating interest. The accumulation of these favorite names by institutional traders and money managers continued over specific periods of time. They knew to be accumulating at these levels because the public's common belief in nervousness and declining stock prices led to these capitalizations. When everyone has the same belief, the institutions go contrary. Remember, the public is usually the last to know and is also usually wrong. Fast-forward to 4,500 on the Nasdaq a year-and-a-half later.

Speculation was large and margin debt was increasing. Bio-techs and Internets were flying on wild moves to incredible heights. Volume was strong near the 2 billion mark. This was a record volume of just a few days over the 2 billion mark. Just the opposite was happening in this time period from 1998. In 1998, nobody wanted to own anything. In the first quarter of year 2000, everyone wanted to own anything they could get their hands on. Again, everyone had the same belief that the market was going higher, and everyone wanted in. Institutions began to go contrary again and sold the majority of their positions to the public traders, giving them all they wanted. This is called distribution. Institutions move markets, and as we were nearing the 5,000 level, institutions were distributing their accumulated shares from much lower levels to the public.

Public funds are limited to an extent, and if institutions are no longer buyers at these levels, then there is no one to sell to at higher prices. Once again, the public is wrong, and the cycle begins again. Traders that entered the markets at higher levels are now forced to rethink their strategy as the markets begin to sell down 10-percent, 20-percent, 30-percent, and eventually 40-percent. The distribution of shares by institutions to these traders that were so optimistic above the 4,500 level raised plenty of cash by institutional traders that when it was ready to go back to the buying at lower levels, they could do so.

Who would they be buying these stocks from? Obviously, it was those traders that they sold these stocks to at higher levels. Capitulation set in this time near the 3,000 level, nearly 40-percent off its highs. What happened next was institutional contrary buying from the 3,300 to the 3,000 levels, while traders were panicking and selling stocks that had declined so much in value. As I write this book, we are currently over the 4,200 level in the Nasdaq. That is a 40-percent climb off those lows and guess who profited from these moves? It was institutional traders as well as those traders that understood how to benefit from a macro sense of tape reading. The adages of "buy when there is blood in the streets" continue to hold true. Sell when panic buying sets in, is second in this equation.

THE MICRO VIEW

Application of this macro knowledge to a micro view is both fascinating and necessary if one wants to understand intra-day price movements. As we discussed, beliefs about stock prices change with every up-tick and down-tick. This change in beliefs in our gainer and dumper stocks creates the oscillations that we see within the first few hours of the trading day. As these oscillations narrow, beliefs about the stocks tend to settle in general and tight ranges as traders aren't willing to change or produce a new set of beliefs on unreadable price action that is not supported by any interest. Remember that interest is defined by volume and pace, and if there is very little of either, then it will be harder to ascertain the direction of a stock, especially if we are unable to identify key market players in these stocks.

Now that we understand how the perceived value of a stock can produce a decision on whether to enter or exit the issue, let's apply a few micro scenarios of stock moves. Stocks that are being accumulated tend to be presented in a fashion of steady buying and no major pullbacks. A continued volume increase on buying and very little selling volume on advances would show that buyers are still stronger than sellers, as traders are still willing to bid the stock higher. If there is any increase in strong selling volume, accumulation would be signaled by the strong selling being absorbed with no major price pullback. In this case of accumulation, most of the selling is simply done by online traders or daytraders that are looking for faster profits.

Institutional selling is generally not included in this scenario as the stock continues to be based on steady volume and move higher on some increasing volume. The opposite of this case in distribution is when stocks move lower on slow selling and very little buying enthusiasm. No institutional buyers are involved, and any online traders or daytraders that may buy are easily absorbed by the institutional sellers of the stock.

We tend to speculate that accumulation is occurring in advance of expected news or other catalyst events that will move the stock higher. We tend to speculate that distribution is in advance of an expected negative catalyst or negative rumors. Many times, we will not find out the true reason for such moves at all. Other times, we will receive the news or reason either the following day or within the week. Although I don't believe in conspiracy theories or market manipulation to the extent that many would like us to believe, accumulation and distribution can be observed in obvious circumstances.

ENGA of late is a perfect example. It moved higher from near 11 to 14 on no news and steady volume. The next morning it announced news that made the stock gap higher by 3 points in pre-market.

What do you suppose happened next? Right, those that accumulated at the levels nearer 11 are now distributing the stock to those retail buyers that are buying the news either on the gap up or on the first climb. The stock sold back down near 11 in the next two days. Those that bought the gap and got stuck in on the news probably sold nearer this 11 to 12 level as they realized they fell for this move. This is assuming they did not keep a stop discipline.

My favorite news event is the stock upgrade. Many times, I will see a stock upgraded by a brokerage house only to see him sitting on the Ask of the stock filling clients' orders. There are two ways to interpret this. First of all, he has accumulated shares at much lower levels and wants to sell the shares to the public on the upgrade. This would make sense because if the firm was interested in continuing to accumulate shares at lower prices, why would they upgrade the stock and cause a price jump in which they would have to pay at higher prices? The second way to interpret this is that they are in a stock at lower levels and want to profit on the upgrade news but also want to provide some liquidity to clients' orders. If they have several large clients that want in the stock, they can facilitate more orders of this stock by soaking up retail buying, in essence selling their own inventory to retail traders, and then transferring their clients' order to buy at a lower price to their own account to cover the shares they sold at the higher price. More on this later.

THE PRICE SPIKE–PANIC SELLING PRINCIPLES

Another principle of tape reading has to do with the panic selling or price spike of an individual stock. Increasing volume and a price advance would signal a continuing uptrend of the stock. This is relatively obvious as increasing prices bring in more buyers and possible short covering. The more buying, the better the chance the stock has to move higher. However, as volume decreases and the price advance slows, this signals the end of the move as the buying begins to wane. This is what we refer to as the top of an oscillation. This is where we elect to go short or begin to practice our exit strategy for long positions.

On the opposite end is large volume and price declines. This would suggest a continued downtrend as selling begins to create nervousness to those that are long and they also begin to sell, as they can't stomach more loss than they already have experienced. Remember that beliefs of the value of a stock determine a reaction. In this case, at each down-tick, the belief that more loss will cause more pain will make a trader exit at these lower prices so as not to lose more money. As selling pressure begins to wane on lessening volume, this is a sign that we are at the bottom of the oscillation.

Application of this knowledge on the micro level is fascinating as we begin to look for that belief in the stock that is common. On an advancing issue where volume comes in very heavy and the price advance is fast, we have to assume once again that these late-to-the-party retail traders are caught up in the excitement of the stock. Who are they buying the stock from? Right, those in from lower levels before this price spike. As the price spike signals the possible end of the move, smart traders will look to exit the long positions into this strength.

If retail traders are the last buyers of the move on this price spike, then they will have no choice but to sell at lower levels as the "real" buying is not willing to take this stock higher. This distribution means a resistance level has been set in on the price spike and the stock begins to pull back on both the distribution as well as the frustration selling by those that bought the stock near the top of the oscillation. We profit by either being in the stock at lower levels and selling into this strength or by waiting for the buying pressure to wane and for volume to decrease and attempt a short trade. Again, it is very important that we know our execution abilities.

I have seen stocks like BAMM that go from 4 to 40, or AVCO that went from 3 to 30. Although these stocks obviously exhibited a waning buying pressure at some point in the move to higher levels, trying to short those tops were both dangerous and, for a few, career ending. Just because a stock pauses and the signal for the end is near, executing that short or exiting that long position has to be understood from an execution risk standpoint. Understanding this tape reading information is beneficial but will not provide 100-percent in accuracy. In those times that it does not provide an accurate read and we enter the position, we have to be able to exit that position with the least amount of loss as possible. Know your execution abilities when reading the tape.

Again, the opposite side of the price spike is the panic selling. Just as we had in the explanation of the market capitulation, individual stocks have fast selling that signal that the bottom of the oscillation is about to occur. The common belief that this stock is not going to stop falling creates panic selling as everyone scrambles to exit with a least amount of loss, or by those that do not want to deplete any remaining profits left over in the stock that they bought at lower levels. Nothing is more frustrating than seeing a multi-point gain turn into a small profit or, worse, a loss. As the selling of the stock increases in pace and then the volume begins to decline while selling pace starts to wane, it is at this point that we begin to look for a reversal and for the stock to reverse and move higher.

This point in time would be a suggestion for an entry for a long position or to cover the short position if you read it in this fashion. Together with the understanding of the gainer and dumper group and how to play their overreactions, understanding the reasons for how and why stocks move in this fashion should provide a better understanding of when to enter and exit trades. Bottoms or tops of oscillations are key areas to identify, and by reading the specific price action in such a way relative to increases and decreases in volume and price direction, this will aid you in knowing when those key areas occur.

When playing such tops and bottoms of oscillations, it is important to understand that when oscillations narrow and momentum in stocks slow, the identification of entry and exit areas becomes more difficult. If the momentum is slower, there is no increase or decrease in volume and price spikes or panic selling that we can gauge entries and exits for. In these situations, our trading becomes a relatively lower percentage. During this period when market pace slows, traders tend to guess on the direction of stocks since there is no readability in the momentum. Stocks tend to sit in narrow ranges, not providing much interest for buyers or sellers to enter the stock.

Now Market Makers are usually just making the spread on slow buying. There is no active directional participation from which to trade.

Therefore, for playing the tops and bottoms of oscillations, there has to be an identifiable momentum by which to ascertain points when the stocks pause at specific levels and have cause for a meaningful reversal. I say meaningful in the sense that the stock will offer enough opportunity to risk a trade on the stock. If the potential is outweighed by the risk, either in limited potential or by execution risk, then the reason for the trade becomes less intriguing, or we would back off this trade.

One more note on slowing momentum is that we often see slow drifting of a stock in either direction. Again, with this accumulation or distribution, we can identify key players; trading this kind of momentum isn't necessarily a negative. However, if we were looking for momentum trading, then watching a stock slowly selling lower would negate the reason for the identification. For us to risk a bottom oscillation trade, we want to identify the point by which fast selling turns into a pause and reversal. On slow momentum, the stock always looks paused and therefore finding the real bottom is much more difficult to ascertain. Thus, if we want to understand how to read slower momentum stocks, we are forced to look into the deeper issues of tape reading.

THE MARKET MAKER EFFECT

To move deeper into tape reading, we have to understand how to view key players at specific price levels. This is a necessity of trading slower momentum stocks because we are not relying on fast momentum to offer us profits. Instead, we are relying on information about perceived intentions of what Market Makers are doing.Understand that Market Makers and institutional traders are not going to be too hip on showing us their intentions. Otherwise, their intentions would never be fulfilled because traders could potentially ruin their plans for orderly distribution or accumulation. These traders, when accumulating or distributing orders for themselves or their clients, want the stock to move orderly so that they are not paying too much for the stock, nor selling at prices that are too low.

If they flashed intentions to buy 1 million shares of stock and traders knew this, then people would be buying like crazy at this point in anticipation that this 1-million buy order would push the price up as well. This would make the institutional trader have to buy one million shares at a higher dollar cost average. On 1 million shares, this can cut into profits in a big way. Therefore, they are very concerned to mask their intentions and for the most part, we don't know the exact intention. Even if we see a few things happening that suggest a Market Maker is a net buyer or seller, we never know how much of the order he still has to fill or if he's already done. Therefore, we have to watch for a combination of basic tape-reading principles according to the idea of accumulation and distribution in conjunction with what a specific Market Maker may or may not be doing.

Previously, I discussed a Market Maker or institutional trader that was willing to facilitate an order for clients by becoming support or resistance at key price levels. I noted the example of the upgrade in which a Market Maker would sit on the Ask, sell shares out of his own inventory to retail traders, and then transfer the clients' order to the Market Maker inventory to cover those shares sold. In this scenario, everybody wins. Let me explain why. If you are a fund manager that wants to sell 200,000 shares of XYZ stock, you don't want to go on the open market to buy at uncertain prices. Nor do you want to display your intention to buy this much in stock to other traders. Otherwise, they may see this order and try to get in the stock as well. This pushes up the price of the stock, and you will pay more for the stock by not hiding the true intention in some manner. Many use INCA in this case to facilitate large orders, but for the purposes of tape reading, the following information is useful.

You want to sell 200,000 shares of stock and feel that if you use INCA or some other trading service to mask this intention, you may not get the price you want. Therefore, you will call your favorite Market Maker to facilitate this order for you. What he will do is agree with you on the price or prices at which to transact this order for 200,000 shares.

To make this explanation simple, let's suppose that the stock is trading at 40 on the Bid price by 40.05 on the Ask price. Your quote screen would show 40 × 40.05. The Market Maker feels he can reasonably facilitate your order for 200,000 at 40. If this price is agreed upon, the Market Maker will now attempt to sell 200,000 shares at 40.05. This would identify the Market Maker to those that are able to see this on the Level 2 screen as the ax of the stock.

This is because the Market Maker is not letting the stock trade higher than 40.05 before he fills his order of 200,000 shares. The reason he wants to sell 200,000 shares at 40.05 is because he will be buying your sell order for 200,000 shares at 40. If he buys 200,000 at 40 and sells that same amount at 40.05, then he stands to profit a gain of $10,000 (200,000 x .05) for his trouble and risk involved in facilitating the order for you at 40. If he sits on the Ask at 40.05 and absorbs all the buying, once he gets to 200,000 shares, he will then transfer the block from your sell order to his account. Covering the 200,000 he just sold and a block of 200,000 shares will cross the tape or possibly in some other combinations, such as four blocks of 50,000 each, all at the price of 40. Normally, the transferred blocks will be at the inside Bid price or sometimes lower.

Once a trader identifies the Market Maker as the ax and then sees these blocks move across the tape, that trader would expect them to lift off the Ask and for the stock to move higher. This makes sense because the Market Maker is not a true seller of the stock, meaning he doesn't want it to go lower, and that the stock should rise as soon as he lifts off the inside Ask if he is the only real seller at the price level of 40.0625. He was not a real seller and was simply facilitating an order for his client that was beneficial to him because he sold his stock at 40. If the stock moved to 39.50 during this facilitation, he wouldn't have cared. They both agreed on 40 as the price. Because the Market Maker agreed on 40, his risk is that his absorbing the buying would create nervousness and the stock would fall. If the stock had fallen below 40, then he would be selling stock at a lower price than he bought it from the client. In this case, the Market Maker loses money on the trade, assuming the majority of the shares sold is under 40.

This is the risk Market Makers take and the reason that they are compensated for their trouble by profiting from the spread. Many wonder why the Market Maker would accept such a risk. The reason is that the commissions and fees derived from these numerous orders from big clients result in a lot of trading profits over time. The institutional traders and fund managers will enjoy the collaboration in that they know they can rely on the Market Maker to facilitate their order at better prices than they feel they can obtain, and the Market Maker profits by continuing to make the spread on these orders. It is a partnership of sorts in which both gain in the transaction. As for tape reading, this is why we want to identify the ax of a stock in such a case.

Remember that if a stock is slow-momentum and under accumulation, we will want to figure out whom the net buyer of the stock is that is accumulating and also any ax of the stock that may be hindering the climb. If we enter into a position on a slow stock and can identify the ax and the net seller, if there is any action in either of these two participants that would negatively affect the price against me, I would be more inclined to exit the position with surest profits. If one or both of these participants continue to raise their Bids and offers in an orderly manner, then the continued accumulation may not be over, and I may want to hold longer. Either way, this type of tape reading is a very beneficial way to gauge the direction of a slow-momentum stock and provide more viable trades to your trading plan.

The basic setup in a slower stock is to: watch for the ax at the inside Ask price to be identified by absorbing the buying, then look for blocks to cross the tape at or below the inside Bid price, and then watch for the ax to lift off the Ask. If this happens, you may elect to hold the stock if you are in from lower levels or you can enter into the stock for a quick scalp-type move.

The opposite case is true for a Market Maker that has been identified as providing support in a stock. Suppose you, as a fund manager, come to me, the Market Maker, and want to buy 10,000 shares of stock. I will facilitate this order for you at 40.05, and you agree to this price. I will then go on the Bid at 40 and buy 10,000 shares worth at 40 from retail traders. Once the 10,000 shares are bought, I will then sell you my 10,000 shares at 40.05, basically transferring your buy order to my account and profiting $500 (10,000 × .05) for my trouble. Once I transfer your order to my account, you will see a block of 10,000 across the tape at the Ask price and for me to drop off the best Bid. If a trader is short the stock in this case, he will be glad to see that I am not a true buyer of the stock (providing support) and when I drop off the Bid, this might provide more downside potential.

The most common question is why doesn't the ax just lift his price and sell at higher levels. This is quite a simple answer if we understand the reasons of why the ax is really the ax. The ax is not a Market Maker that wants the price lower so he can buy at cheaper levels. This is often a very wrong comment that is made in many chat rooms. Obviously, if the Market Maker wants to accumulate shares, the lower average price, the better, but for purposes of tape reading, the answer is easier to explain. If I agree to buy your shares at 40 and I believe that I will not have any trouble filling this order at 40.05 for 200,000 shares, I will stay right here to assure myself that I fill the whole order and not risk the stock moving lower, creating a loss.

If I move up a level higher, I will be competing with other market participants at those prices to sell, and in this case, I may not be able to fill the whole 200,000-stock order. My initial purpose is to facilitate the order in a fast, beneficial, and relatively certain manner. The purpose isn't to get greedy and see how many more .15's I can squeeze out of the order for my own benefit. Obviously, if I can I will, but if higher price levels look like too much competition to fill the order, I will stay where I can assure myself I can fill the whole order. This action identifies a key player or ax in this scenario. This is only something a trader can view by watching a Level 2 screen relative to the Time of Sales information that comes across the tape.

Again, tape reading isn't just watching prices going across the ticker. One has to understand who is doing the buying and selling and for what purpose. On the macro view, institutions are usually buying low and selling to retail traders and vice versa. They are selling at the highs when the markets are showing signs of a panic buying and then accumulating shares on panic selling. On the micro view, we are looking for pace and price action relative to increases and decreases in volume and price direction. We are also looking for block trades to cross the tape and identify who the supporting Market Makers are or who the identified ax is. We are trying to figure out what those blocks mean and how can we either profit more by doing so or taking surest profits if what we believe is a negative on specific price action.

Tape reading goes far deeper in understanding than just reading the ticker tape buys and sells ratio. Learning to read the tape in relation to the previous information provided will give you a much better sense of why markets and stocks move and how to best profit from this understanding.

12 CHAPTER

RULES OF A TRADER

When traders move from the world of investing to the realm of short-term trading, the psychology and mindset behind each approach tends to become mixed and, if not separated, can cause problems while carrying out your trading plan. However, although the shift from investing to this new way of trading demands some changes in strategy, some common traits need to be reiterated relating to money management and a strict stop loss regiment. When I first began trading for a living, the advice by those I was most closely associated with provided the only rules that pertained to investing. Two of the most detrimental phrases were that "it is only a loss when you sell it" and "stocks always come back." Although these statements do have some truth to their reasoning in certain issues, the application of this to active trading is the primary cause of failure to many aspiring traders.

The mainstay of investing has been to trade the markets in the fashion of Warren Buffett. Buy strong companies and hold the stocks for years. Although I have very little argument from such a strategy that has obviously worked well over the long term for him and his shareholders, this type of reasoning can crush the active trader. This mainly stems from the fact that when we trade short-term, we are trading stock symbols, not companies. We are trading the reactions that traders have to price movements for numerous reasons. Nothing of this has to do with long-term fundamentals, P/E ratios, and valuations. Traders are more tuned in to reasons why stocks move in the absolute short term. This can be from seconds to minutes in some cases and in others lasting several days.

However, rarely is an active trader's position held for more than a couple days. The active trader looks for the points in time when there is a disagreement in the perceived value of a stock, causing the greed and fear variables to enter into the stocks movement. Although perceived value is always going to differ and give basis to a stock market's existence, the prevailing price will always be in agreement. Simply put, the current price of the stock is right where it should be. Whether someone thinks that is too high or low will always be a disagreement.

For example, in 1999 we had two opposing views on Amazon.com (AMZN). Amazon was trading somewhere in the 200's and an ongoing price target war between two analysts was taking place. One analyst downgraded the stock with a price target of $50, while the other analyst upgraded the stock with a price target of $400. People often refer to a stock as undervalued or overvalued; the real answer is that a stock is neither. The current price of the stock is the absolute price and therefore its value is the current price. Perceived value will continue to differ, causing traders to buy and sell stocks while creating the necessary fluctuations for momentum traders to capitalize. If everyone agreed on value, then stocks wouldn't move, as they would sit at that value until something in the company's "formula" changed to make the value different.

Since momentum traders are making decisions based on this disagreement of value, they have to trade with the assumption that "the stock won't always come back to their price." This assumption will demand that a trader cut his loss immediately, thus going against the phrase that a loss is only a loss until you sell it.

Momentum traders need to realize the need for taking losses is a positive rather than a negative aspect of trading. Not all stocks do come back and, in some cases, wipe out a trader's portfolio in as little as one trade if they do not keep their losses small. The most frustrating occurrence for a trader is to sell for a small loss and then see the stock turn and eventually offer a profit. However, for as many times as this happens, again, it only takes one stock that doesn't come back to offer a profit that wipes out a trader's portfolio. Taking small losses is known as a strict stop loss regiment.

STOP LOSS DISCIPLINE

Stops will manifest themselves in a few ways: mental stops, trailing stops, and auto stops. Each has their place and importance, as well as their drawbacks. When I first began trading, I had to use purely mental stops to execute my decisions. This meant that I was unable to place a live order into the market with my broker that would be executed once the price hit my stop. I had to simply pick my point of stop loss and once the price was there, I had to execute that order at that specific period of time. However, during the SOES period when they still ruled the execution world, it wasn't much of a problem as Market Makers were showing liability sizes that made executing against them fairly easy. Therefore, I never felt the need for having to place a live order for a stop loss. I simply had to pick the point when I wanted to exit and, a good percentage of the time, my exit was executed at or very near my desired price.

Today, however, mental stops demand a higher degree of Level 2 understanding, as well as execution routing, since it's not as easy as just entering the SOES order. With liability requirements requiring Market Makers to execute a minimum of 100 shares, the way we route our orders has to be taken into effect. Without a Level 2 screen, we do not know which Market Makers or ECNs are showing with regards to specific sizes. This makes mental stops a bit more difficult when we have to make a split-second decision about keeping a mental stop.

More to this point, mental stops aren't much of a consideration for those that are efficient at executing their trades. Most traders I know that are efficient at executing all use mental stops and either exit into strength or pick the best route at or slightly below inside prices. There really is not much of a need for auto stops when a trader can automatically keep their mental stop at the best price that they feel they can exit at.

The benefits to using mental stops are that you can begin to trade in a more "at-the-moment" manner. This means that as the stock moves or doesn't move, your belief system of the trade can dictate the exit strategy and you can then exit as you see fit. Not having to enter in a stop order and then cancel and re-enter may save you some time in the approach to the exit. Your mind is more free to assess the stock at specific points in time when your belief system changes and you can exit the trade accordingly.

The negative side to this is obviously the ability to exit your trade if you are feeling somewhat underconfident about your execution skills. I find the reason many traders give for not entering a trade is the fear that they won't be able to exit if they have to at a reasonable price. With mental stops, this fear will not be alleviated until one has confidence in one's execution ability to keep that tight stop loss. As for developing this confidence, simply trading safe stocks from an execution standpoint or trading and watching fewer stocks at a time will help to alleviate the problem. If one trades a stock with a wide spread that jumps up and down in half-point increments, the execution risk is high, no matter how good one's execution ability is. If a trader is trading a tight spread stock with stable moves, then keeping a tight stop loss is much easier to do. The obvious option for those that are uncertain of their execution ability is the use of an auto stop.

Auto stops simply let a trader enter in a price to exit, should the price of the stock move to this price. If the price is hit, the trade is executed and the trader is out of the trade with minimal execution effort. Although I see auto stops as beneficial in certain cases, I personally find them to be more of a hassle than a benefit. Let's discuss ways in which an auto stop will not be beneficial.

Market Makers have their own agendas to stock moves, none of which has to do with executing auto stop orders solely for the purpose that they force you to lose money or give back profit. Stocks move because of buying and selling pressure due to "fear and greed," not because there are "x" amount of stop orders at certain price levels. Market Makers do not drop their bids to take these out, nor do they conspire to make this event happen. However, as the stock moves to the price of the auto stop, chances are that it will be executed a high percentage of the time. Sometimes this is what we wanted, sometimes not.

In the case that the stock is selling down relatively fast, maybe too fast to keep a mental stop at this price, this auto stop may be good. However, if the stock drops to the price of your auto stop but no real selling hits the stock, you are executed when the stock is really no longer falling. In the latter case, the mental stop is more useful. In the former case, if the auto stop is executed, then maybe the auto stop is the best choice. I also know that auto stops work best in cases when a trader absolutely has to leave the computer for whatever reason, but they do not want to close the position. Whether I agree with this process or not, I have no real preference. I tend to close all positions that I am not watching, but in some cases, I can see where an auto stop wouldn't be a negative thing. Having to leave a position that is showing relative stability isn't that bad of an idea as long as it is known that anything can happen while you are away. Traders like myself tend to develop iron bladders for the less "pressing" emergencies.

Moving back to the reality of the issue, executing both entries and exits is not a mechanical idea. It is something that has to be watched and executed in a fashion that does not go against your trading plan. There are cases where one or the other will work best, but it is up to your progress and understanding to know in what cases which one will work best. A simple mechanical approach to executing relating to a lack of understanding of how stocks are executed will not allow this progress to develop.

TRAILING STOPS

In the previous paragraphs, I have been mainly talking about stops when a trade moves against you. The next kind of stop relates to when the stock is moving in your direction. This is called the trailing stop. The trailing stop again can be mental or auto depending on both the methodology behind the trade as well as your reasonable ability to execute the exit. Trailing stops simply refer to moving the stop price in the direction that the stock is moving to lock in better profits.

For example, if I bought a stock at 40 and it was trading at 41, I may want to trail my stop higher to 40.50 in case it pulled back. This way I won't give up more than a half-point in profits. If it climbed to 42, I again may trail my stop to 41.50. Eventually, one of two things will happen. Either my beliefs will change about the value of the stock, that it is too high, and I will sell the stock at this price level or the stock will pullback on its own profit-taking and hit my trailed stop. Either one of these scenarios enables me to lock in better profits as the stock moves in my direction while taking reasonable profits along the way. Obviously, if I bought the stock at 40 and it fell below that price or whatever my stop price was, then I would execute the stop loss instead of initiating a trailing stop. This is clear since the stock no longer exhibited a performance consistent with my beliefs, so I would exit the trade with a small loss.

Now that we've gone over a few of the ideas and mechanics of stops, we need to discuss the psychology behind why stops are so hard to keep for newer traders and, in some cases, experienced traders as well. I have seen so many traders in my own room and heard about many others that have ended their careers because of that one stock that "had to come back" but never did. Eventually, the pain of loss became so great or worse, yet a margin call came, and they had to quit trading before they ever had a chance to see if they really had the abilities to become good traders. It is said that 70-percent of daytraders fail. A percentage of this failure rate is due to the inability to keep a tight stop loss. It only takes one bad trade to wipe out a portfolio. Don't let this happen to you.

A stop loss should never be seen as a negative thing as long as it is taken in the right steps of the trading process. As long as the stop price is determined and executed, the stop loss can be taken to ensure that you could come and trade another day. If the stop loss is more than desired because the previous stop price was overlooked or missed and not executed, then this is a personal flaw more often than not. Although I say that stops are the sole responsibility of the trader, I understand that at some points in time they are out of control of the individual. In these cases, we may have a technological glitch that removes our connection to the markets and by the time either a broker is contacted or the connection is restored, the trade has moved past your stop price. Although I understand this can happen, and it has happened to me, this is not a part of the stop loss process that we must focus on.

However, should this type of uncontrollable trading occur, there is a smart way to go about handling this case. If you are in a trade and the connection to the markets is lost, the idea is to stay calm and follow a few steps. First, go to your backup connection if you have one while you are calling your broker. Depending on which broker you use, you may or may not get the information you need to stay in the trade. If your broker is good about feeding information so that you can determine the continued momentum, you may want to stay in the trade until you can restore your connection or the trade pauses and momentum slows. If your broker is not good at this, then your only choice is to exit the trade. Many times I have seen traders in the MTrader chat room lose their quotes but not their ISP connection to the room and have other experienced traders watch the momentum and trade as you restore your connection. If you do not have this sort of support, it is normally best to exit your trade until the connection is restored and stable.

Going beyond the technological problem of not being able to keep a small stop loss is the emotional part. Many newer traders tend to view a loss as negative impact on their trading portfolio or take it personally as a negative reflection on their ability to trade. Many traders seem to believe that lost money is lost self-worth. This couldn't be further from the truth. A small stop loss taken is a sign of a disciplined trading program that one adheres to. It both instills confidence in your trading ability from an execution standpoint and enhances your reasoning for trading. When one goes back through one's trading journals and sees how much money is lost due to wider than desired stop losses, he or she will be amazed by the difference.

The other side of the issue is that many will key on those trades that came out as profitable simply by holding the stock and letting it come back to profitability. Again, this may work for you 9 times out of 10, but if the tenth time does not work out, you stand the chance to lose the profits from the previous nine times. Also, a strict stop loss regiment employed in this fashion will begin to tell you about your entry and exit points relative to timing and execution ability. This simply means that if you are taking numerous small stop losses while not providing enough gains, you are doing one of a couple things. You are either not entering close enough to the best price for the reversal or trade direction (chasing) or you are simply trading a plan that is not working for you. Taking 100 stops and losing $5,000 versus taking one blown stop and losing $5,000 will enable you to better assess your trading plan with more practice and experience under your trading guidelines. One trade won't allow you to know whether this trading plan is working or not. Trading more actively and assessing the win/loss and profit/loss ratio on this idea will give you a sense of how effective the plan is. Again, realize this is a momentum trader's plan and not an investor's plan, where one or two trades a year may be normal.

When a trader can begin to understand that a small stop loss or predetermined stop loss is a function of a trading plan, then they begin to see stop losses as a positive. This shift of psychology within a trader will ultimately help them to either achieve success or come to the realization that this method simply is not working for them. Acceptance of a small loss comes from a lot of personal change in many traders. Ego in a trader can play a huge role in not coming to this acceptance right away. Many traders feel that the reason they are in the trade is because they are right, and the market and everyone else is wrong. Therefore, they will cling to the issue until bankruptcy to prove themselves right. Unfortunately, you can see the detriment that this serves to traders. Getting rid of one's ego and stubbornness to prevent holding a losing trade and cut the losses immediately is a big step toward understanding stop loss executions. I simply look at a stop loss as a way to protect my capital from larger losses.

I know an investor that bought Sunbeam Corp (SOC) in the teens before it made the run over 50. As it moved over 50 several months later, I told him to keep a stop loss near 50 to lock in profits. A nearly 300-percent gain in less than two years on your money is certainly nothing to give up because of external hope that the stock will continue. However, negativity dumped the trade to low 30s and eventually to under $10 a share over the course of the next couple of years. Unfortunately this 300-percent gain turned into a tax write-off. Risks are involved both in investing and momentum trading. Keeping a stop, trailing, auto, or mental will serve you best as you continue. Ego and hope will not allow one to continue a consistent trading plan over time.

MONEY MANAGEMENT

Although the idea of money management to me is one of the most important aspects of trading, it is surprisingly how little it is discussed in many trading forums. My idea of money management is being able to keep losses small no matter how much money is being placed into the trade. Some traders tend to think in terms of lot size per trade, while others tend to think more in percentage terms. Let's look at each issue separately, as I feel both have their merits depending on what style of trading you have.

First, let's discuss the share lot size. Many traders, as they become efficient with their trading executions, look to increase their size position into the trade. This share size tends to not change with respect to stock price, meaning that traders will trade 1,000 shares whether the stock is $2 a share or $100 a share. Obviously, the comfort level of trading 1,000 shares will come in time to newer traders, while an experienced trader will think nothing of it. Notice that in this scenario, a trader will risk either $2,000 or $100,000. Although the share lot is the same, the percentage of the portfolio has obviously changed dramatically. For purposes of this discussion on money management, I will assume that trading 1,000 shares from an execution standpoint is relatively easy and does not pose a problem to take a wider than expected loss. However, assuming that a trader sees a trading opportunity in a more moderate to high-risk scenario, they will simply drop their share allotment to the trade.

In this case, instead of trading 1,000 shares, they may only trade 500 shares, capitalizing on the move but not opening them to more portfolio risk, should the trade provide too much difficulty in the execution phase. This change in thinking towards each trade can only be assessed from a personal viewpoint in the trader's willingness to add this extra risk and playing smaller shares. Many times I see this scenario in my own trading. However, times occur when I see this in other's trading and I would not employ this strategy. There is no right or wrong as traders are different and each decision is made on their own merits as a trader. The market will ultimately decide if the trade was right or wrong, but it will be the responsibility of the trader to execute the exit strategy.

Each trader must determine how tight to keep his stops and how much of a percentage of his portfolio he is willing to risk on any one trade. One trader may feel comfortable with keeping a .15-point stop loss, while another feels comfortable with .40 of a point. This is all determined by portfolio size and a willingness to lose a certain percentage of your portfolio on any one trade.

For instance, if your portfolio size is $50K, you are in a trade with 1,000 shares at $50 per share, and your stop is .25 of a point, then your loss potential is $250 plus commissions. If your portfolio size is only $25K, then your loss potential is still $250 but twice the percentage loss of your total portfolio. Market conditions may require you to loosen up your stops at times, but the number of shares should be adjusted to fit the total amount of loss you are willing to accept from your entire portfolio. You may want to only purchase 500 shares instead of 1,000 if your portfolio size is 25K on a $50 stock to keep the total percentages in line with your percentage loss program.

However, that being said, I am a firm believer in keeping your stops tight. After all, if the momentum has shifted against you, then the reason you originally entered the trade is no longer valid. This ensures that a good stop loss regiment will keep your total losses small. This assumes that you have the character and strength in your own trading plan to execute the stop loss when it needs to be stopped out, not changing the plan in midstream. Money management is a beautiful thing when employed in the right fashion for momentum traders. It helps to alleviate taking huge chunks out of your portfolio.

The learning curve can be fierce and your greatest resources include time and money. Fortunately, sometimes these are mutually exclusive, but often they are not. Give yourself enough time to let the trading plan work. Taking huge chunks out of your trading portfolio early in the learning process will not allow for this learning period to be long enough to catch on to the gist of the trading strategy. Obviously, if you are trading a small portfolio under $10,000, you have a harder road ahead of you in terms of share size and different price levels of stocks. However, whether you have $10,000 or $1,000,000, the principles of stop loss and money management must still be adhered to.

Be strong enough to accept the loss as a matter of safety, not personal negativity and disgust. If you can't get rid of the ego or the inability to execute stop losses when you know they should be taken, you may want to reconsider your choice to continue trading. You will save a lot of time, frustration, and money by doing so. Give yourself a chance and employ the described discipline in this chapter that best fits your abilities.

GOLDEN RULES OF TRADING

Any trader's system has to employ some kind of rules for themselves. The most important aspect is learning to execute these rules and, surprisingly enough, knowing when to break those rules. For me, break-ing these rules resides in the part of trading when one moves from mechanical trading to including a more intuitive sense of the markets. Although everyone has their special set of rules, I have listed those by which I trade everyday. These Golden Rules of Trading have been devel-oped by me over the years and should be memorized by the student. I suggest you print them on a poster and put them on the wall where you trade. The breaking of trading rules for the most part leads to confusion and losses. You will no longer be confident and exercise good judgment.

I have had students toss out the rules by "trying things." When you have fast profits, there is the temptation to experiment with them. If you are successful, at first it only reinforces bad habits. The losses will come fast and I have seen traders lose nearly all they have. If you do not know why you are losing, you are in serious trouble. I look at losses as tuition if I learn. I try to not get upset if I have followed the rules and executed a high percentage trade correctly. Every trader must deal with losses. Getting over the emotional part of trading, especially in a loss, is the most important concept to master. Do not be tempted into a "forced trade" to try to make up a recent loss; patience is your friend. Take only what the market offers.

GOLDEN RULE #1: CLEAR YOUR SPREAD

MACR Bid 9.20 Ask 9.25 Vol 433600 High 9.25 Low 9 Current 9.20
Clearing your spread would mean buying MACR at 9.25 and have enough buying occur as the bid up-ticks from 9.20 to 9.25. If you had to sell at this point at 9.25, you would get out even with the only cost being your commission. You have purchased opportunity. Do not fall into the trap I see all the time of predicting the price it will go through. Deal with the here and now and not with the pie in the sky. You have succeeded in your trade when the spread is cleared; that is your goal. The minute the buying stops and the exact opposite begins to occur, I sell! I do not care what the price is. What you have made is irrelevant.

The reason you bought the stock is no longer true when selling starts if you went long. Remember that traders begin to trade on a belief sys-tem that says the stock will move in a desired direction from where they entered. Once the belief system throws a change into this expectation, the exit strategy must be automatically executed. Should the belief system not demand an automatic execution of the exit strategy, the belief sys-tem fails to be something that we can rely on. If you can't rely on yourself in trading, then you are setting yourself up for certain failure. I often see the following comments:

"I sold it; now look at it. It's 5 points higher from where I sold it. I am a terrible trader." or "Hey, use me as a contrary. If I buy it, you guys short it. Heck, I should just do the opposite of what I think and I'd make a ton of money."

If this is your thinking or if you have ever thought in this manner, either change it or stop trading right now. If you can't rely on your own belief system, then there is no reason to trade on the stock market on an active basis. It would be best to put your money in mutual funds or U.S. Treasuries so you don't have to think about it. In this rule, once the stock clears your spread, your stop loss target should be made and exit into the price area where your belief system changes. Anything that happens after that, whether profit is missed out on or not, is left to the other traders. You took out of the trade what you could and you profited or lost from it. Don't let this hindsight trading mindset ruin your trading plan.

GOLDEN RULE #2: TRADE THE RULE, NOT THE EXCEPTION

Once you have adopted rules of trading, the stocks that present themselves for a trade *must* fit into the guidelines of your rules. This is what a trading model means. Twenty-twenty hindsight is the biggest cause for breaking rules. Five seconds after a stock has started either up or down, a trader always says to him- or herself, "I should have known it would do this!" The more a stock moves up, the worse you feel for not "trying" the trade. Many times I have purchased a stock, cleared my spread, and sold at the first hint of selling, making .25 of a point. The stock would go down as I expected and then start up another dollar. Unless you know that a large percentage of the time the trade does that, you will be tempted to stay in stocks that erase your profits.

Some stocks can fall quite rapidly, leaving you with huge losses. I have seen traders lose months' worth of profits in one of these trades. You are purchasing insurance against that happening by selling as soon as the reason for the purchase is no longer valid. Know how the trade usually reacts by carefully tracking your trades and patterns. Find the general patterns that occur with every type of momentum stock. The ones that react predictably are the rule, and the ones that don't are the exception. Know the rule and let the exception go. An exception will reinforce bad trading habits, especially if that trade was profitable. Quite often, I see traders who make huge one-time profits breaking rules, only to be

down significantly shortly thereafter. My rules of trading have successfully preserved my profits through many market changes.

GOLDEN RULE #3: STAY AWAY FROM ILLIQUID STOCKS

Illiquid stocks generally have high spreads and move extremely fast on
low volume. What goes up fast will go down faster. If you are on the
wrong side of an illiquid trade, your losses can be excessive. My only
exception is if I see a news story a few minutes before the market close,
and I know the story was exceptional, I may be more prone for a buy and
exit into strength in the after-market or pre-market the next day.

Recently, a news story hit the wires on a low-volume stock and I
advised a student to stay out. The stock went up $3, which was the excep-
tion. He was lamenting all day long that he did not do a market buy at
the beginning. The stock moved so fast from the initial rally price that a
market buy is the only way he could have gotten in. Use extreme caution on market buys. When you do trade with a market buy, you are trust-
ing your broker to execute in a timely manner. In a fast-moving stock,
your execution can be several minutes from the time you place the
order. You may actually buy at the top of the rally and not know it due
to delays. By the time you confirm the order, you are down the $3. I
know; I have done it, only once. I learned fast.

Sometimes a funnel effect occurs with fast-moving stocks as the
order queue fills up and prevents you from doing a fast market buy.
Everyone wants in at once. My advice is don't trade illiquid issues that
can be just that. Loss control is the most valuable tool for any trader.

Almost every illiquid stock that has any movement in it at all has
very large spreads of .50 to one full point. Stay away from stocks like this
at all costs unless it is one that has just invented the cure for cancer in
the last 10 minutes!

GOLDEN RULE #4: USE CAUTION WITH STOCKS WITH SPREADS OVER .25

This rule is in place to limit your losses. Any stock that changes the
spread dramatically should be avoided. I have been in trades that can be
under heavy buying when the market maker drops the bid .35 as he sees
selling orders hammering his bid price. Remember if he isn't a true buyer
of the stock, he won't be too willing to buy a lot of that stock at inside
price levels. When I see this, I exit immediately and never trade that stock

again. .35 plus .15 original spread cost me .50 a point loss. Any selling at all and you will be down one dollar in a hurry.

DATM BID 38.50 ASK 39.50 HIGH 39.50 LOW 36.90 CURRENT 38.50
MACR BID 9.20 ASK 9.25 HIGH 9.25 LOW 9 CURRENT 9.20

Notice the spread on DATM above is one full point, and the volume is only 92K. This is typically a trade to stay away from. If you buy DATM at 39.50 thinking it may go up, and the buying stops and selling comes in, even without a down-tick, you are already down one full point. If you had 500 shares of this stock, you would be down $500 from the start. On the other hand with MACR, if you bought at 9.25 and selling came in, you would only lose .05 before the down-tick. If you bought 1,000 shares, that is only a loss of $50, quite a difference.

GOLDEN RULE #5: KNOW WHY YOU GOT INTO A TRADE AND GET OUT WHEN THAT REASON IS NO LONGER VALID

This rule is probably one of the most difficult to teach as it involves ego with each trader. It is especially difficult early on in a trade to admit the stock is heading in the opposite direction you expected. I have seen traders paralyzed to inaction when the buying turns to selling. This is especially true when you have profits in a trade, but the profits are not as great as you had hoped.

When selling starts, your insurance policy against a fast and continual retreat down is your sell. When the trade dips down and starts back up to a higher price (stair-stepping), 20/20 hindsight always seduces you to hold the next trade and not take early profits. Only hold through stair-stepping if you know that a high percentage of the time, the type of momentum trade you are in usually stair-steps in your favor. I cannot emphasize enough, selling the trade is your insurance policy (see Figure 12-1).

Notice that USCS made three bottoms, the first at 24, the second at 20.25, and the third at 18.35. I recently had a student who purchased this stock at the first bottom, made .15, and then bought it again at the second bottom. Notice it did not bounce from the second bottom and the logical exit point was .15 below his entry. The reason he bought the stock was no longer there, it was no longer getting bought, and the selling came in. He did not sell and lost nearly $1,000 when he finally exited the trade at the third bottom. Know why you bought and when that reason is no longer there, exit the trade at your predetermined exit point *every time*.

FIGURE 12-1

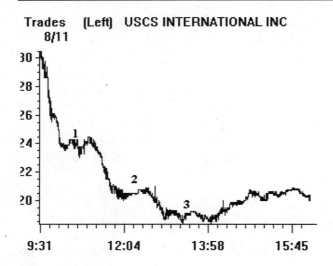

Trades   (Left)   USCS INTERNATIONAL INC
   8/11

GOLDEN RULE #6: PAPER TRADE UNTIL
YOUR SYSTEM TRADES ABOVE 90-PERCENT

Traders with small portfolios cannot afford many losses. Their system of trading must allow them tremendous gains to make a living. Paper trading is an exercise in patience and in the long run keeps the money in the proper pocket: the traders. Every time I try something new without paper trading first, I lose no matter how good it sounds in theory. If it is a solid method, it will hold up over time. I have known traders who were addicted to trading and were continually trying new methods. They wound up confused, frustrated, and broke.

When traders begin to move away from paper trading to using real money, the problem is that they have a fear of pressing the execute button because real money is now involved in the trading plan. From this, we teach our traders to use small shares in the beginning. This does two things. First, it does not offer much loss potential for those trades that turn out to be negative. Secondly, it enables a trader to get over the fear of pressing the buy and sell buttons. In doing so, traders can begin to both practice their execution ability as well as eliminate some of the emotional fears of trading. It is a long process to become proficient at executing and even longer to control one's emotions. Trading small shares in the beginning will help.

GOLDEN RULE #7: TAKE PROFITS WHEN YOU HAVE THEM!

Although I have found it generally true that more profits can be made from a stock if you ride out the selling on a stock that is going up, those that reverse and continue down can do so at such a rapid pace that the losses can be excessive. One of the biggest faults traders continually have is to second-guess a stock's movement. They continually second-guess their trades by allowing 20/20 hindsight to dictate their trading. The second after a stock moves in a certain direction, a trader will say to himself, "I should have known it would do that!" Remember you can only go with the flow at the moment. If a stock is selling at $10 per share, you cannot know if the next low is 3 or the next high is 20. Daytraders live in the moment. I take my small profits and wave good-bye no matter what the next direction is. I have never been sorry.

FORE is such an example (see Figure 12-2). I had a student who shorted FORE on $\frac{8}{12}$ at the open. He exited the trade when the selling stopped and made .05 of a point. Not much of a profit, but he stuck to the rules and avoided staying with the trade. He missed out on a 1.5 point rise and saved himself from making a $1,500 mistake. I make my

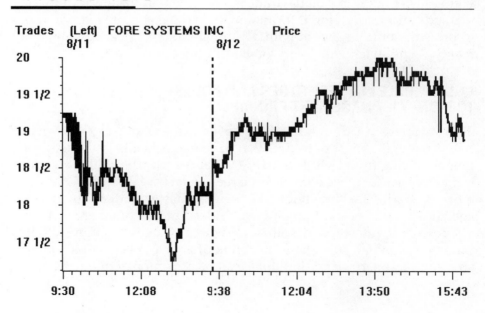

F I G U R E   1 2 - 2

profits in the same manner as a taxi driver makes his, one trade at a time and in small percentages. I am happy with .25 to .50 point gains, as they add up quickly.

GOLDEN RULE #8: WRITE DOWN THE TIME
TO THE NEAREST MINUTE YOU PLACED YOUR TRADE

This rule is intended for those who use broker expectation systems. Brokers are human and they make mistakes. I have had trades executed 10 minutes after I placed a market sell! I called my broker and complained, giving him the time I placed it. Not only can you get a better execution price, but you can test the quickness of your broker's services. If the stock is going down rapidly, you can lose a lot with slow executions. You should have a reasonable idea of how long it takes to execute your trades with each of the different stock exchanges.

GOLDEN RULE #9: KNOW THY SOURCE

As you begin active trading, never rely solely on the advice of others. Plenty of self-proclaimed trading gurus out there are nothing but stock hypers with less than stellar intentions to separate you from your money. Remember that everyone has their way of trading; it is up to you develop yours. Listening to reputable traders will give you insight into trading methods and underlying information, but in the end, it is you that has to press the buttons. Learn with a bit of skepticism to keep yourself in reality. Apply what works for you and throw out the rest.

GOLDEN RULE #10: KEEP STOPS AND ADHERE
TO MONEY MANAGEMENT PRINCIPLES

Stop losses again are your insurance policy to alleviating more downside risk. Although I know of traders that have made profits in the six-figure range, starting from as little as $10,000, I also know the ability to do this is much easier for those who have a large capital base. However, the more money a trader has does not make them a smarter trader. Money management principles and the complete understanding of margin rules are a necessity. If you come to a situation where you get a margin call, this can wipe out your portfolio in the blink of an eye. Keep stops manageable and reasonable, and don't place all of your money in one trade.

GOLDEN RULE #11: KNOW THY ABILITIES

The ability to make money here and there on unsafe stocks such as IPO issues and low float runners will ultimately kill you on one or two trades. There is no way to safely trade fast-moving stocks or exceptions. Enough safe opportunities occur during the trading day that we need not have to risk our capital base on high-risk trading.

GOLDEN RULE #12: OVERNIGHT GAP PLAYS ARE TO BE TRADED ONLY WITH RISK CAPITAL

Overnight gap plays assume much risk. There has to be a stable to strong market in the morning and even this doesn't guarantee a gap up. My best examples of this were on SDLI and RBAK in June of 2000, shown in Figures 12-2 and 12-3.

The market looked fairly positive in pre-market conditions, but both RBAK and SDLI gap plays traded lower by better than 5 points. A 5-point hit in one trade is unacceptable in momentum trading and could very well take a huge chunk out of the trading portfolio. The risk is higher, so if you are playing with a limited capital base to begin with, be sure to trade what you have control over, not trading overnight risk.

GOLDEN RULE #13: ACCEPT RESPONSIBILITY FOR YOUR TRADING

No one has told you to trade the markets, nor are they making you buy and sell stocks. The ultimate decision to trade is yours and yours alone. Profits can be enjoyed by you and losses have to be accepted by you. When you begin blaming others for your mistakes, whether it includes Market Makers, brokers, or those with "tips," you are displacing blame to an area where it doesn't belong. Responsibility in your trading stays with you always. If you ultimately need to leave trading, then you will be able to tell yourself that you made all the necessary moves to progress and it just didn't work out. If you succeed, you can relish the fact that it was solely you that made this opportunity happen. Teachers and colleagues will help you through the process, but win or lose, the trading is yours.

GOLDEN RULE #14: HAVE THE STRENGTH TO QUIT WHEN IT'S CLEAR IT'S NOT WORKING

I have seen a few traders in the room lose their entire portfolios, save another $5,000, lose it again, and complete the cycle again. Have enough character to know when enough is enough. Trading isn't for everyone. There needs to be enough inner strength within you to know when it is time to pursue other avenues in life. At the very least, you leave with an increased sense of market awareness that you didn't have when you first began this journey.

13 CHAPTER

PERSONAL ACCOUNTABILITY AND TRADING ATTITUDE

One of the most common errors that traders can face in trading is following their egos. Ego is one of the most destructive forces within a trader's mindset when trading. One's ego manifests itself in a way that everyone else is wrong and, given enough time, they will realize it. Egos will also lead traders to believe that events in the market that offer a negative response, whether in a wider than accepted loss or uncontrollable trade, are someone else's fault. The lack of accountability by a trader because of their inflated egos eventually gets the better of them. The market will always find a way to crush someone's ego either by a huge loss or by a string of losses when traders fail to admit they are wrong and take accountability for being wrong by cutting losses immediately.

No matter how logical traders try to make the market seem, there is one common theme: that the market does what it does. The more sense a person tries to make out of the situations that occur in the market everyday, the more confused they become, unless there is a real understanding about several issues of the market. Market Makers have agendas each and everyday. Institutions have their plans laid out. Market technicians, analysts, fund managers, hedge fund owners, insurance companies, and many more participants have many opinions about the market's valuation and where stocks and the market indices should be. There is clearly no way to ascertain each and everyday what is happening in the market as it is happening. This lack of certainty creates a lot of fear and stress in newer traders.

Throughout our youth, we have been taught to seek the truth, to see something that happens and try to explain it. The market doesn't work in such a way. Traders see something happen and they have to react before the information is "figured out." Throughout this book, we have seen numerous examples of when the street finally figures out a trend or a stock move, it is nearly over. Continuously trying to figure out why things happened can certainly benefit us for the future, but in the sense that trading is "of the moment," constant guesswork about what just happened leads many traders on the wrong path. They are so adamant about what just occurred that they are willing to accept any and all explanations about that event.

Seeking this truth isn't necessarily a negative thing, but what people come up with to explain these events is certainly suspect at best. Literally thousands of false interpretations are made about the market every year. Those traders that don't know any better simply believe this information on faith because the information seems logical. It is a trader's job to set forth goals to learn about market information in a manner in which they can filter out the misinformation from the market.

When traders first realize that the information that they were given is wrong, it normally is at the point when a loss is made on a trade. The trader blames the source of the information or some other external force as to why a negative result came about from the information that they perceived to be true. Instead of finding out the reality of the situation, the trader displaces responsibility and accountability elsewhere. In this process, a trader learns nothing and progresses no further in his own trading. Put accountability where it belongs, within you.

The market is never wrong. I start examining a person's ego when I see a trader in a losing position that is clearly against the trend or the market and they refuse to acknowledge the loss of the trade. Their mindset is such that they are right and the market is wrong. If anyone thinks they are larger than the market, that they are smarter or more correct than the market, they had better re-evaluate their egos or cease to participate in the market. Conversely, the market doesn't know who you are. It doesn't know how much you owe on your car, house, or boat. It doesn't know that you have three kids and a spouse to support. It doesn't know, nor does it care. The market simply exists to exchange money from the losers to the winners.

Which scenario happens the most over time is up to you and how you decide to trade it. It depends on whether your stubbornness in incorrect thinking is corrected or if you can't accept loss no matter how much is lost in a losing position. The market will reward those traders that can stick to a discipline that works for them and punish those that fail to develop and adhere to a set of guidelines. With the market so unforgiving in this fashion, the accountability has to be within you. You need to trust yourself and your abilities. If you succeed, you have no one to thank but yourself. If you fail, you have no one else to blame. Trading decisions reside in you. Learn to develop this trust in yourself and stay accountable for all your decisions and actions.

When a trader begins to trust in him- or herself, to take responsibility for the trade, he or she can begin to work much better on stop loss issues as well. We talked earlier about fear and the inability to keep a stop loss. Although there are technological limitations to keeping a stop loss, the most important is the inability to act upon a stop loss price. Many newer traders do this for fear of loss and shame that they associate with a loss. Seasoned traders view a stop loss as a positive as it protects their capital base from wider than desired losses. The transition from fear of loss to an emotionless loss taken to prevent this possibility of a wider decrease in portfolio funds stems from taking responsibility in the trade. They no longer respond to the ego in the trade, but rather they employ a mindless stop response to exit the trade immediately. When exiting the trade for a loss, there is no sense of shame, loss, frustration, or anger. There is just a sense of complacency that the trade didn't offer a wider than desired loss, and the next opportunity that comes along is taken. The more accountable a trader becomes to himself, the more he is able to learn about his own methodologies and even more about himself as a trader.

If a trader responds well to a trading discipline and matches its criteria for exit and entry without emotion or lack of accountability, he can begin to assess its validity on its own merits. He can decide how much loss and profit the method employed was actually doing. The results are right there to be reviewed. No emotions are attached to the profit or loss made, and therefore the viability of a trader using this method can be assessed. If the methodology is showing a reasonable trading style with good discipline principles, the next step in a trader's progress is to move to his mechanical approach to his intuitive approach. A lack of accountability whether through an ego or other emotional barrier will limit a trader's feel in the markets. This lack of feel either in the overall market trend or in a stock itself will ultimately be a detriment to a trader's progress.

If a trade is relatively safe, the setup is the same, and all other variables point to a buy, the trader needs to define that feeling within himself of why that trade wasn't entered. Many call this approach an

intuitive one. In order to profit over the long term, a trader has to bring
the results of a trade to a level where it is a decision that is manifested
from within. The trader acts on his own belief and exits in the same fashion. Many years of mechanical understanding, being around other
traders, feeling the markets, and participating develops this mechanical
approach and ties it into impulses that the mind can develop for a trader
to follow. If this is cluttered with external negative information such as
Market Maker manipulation and the evilness of the market itself, a
trader does not stand a chance from learning the true and underlying reasons for what has just happened to him. A person can't move along life
blaming everyone else and everything else for personal loss. There is no
difference in trading. The responsibility lies within each trader individ-
ually and his actions must demand a response from this responsibility.

TRADING ATTITUDE

It is uncanny how many traders refuse to accept the trend that is occurring either in the market or in their respective positions. They fight these
trends over and over until the position takes too much of a loss to bear
and they exit with that realized loss. Worse yet, I see traders holding losing positions, waiting for the market to return this position to profitability. The first scenario stems from breaking the rules of stop loss
management, while the latter scenario stems from simple ego. They feel
the market is wrong and, given enough time, the market will come to its
senses. Either way, they have a constant struggle within the markets as
well as within themselves that hinders progress. Instead of following
their beliefs on trends and taking small losses or riding gains, they simply enter a position at a specific time period. If the trade goes their way,
they believe themselves to be great traders, that what happened was
exactly what was expected. If they are wrong, they do not exit but rather
tell themselves the position will at some point become profitable anyway
because they know better.

Tell that to those holding CORL and BAMM in the '40s and ETYS
from the '70s. Rather than fighting the trend, a trader needs to know how
to change with the market and follow the trend. During times when your
indicators are proving you wrong is the time to exit. Although I certainly
believe strongly in a trader's intuition, there has to be a point that the
trader takes action to stop the bleeding even if the belief is strong
enough. There is no sense in owning a position that has wiped out
50 pecent of your portfolio because of a strong feeling, especially if your

market indicators are showing you something that confirms the reason to exit.

Changing with the market comes from many years of experience. Newer traders have the most difficult time changing with the market because they do not have a feel for the markets. There is no experience of market moves, no understanding of what drives markets, and no abilities to follow their beliefs based on limited knowledge. Many professional traders have a feel of where the market is headed and are able to build upon positions based on this feel. Before traders can understand this level of feeling, they must spend years working on the mechanical ideas presented to them within their trading system. Whether it is short-term trading or even investing, there has to be an understanding and experience derived from a trader's interaction from the markets. The more familiar the mechanics become over time, the more a trader can act automatically on market opportunities.

Markets change constantly. It is a dynamic environment that shows changing indicators, patterns, and moves, but it is based on a few common things. These are things like fear, greed, panic, and disagreement of value. These underlying aspects to the markets cause volatility and constant change. Traders will continue to trade their patterns and indicators until they no longer work. In this sense, a trader will cease to exist if he does not learn to adapt to the changing of his patterns and indicators relative to his belief system. A trader must be just as dynamic as the market but with a set of rules that enables him to profit handsomely when he is right and cut losses immediately when he is wrong.

Traders gain this ability by years of hard work. The notion that a trader can trade for one or two hours a day and play golf the rest of the day sounds nice, but if a trader really wants to be consistent over time, he needs to dedicate himself to his progress. The idea is not to become a part of the market, but rather to let the market become a part of you. Once the market is inside you, you will gain that feeling that is needed to change with the markets. Getting to this point takes many years to do so and it is a process that never ends due to the dynamic nature of the market.

You can become more in touch with the mechanical sides of trading in some very simple ways while you are learning. Once you begin to make the mechanical side of your trading more automated, the bridge to your mental state can start to develop. The most obvious start is for a trader to associate himself with better traders. At the beginning, this isn't a very hard step. However, I am surprised at how many traders come into the trading game with their pre-conceived ideas and are unwilling to accept any information from colleagues. They figured that they had been around the markets long enough that they had nothing to learn or be taught. They found out months later that they needed to expand their willingness to participate with those more knowledgeable than them.

The idea behind this association is to build a trust with that individual to teach you the mechanics behind trading and to correct any misinformation behind market moves or other aspects of trading that is suspect in chat rooms or bulletin boards. Once a trader begins to understand relatively simple aspects of trading, they have a foundation by which to accept or reject further information stemming from their current knowledge base. Once they get a reasonable sense of the markets, they need to begin to build some expectations for the future both within themselves as well as their chosen system.

Many traders fail to plan their strategy in the beginning. This can be seen in poor planning of their capital base or their willingness to jump right in the market with their money without understanding why they are entering the market in the first place. Remember that there are no minor leagues in trading. You step up to the plate with your money in hand and the best traders in the world are happy to take it if you let them. Market Makers and professional traders are trained over many years to trade the markets. They have more knowledge than you and are able to capitalize richly on this knowledge. This is where a trader must again devote and commit to trading as a profession. A trader must carefully track his or her system on a daily basis. There needs to be a foundation for the system being utilized that fits you and how you feel about the markets. Regardless if the trading system is scalping, short-term trading, or momentum trading, you must carefully keep track of the way that system provides opportunity throughout the day. A trader needs to get a feel for different periods of the day as some may provide more opportunity than others.

When tracking the macro-momentum of the markets, I want to know if the market has been moving up or down. I want to determine the breadth of the market relative to the total volume. If I see a strong move to the upside but there is no volume conviction, then I will be more cautious the next day to see if that market move can be confirmed. Conversely, if the market is falling fast on low volume, then I'm more inclined to not trust its true direction. If the underlying market indicators such as breadth and volume support what the stock move showed, I'm more inclined to trust it. If not, then I'm looking to see something that will confirm it. If there is nothing to confirm the trend, then I'm skeptical at best for any positions that I may be holding. Each day I look at the macro by how strong the market pace is relative to the move that is being made at that point in time. I want to know how strong the buying and selling is near the open, mid-day, and into the close. Furthermore, I want to apply this to my patterns to see if there is a correlated affect on my patterns.

For example, I want to know whether my gainer category is showing me enough strength in the market to be aggressive when looking for bottoms or if I should be more inclined to go short. I want to know if the trend is selling so that if the gainer category is strong, but the macro is showing me negativity, I can be more cautious. If the market ends the day on strong selling and the next morning I don't see a lot of value buying, I will be expecting more selling the next morning that would make me cautious to be aggressive early in the gainer group. Unless the stocks are gapping down the next morning on strong pre-market volume that may bring in value buying at the open, I will be looking to short into any runs on stocks and continue to follow the downtrend on this selling. Conversely, if the macro ended the day positively and my gainer pattern is showing me signs of strength, then I will be more inclined to be aggressive off the bottoms early and back off shorting the group. What I am doing is finding the macro flow of the market and applying it to the more micro sense of stock action to participate. When I'm right and the stock is following the flow that I am experiencing from tracking the patterns and the macro, I will be rewarded. If, for some reason, the market is not showing me what I believe to be true, I will not fight the market, but rather take a stop loss immediately to protect my capital until I am able to get back into the feel for the trend again.

If you notice that I am not being stubborn in my trend decisions, I am changing with the market trend as it changes, profiting from the following of the trend. The dumper pattern will also show me signs of a change. When the pattern is strong and when stocks are making only one bottom early and then rising fast in the morning or even slowly throughout the day, I will be more aggressive on the bottoms and back off shorting this category. When the pattern shows me a weakness, either due to real nervousness in the market or continuous multi-bottoms, I will be more inclined to back off the first bottoms and look to go short if value buyers aren't attacking these negative overreactions to the downside. In times of great speculation and nervousness, stocks can be cut in half on one of these overreactions.

I want to track this pattern to see how confident value buyers are in these time periods so that I can develop a feel for whether the stock will begin a rise early or show more weakness. By developing this experience and knowledge on how specific categories and patterns are reacting relative to their respective markets, I can begin to take the mechanical approach of this tracking and apply it to the feel that I derive from years of watching these patterns and indicators. If we simply trade the markets for two hours a day, we do not develop this feel. Conversely, if we do not trade these markets consistently, we lose that feel as we are unable to change with the markets because we aren't giving our attention and time to doing so.

I talked with one trader who recently returned from a three-month vacation after having one of his most successful years of trading. He came back after this vacation and had a real problem trying to develop this feel for the market again. He felt that the market dynamics had changed so much in three months that the market was no longer a part of him and he had to redevelop this relationship with the market. Time and commitment to the markets are essential to keep the edge of this market feel as well as to allow it to expand in order to aid in your progress as a trader.

Understanding your patterns and how they may relate to the macro trend in the markets allows you to pick your entry and exit points accordingly. There are days that you can feel when to enter the market and get the best intra-day price available. When you are wrong, you simply take the loss and re-evaluate what the market is telling you to do. When you are right, you continue with your feel until the feel changes and you need to exit the position. This is true for both long and short positions in the market. Knowing when to enter and exit will eventually be defined upon your experience of the market and the automated process of acting on these feelings. The feelings are derived from years of experience trading the markets, so trust them. Act on them.

When you just can't seem to get in sync with the markets, when your indicators are constantly stopping you out of trades, and your beliefs are in conflict with what the reality of the market is, this is a good time to step back from your trading to re-evaluate. Many traders I know surprisingly get more aggressive in these time periods trying to get the feel for the market. They are trying to win back those losses with more aggressive trading. The problem is that the underlying cause for the losses hasn't been rectified. Until this problem finds itself a solution, the same mistakes will be made, leading to more loss. If the market is extremely narrow or the indicators are not confirming your beliefs, this is a time to be more passive in your trading. If there is uncertainty within you and your trading plan, the idea is step back and find the problem. Take a step back and find that zone again where the market is once again a part of you. Until this time, do not be aggressive.

When you can feel yourself in sync with the markets in such a way that the indicators and beliefs within yourself are working together in tandem, this is the time to be aggressive. This is the time to let the automation of what you know to be true come out in the markets and take advantage of the opportunities being presented. This type of trading environment is incredibly exciting as you begin to reap rewards for your patience. Obviously, not every trade will yield a profit, but the trends will be followed and the profits built up over time should outweigh the losses being taken in catching that trend. However, there is that fear of the reappearance of the ego, the idea that nothing can hurt you and this can lead to reckless trading again. I've often found myself trading very well at certain times, but I've had to almost step back and ask myself if this is just too much at one time.

I've had to beat my ego back into submission to keep my concentration on the markets, to enjoy the game of trading rather than the rewards it was bringing me. I know that if I get out of control, the market will find its way to retake the profits that I had just made. I don't know if I've ever been too aggressive in the market, but I'm aware of the troubles that it can cause when I'm losing aggressively, as well as profiting aggressively. Obviously, the latter I can deal with better, but I must be aware to keep my mind clear on why I was profiting in this manner so as not to clutter the reasons for this progress and not end its ability to keep me going in this direction.

This is a purely mental state that pure mechanical traders will fail to understand. In most cases, newer traders using a purely mechanical approach will end up losing their hard-earned profits in this manner as they feel invincible from the markets. They will increase lot sizes, trade out of the feel, break rules, and end up losing most of what they made from market prior to this. Know when to be aggressive and when to be passive. Developing this feel from years of understanding the mechanical system will aid in this progress.

14 CHAPTER

MOMENTUM INVESTING

In this section, I will discuss what I call the best of both worlds. It combines the short-term techniques of momentum trading with long-term methods of investing. It is meant to be completely separate from the previous chapters and can be used to fine-tune your long-term trades. Many people think just because I am a short-term momentum trader that I have no interest in long-term trading. Nothing could be further from the truth.

HOW AND WHY I BEGAN THIS LONGER-TERM APPROACH

A few months ago I went looking for a manager to handle my retirement account as I was too busy to give it much attention and I was tired of gaining only money market percentage increases. After interviewing a few, and asking how they did compared to the Standard & Poor's 500, I soon realized that they intended to diversify me under the table with the same type of general plan with minimal gains that they have touted for many years. After mulling over the expenses and their lack of real direction, I decided to simply do a few longer-term momentum trades per year on my own and reasoned that I should come out better than what I was being offered. So began my long-term trading career.

As a momentum trader, I am in a very good position to spot daily momentum and can use my flexibility to gain profits. Most money-managed funds lack flexibility and so they wind up diversifying until the profits are watered down by the accumulation of dogs. They really make money based on their reasons for the trades and not the trades themselves. They have golden tongues for investment spiel, but most cannot beat the S&P index. The ones that do usually get into cycles before they occur but are then destined to ride them down as interest wanes and profits fade.

A recent example of this was seen in the biotech sector. After rising to phenomenal heights, it hit the skids, wiping out profits fast and furiously. "Why not sell the high?" you ask. Few money managers can time the market that well, and most hold long-term. The more they trade, the higher they drive up commissions, expenses, and tax liabilities, so they are forced into an inflexible long-term approach. They depend on a "rising tide floating all boats." So I strongly feel that anyone willing to educate themselves about momentum and to actively take charge of their own investments will have much more profitable results as they take advantage of the market momentum.

I needed to overcome a few pitfalls in making the transition from daytrading to momentum investing. It was a time of trial and error getting the right combinations together and finding my way into this new territory. The first thing I realized is that my daytrading background oriented me too closely to the short term. I had to constantly fight the impulse to take .50-point profits. I had to learn to let my stocks breathe and develop more slowly into larger potential. I was in it, after all, for the long term. The second thing I found was that some of my long-term trades were no longer breathing and needed some mouth-to-mouth resuscitation. I had to learn to identify and separate those plays developing slowly from those going nowhere.

I find investing in momentum plays just as exciting and emotional as daytrading. I have found a new respect for the investor who is able to buy and hold and not obsess over their portfolio. Because of the momentum trader in me, I can be obsessive at times, so I play very small shares to ensure I don't obsess over every trade. In this market with all its fluctuations and uncertainty, I now feel the daytraders have it much easier than the investors. They are in and out of trades within a few hours, ending the day in cash, and don't care what the market does the next day. Investing ain't easy!

I came to the conclusion rather quickly though that momentum plays were the most profitable way to trade my retirement account while still not over-burdening my time. I began trading a couple times a week and increasing my portfolio at a rate where my gains after a couple months exceeded what I was hoping for at the end of the year.

THE PRINCIPLES OF MOMENTUM IN INVESTING

When stocks move, they tend to oscillate up and down in waves. We call these waves "momentum." The waves do not move uniformly, however. They will either oscillate in an up-turning trend, making gradual new highs and higher lows, or they will oscillate in a downward trend, making gradual new lows with each turn. Imagine it is like a ball making tiny bounces up a staircase, and then down a staircase. In daytrading, we are taking advantage of each bounce the ball makes. In momentum investing, we are taking that time frame a bit longer, and taking advantage of the staircase, rather than each bounce of the ball. Momentum investing is similar to the principles of momentum trading, taking advantage of short-term movements. The exception being you let your trades ride until they run out of steam or until you have sufficient profits. You ride the trade until the ball loses momentum and arrives at the top of the staircase.

To accurately judge this momentum, a momentum player must be aware of the general principles of momentum: selling creates value . . . value creates buying . . . buyers create profits . . . profits create selling. The quicker the action occurs, the more predictable the action. Stocks do not move on their own; people move stocks as they react to potential. The faster the potential presents itself, the faster the reactions will occur. I call it the principle of "time and movement," as previously discussed in the book.

The principle of "time and movement," which is the basis of momentum trading, means that generally when you see 20-percent or more in a short period of time, that movement will then be counteracted to, also within a short-term period of time. The faster a stock moves up or down by 20-percent, the more predictable it becomes in its actions and counteractions, and it is then described as having momentum. This principle applies to both daytrading and longer-term momentum plays on different time-scales.

So we first identify momentum in a large movement up or down. This creates increasing incentive, and near the 20-percent mark, we look for reactions to that incentive. We then jump onto that wave for as long as it flows. At the tops, as profit-taking incentive increases, we then have a choice to sell or hold for an even longer-term trend. Understanding the principles of "time and movement" and momentum will help you to make your decisions.

For example, when the Nasdaq hit its recent bottom after the crash at 3040, I began looking for reactions to the growing incentive in the values created. I then began adding positions as I identified momentum coming into individual stocks and the buyers coming in stronger during the day's trading, indicating the counter-reaction was beginning. Cisco, (CSCO) is a stable market leader and often a good one to watch for general market indication (see Figure 14-1). At the market bottom, CSCO came off a low of 50 and climbed nicely up to $60 in a few days on one heck of a nice rally.

Value hunters reacted to the value that was created in a short period of time during its quick drop to 50. At 60 then, we have a choice of exiting with the profits of the short-term momentum or holding as a long-term investment.

A few further keys can be used to unlock your understanding of momentum stocks, such as trading volume, the news event that began the momentum, the intra-day range, the gap up on the day of the news if it began prior to the market open, and also the ending value in com-

F I G U R E   1 4 - 1

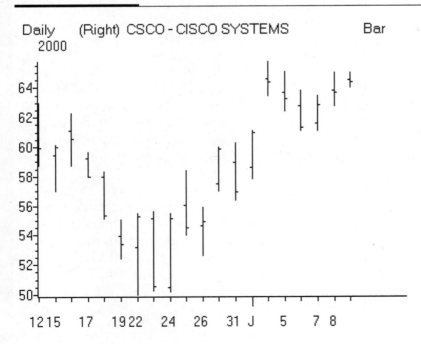

parison with the high and low. This criteria is the same as for daytrades in the Gainer category, as discussed earlier.

MOMENTUM INVESTMENT CANDIDATES

It is important to compare daily charts of the stocks you are considering with a daily chart of the market to assess whether they are market followers or acting on their own momentum. We want only those stocks that are participating in the general market and moving with the general market direction. For example, if the market has pulled back and I am seeing the first day of good buying with many of my leaders ending the day strong, I will look at charts for stocks that were obviously pulling back and climbing right in line with the market. I call them "participators," and they become good candidates to buy if you expect the market momentum to continue upward for a day or two. I like to do scans that pick the bottom dwellers on the first day they end above the mid-range point with increased volume.

Those are candidates to do well if the market is inclining, because value has been found by traders.

When considering a long-term investment, it is necessary to first establish a long-term bias. In other words, is the market climbing in the next few years or declining? That is your first and most important decision to make, and no one knows for sure. You can look at the history of the stock market and build a better case for an inclining market than for a declining one. In momentum investing, we begin exactly the same way, with an established bias. The short-term trend must also be determined when entering positions and the further you miss the upward momentum, the longer you have to wait for your positions to turn around and participate in the inclining market. When you enter a long position because the stock is under momentum, should the market then turn against you, the stock will also turn against you and you will be forced to ride it down until the market turns once again. But it will come back, if it is a market participator, when the market comes back. The nice thing about an investor is they have time to wait it out. It will lock up your capital, however, if you accumulate too many positions at market tops.

Once you enter your position, you are now an investor. One thing you must get in your head at the very outset is that you have a good stock with positive momentum. If the market dips, your stock will go down, but when the market recovers, your stock will too. This position should be a very small part of your total portfolio. The law of participation means that your stock will follow the leaders and the general market. If the market dips, your stock will dip. If the market climbs, your stock should also climb. Once you find that your stock is not participating with the market, exit the trade. Small shares will protect you against excessive losses. Do not fall into the trap of tying up daytrading money by listening to the lure of the investor. Hindsight is your worst enemy as you regularly see stocks such as Qualcomm (QCOM) that move up incredibly in one year. You will tend to think long-term investing is easier than daytrading, and it is not easier or as profitable.

I only enter small positions at one time, to protect the bulk of my capital, and it has worked for me very well. I like to invest very small shares (around 200) per trade and keep my investment risk small, but I expect at least 10-percent gains per trade. Many times the momentum will be much greater than expected and often the gain far exceeds my expectations. Online traders have brought a lot more opportunity into our market and as their numbers grow, so does the momentum they create. In June of 2000, I advised my traders that Rambus (RMBS) had strong-enough momentum to carry it from 57 to a target of over 100 within the next few days. A few days later RMBS was trading at 138 (see Figure 14-2).

Those types of trades are whipped cream, but they are a product of being in a good trade to begin with. I do not trade everyday, and I only move when the market looks consistent. All I really need are a few good trades per month to make very good percentages, far beyond what any mutual fund would make for me.

I will normally enter a trade at the end of the day in the last 10 minutes of trading. I have all day to evaluate the merit of the reason for the momentum and estimate who is in the trade. Daytraders will take profits on the next day and cause an initial short-term downturn at open, so many times I will be forced to absorb some selling before the institutional traders begin to climb on board for a nice steady climb. It is important to evaluate the action by looking at a long-term chart and not get obsessed with the short-term oscillations, which is a problem for me because of my day-trading background. I tend to get obsessive and watch all the small movements, so I have found it beneficial to my long-term goals to not watch the stock at all but simply evaluate where the trade ends the day in relationship to the Low and High, trying to develop a longer-term outlook. I feel protected due to the small amount of shares and the fact that I purchased a good company with an excellent outlook in the next 12 months. Remember the lower priced stocks can be over-

FIGURE 1 4 - 2

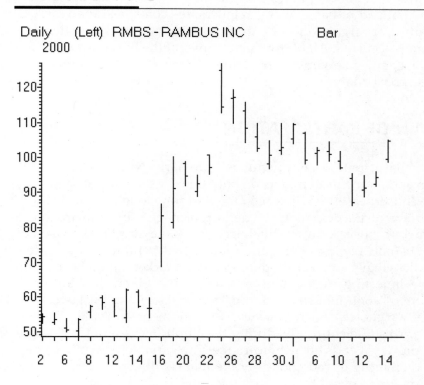

Daily   (Left) RMBS - RAMBUS INC   Bar
     2000

weighted with daytraders and cause some serious volatility and should be avoided when possible.

Always be on the lookout for bargains. As bargains become more obvious, they bring in bargain-hunters. So be aware of "all-time lows" and consider going shopping. The signs of increasing momentum I look for are ending the day well above the mid-range point with a price increase from the previous day and increased volume. Look for sudden increases in volume compared to the previous 200 days. Many times this will begin a nice move to the upside that can be very dramatic and profitable. The more popular a stock is, the better. I always watch for signs of bottoming in key stocks that have had their day in the sun and are now out of favor.

For example, in early 2000 I was watching key stocks in the Dow when the Nasdaq tech rally was in full swing and many stocks had climbed phenomenally. During that time, many Dow stocks were at yearly lows, had solid earnings, and sound business management. I bought a boatload of bank stocks, retailers, telecoms, fast food, and so on, all trading at bargain prices on the ignored Dow and caught the rotation before it occurred. All of my stocks came off the bottoms to provide tremendous gains in a very short period of time. I like to call this common sense chart analysis.

THE LAW OF PARTICIPATION

The law of participation, simply put, is a big party. News events are the invitation and momentum traders do not care why the party started; they are more concerned with who is coming and how long they will stay.

The law of participation by definition begins by anticipating a short-term but consistent move by the market in the direction you expect. A market usually begins a trend and follows that trend for at least a few days. The less likely you feel about the general market trend, the less you should be investing in momentum trades. The bread and butter of momentum is "continuing momentum," which lasts for at least two days. You have two choices when in a successful momentum trade. The first is to exit with sufficient profits during the climb. The second is riding it out until the day it ends below mid-range. The variables you must ascertain when entering a trade not only the market direction, but also the micro-momentum event that caused the move in the first place.

I look at the market in the same way I look at individual stock momentum. If the market ends the day below the mid-range, I assume the market is gaining in negative momentum and I will expect a downward trend to begin. When I see that, I will look at my momentum investment positions and consider taking profits even if the stock is ending the day near the upper end of the price range. Stocks that end in the upper price range indicate upward-continuing momentum, and markets that end in the upper portion of the day's trading range indicate upward-continuing momentum. I like to look at the market in light of where it has been and consider it like a big swinging stock that moves up and down and becomes predictable the farther it swings in the shortest period of time. For example, if I see three days of –200-point drops in the Nasdaq I will be looking for signs of buying and a direction change much more so than three days of –35-point drops. Time and movement applies to markets as it does to stocks.

When the market climbs off recent lows, I will increase my momentum positions and keep the old ones that are still participating, but as the market begins to look frothy, I will begin to raise cash in anticipation of a downturn. Remember the law of momentum, which means as a market climbs, profit taking will increase. The quicker it climbs, the more profit-taking will occur. A frothy market is one in which you begin to see wild swings up and down and should be considered a danger sign. The same thing occurs at the bottoms and you can readily understand it when applied to human behavior. When people become excessively worried or unsure of their actions, they will be more erratic and will change their minds in a hurry. The market will reflect that action because people are the cause of momentum, both up and down.

Once a momentum stock ends the day below the mid-range, it is the first sign of a reversal and a dip. We can never be sure if the dip is the market or the stock and so you have a choice on that day to exit. If the market is strong and ending well with the fresh momentum story stocks ending nearer the highs and your momentum stock is under the middle of the day's trading range, it signals the end of the stock's momentum. Remember we want "participation" and when your stock no longer participates, it is probably under heavy profit-taking because of the climb.

When I enter a fresh momentum position, I will expect some profit-taking, especially with stocks that have good earnings reports because it seems gamblers are always willing to buy into a stock in anticipation of good earnings, and so after the report, they take their profits. This is the time to look at your trade in light of the 200-day chart and consider the long-term upside potential. We have some protection against dips because of our long-term outlook and we should be willing to ride a good company for a few years if need be. Personally, I have found momentum investing to make incredible profits fairly fast.

If you get caught in a long-term momentum position when the market corrects or dumps, you will be forced to ride the position down and wait for a bottom. I was caught in a couple positions when the market reversed and had to absorb some serious losses. But as the market bottomed and buying returned, I doubled my shares and rode the market up, recovering the losses. Remember the reason you bought the stock was because it was a participator and was under upward momentum, which should occur again once the market reverses again.

When I see market bottoms after a big assault by sellers, I will always go shopping for the latest leaders that have been touted by institutions or for solid stocks with solid earnings, growth potential, and good management. Many times you will see a lopsided investing cycle, which over-weighs one market such as technologies. When you see this lop-sidedness, begin to look for action in the beat-up sectors or the forgotten *good* companies. I recently spotted a rotation out of the technologies of the Nasdaq into the brick and mortar companies such as Wal-Mart, Procter and Gamble, and Chase Manhattan and rode some great profits as institutions began to invest in the good earnings companies again.

Long-term momentum can generally be identified by stocks ending the day above the mid-range under higher than normal volume and a good price climb. Be careful for excessive climbs in one day because the higher they go in the shortest amount of time, the more likely it is to get big profit-taking. We are not interested in the daytraders when investing and we will be less inclined to go with cheaper stocks unless we have reason to believe institutions or online investors are interested in the story. We want the big multiple-day gains, not the small intra-day swingers. It is OK if your boat floats out with the tide; it will return as it stays with the flow. When it strays out of the flow, exit the boat.

I have done very well in the last several years by waiting for blood and buying when the blood begins to stop flowing. I have bought when Mexico dumped, Asia dumped, oil dumped, and during most of the big corrections in the Nasdaq and Dow. Remember that when prices end above mid-range with increased volume, it is the signal that upward momentum is occurring.

The strength of momentum investing is that you are willing to ride out the downturns and you do it with very small shares. The easy thing about it is that you relax with a long-term mentality but capture the short-term profits. Build a solid platform before you commit to a trade and have specific expectations. Real momentum is defined by participation with the market. If the market falls, your momentum stocks will fall. If the market climbs, they will climb.

The rules for picking a continuing momentum stock are

1. Find a stock that does not sell off with the other gainers during the trading day.
2. Look for big blocks.
3. Find a stock that ends the day with good buying interest and a minimum of profit-taking indicated by finishing the day well above mid-range.
4. Find a stock that has a good institutional type news event in an institutionally led market or a good online investing-type story if online traders are very busy along with daytraders. Know your market.

THE MARKET'S INFLUENCE ON MOMENTUM INVESTMENTS

Momentum investments will not only react to the individual movements within the stocks themselves, but also to the general moves of the market, the bigger picture. The general market mood and confidence of the market as a whole will make up 80-percent of the influence over momentum stocks. So for continuing momentum plays that span over a few days, it is important that the market behave somewhat consistently in mood. Anytime the market begins to move up and down erratically from one day to the next, momentum plays will also move erratically and become a frustrating proposition at best. So a basic rule of playing multi-day momentum plays is to avoid choppy uncertain markets. Look first for a consistently trending market, and anytime you see it changing unexpectedly, exit your positions until the market stabilizes. Familiarity with the stock market environment is then a key ingredient in understanding the potential for momentum plays.

I like to track the market mood by tracking the stocks that are talked up by institutions, such as IBM, MSFT, INTC, AOL, JDSU, AMAT, ORCL, BRCD, CHKP, and EBAY. Watching these key players keeps me abreast of the Nasdaq. I have one screen devoted to those key stocks and I have found that they will move first ahead of technology trends, allowing me to trade ahead of the market move. You can do the same sort of tracking by watching key players within the NYSE, AMEX, Nasdaq, or any other market.

This is also useful for tracking individual sector movements such as financial stocks, bio-techs, healthcare, the semi-conductor sector, and so on. Just as the market in general will influence the movement of an individual stock, the sector movements will also affect the movements of the stocks. Sectors come into favor and out of favor, according to analyst's views on the sector, recent new technology, current demand within that sector, and so on. The mood and confidence in a stock's sector at any given time will also be a factor in a stock's momentum. Sectors that are currently "hot" will also tend to lead general market direction.

I like to find the representative stocks within the current leading sector and watch them trade throughout the day because it allows me a sneak preview into the coming momentum of the general market and possible market direction changes. For example, I may see afternoon selling within my chosen group of stocks that is of slightly greater intensity than the selling of the previous days in a climbing market. This can be a key indication that profit-taking is sneaking into the market, that the upward-trend is turning, and the next day could very well be down. If, on the other hand, my group of leaders climbs more than in previous days, in a declining market it could be an early tip-off to a market bottom and the signal to go long on sector leaders that are participating. I also regularly note the intra-day lows on these key stocks, how far down they are compared with the open price, and how far up stocks climb off those lows. The significance of this is that any unusual selling down lower than on previous days can also mean that the market may be turning direction.

DEFINING THE MARKET

Generally, the stock market is looked upon as being either a bear or bull market. I would like to clarify the differences and discuss how they will affect your trading. I generally look at the market like a rubber ball bouncing up and down a set of stairs. A bull market, or an inclining market, is one in which the ball bounces up the stairs. A bear market or declining market is one in which the bouncing ball goes down the stairs. With each type of market, you will notice smaller bounces in the opposite direction of the general direction.

For example, during a declining market, each buying spree will be met by more selling and the rises will be less determined. During a bull market, each dip will be met with buying that overcomes each bottom and we will see new highs. The stock market on a daily basis is the rubber ball and it bounces up and down to some low and some high and it generally ends at the low, middle, or high. This bouncing rubber ball is what I call macro-momentum and the stairs would be considered the bull or bear market, inclining or declining. For example, if the market has been moving up for a year, I would consider that to be an inclining market and we make the best money in such environments, especially if we are trading our retirement accounts.

So the day's action will reflect the general direction of the market and dips will get bought when stocks retreat and also when the market retreats. We depend on consistency in the direction of the market to make money playing momentum. So basically we feel that once a trend develops, we play it until it reverses. When a trader is unsure about the general direction of the market, it is best to wait it out.

The bouncing ball or the macro-momentum in which the market is making its moves each day is generally considered by looking at the fresh gainers and second-day gainers for a fresh peek into the momentum for each day. I will only look at stocks that are trading over one million shares of volume that have the best gains. I feel that a market can be best understood by looking at the strongest stocks first and then at the sectors for a consistent interpretation of the daily buying or selling. For example, I know that if my strongest stock is trading at $50 and it only sells down at the open by $1 and then rises off that bottom to climb over 10-percent, the stock and the market is considered to be strong. If the strongest stock that is trading at $50 falls over $4 from the open and only climbs $2, I know that the market is under profit-taking pressure and buyers are dwindling. I ignore buyout stocks because they generally will not retreat very much off the buyout price and generally provide little opportunity.

Once I identify my strongest stock, I look for other "like" trades to follow in that the selling and buying should be somewhat represented by the strongest and the followers should mirror the action. I do not expect the same type of potential because the news event that is causing the momentum in the first place will determine the amount of trading interest and residual climbs for the next few days. That is why it is important to track the news events, see the reactions for a few days, and relate that action to the market you are seeing. Even on down days you can determine the amount of buying interest by watching the stronger and sector stocks that have good volume. I like to judge a market by its participants. For example, I like to see a broad-based buying pattern that signals a more sustainable momentum. I like to see most of the techs rally on days in which the Nasdaq is moving up nicely. If we are recovering off recent lows on a good pullback, I will buy a basket of stocks, eliminate the dogs that do not participate the next day, and keep the strong ones.

The only reason an inclining market will turn into a bear market or declining market is when the overall fundamentals are changing in our economy such as interest rates climbing, governmental problems, or earnings reversals, especially with widely followed stocks such as CSCO. I try to watch my bread-and-butter stocks that continually mirror the market and note any changes on a daily basis. Until we see change and a good reason for it, we must assume we are in a short-term pullback if the market goes down for several days; the upside potential is better the lower the market goes. Sellers create value and buyers create profit-taking. The beginnings of both types of action can be seen in the strong stocks on a daily basis if you know what to look for. Basically, you consider the ending price of each strong stock in relationship to the high and low of the day. Ending below mid-range is a sign of negative momentum, ending above mid-range is a sign of positive momentum, and ending at mid-range is a sign of neutral momentum.

During these short-term pullbacks in an inclining market, I will get more aggressive, expecting a reversal and a continuation of the upward momentum. I judge individual momentum by the ending price in relationship to the high and low of the day and I also judge sectors and the general market by the participants (those stocks with good volume that are mirroring the market). Anytime I find myself in a trade that is down when the rest of the participants are up, I will exit the trade, considering it out of momentum and not participating.

The market is made up of two big entities. One is the Dow and the other is the Nasdaq. The Nasdaq is made up of mostly techs and the Dow is larger, older companies like financials and insurance. Many times they will trade in opposite directions when institutions take their money out of technologies and put it into brick and mortar companies so the differences in each should be kept in mind. I play both markets and look for those types of rotations from one into the other. It is important to watch for sector momentum too because many times you will find the sheep following the leaders and sectors can sustain momentum for days, weeks, or months. You can get a feel for what institutions are doing by watching key stocks that get mentioned time and time again on shows like CNBC by money managers for big firms such as Salomon Smith Barney or Goldman Sachs.

Markets that begin in a positive or negative direction are expected to stay headed in that direction for at least two or three days, allowing room for profits for the momentum investor. When important numbers are coming out or any important stock market event occurs, such as the Feds meeting, I like to remain in cash to keep my risk at a minimum. My thinking is to take consistent profits when I can and get out when there is any uncertainty and I collect my money market profits. A good momentum trader is continually learning which news events move both markets and stocks. Upgrades by important brokers, unexpected earnings gains, stock splits, and negative events in important stocks can all bring consistent moves in both the stocks and the market.

When big companies are releasing earnings, it can move the market up or down depending on how important the sector is and how many institutions are invested. Many times an important stock will release unexpected upside earnings, and other stocks in the sector begin to move up in sympathy with the reporting stock, which can set up a sector move that can last through earnings season. The market reacts big with anything unexpected and a smart trader will look for opportunity. I like to apply common sense to the stock market and find it to be important when assessing potential in the market and with trades. Some of our best money managers possess tremendous common sense in their investment approach.

When I consider the stock market each day, I will look at the low, then the high, and where the market ends the day in relationship to them. If the market ends at or near the highs, I consider it to have buying momentum even if it is ending negative on the day. The best upward momentum markets end near the highs and in positive territory. Remember the law of time and movement applies to markets as well as stocks and if a market climbs 500 points in two days, it will be due for some profit-taking and it would be wise to take your profits off the table when the market is looking like it is opening down. When markets open negatively by looking at the futures of either the Dow or Nasdaq, I consider them to be under negative momentum and if they look like they are opening up, I consider the momentum to be positive. A quick look at CNBC 15 minutes prior to the market open can establish the outlook because they post the futures all day long.

As the day ends, the stocks that have the best momentum going into tomorrow's market are the ones that are near the highs of the day and have good buying pace. Those are my candidates for holding long-term investments with small shares. I will not enter any long-term positions when the market is in severe up and down patterns, which is called a "frothy market." If I feel there is a chance of the market reversing, I will not risk my capital with new positions. Remember the rule of momentum in that "time and movement" also applies to the general market, which means the farther the market climbs in the fastest amount of time, the more likely it is to reverse. This applies to the bottoms or dips as well as the tops.

I generally like to look at the news regarding the momentum and only consider the long-term implications. I need the news to carry some weight and impact earnings dramatically when possible. I like to look for sector momentum that indicates institutional or online trader momentum. I also look for turnaround stories. I do not like to play stocks that are up a huge percentage because of the incentive for profit-taking.

I will always look at a long-term momentum play via a 200-day chart. I like to apply common sense to what the chart tells me. For example, if the yearly high was 240 and the stock is trading at 120 and I get a good earnings story, I will expect the potential to be about half-way up to 240, at least, which would put a target at about 180. I look at long-term charts much like I see narrowing oscillations during a trading day. I look at the low and then the high and consider the momentum will carry a stock off the low up to but not over the high. Remember though that the stock must be under positive momentum or you will forever be chasing stocks that look like they might be bottoming.

News almost always begins the momentum, so look for upgrades, earnings stories, or sector stories. Many times you will see a stock that blows away earnings expectations early in the "earnings season." Watch the fellow sector stocks because many times institutions will begin pouring money in other sector-related issues that can be the beginning of a huge move in anticipation of unexpected increased revenues and earnings. Be careful about chasing increased revenues because many times companies will report 100-percent increased revenues, but they spent 120-percent in advertising and expansion costs to get those extra revenues. Earnings are the biggie and a smart trader should always consider how the earnings were increased and how bright the forward-going future looks. Many times companies will try to doctor the results by selling some assets and applying the proceeds to their earnings. Try to identify real earnings by cutting costs or increased product demand and smart managerial practices. Try to apply earnings like it was your own hot dog stand and consider your market share, overhead, product demand, expansion potential, the related costs, and the outlook down the road. Try to identify the leaders in each sector because these will be the ones the institutions will normally buy.

I find it very helpful to listen to CNBC and read financial papers to get a feeling of which types of stocks and sectors institutions are interested in. A big keyword with institutions is "undervalued" and many times you will hear the same stocks mentioned over and over as favorites. One such example was Cisco (CSCO) before the big drop, and you can almost chart the institutions by the movement of that one stock. Lately I have been following Juniper Networks Inc. (JNPR) and Ciena Corp. (CIEN).

INTERPRETING THE MARKET

I like to apply simple expressions to give an interpretation of what I am seeing during each trading day. I am interested in repeating actions and patterns that would signal consistent behavior for the next few days. For example, when I see all the buying moves during the day countered by immediate and equal selling, causing narrow movements, small climbs, and small drops, I will state that there is a war between buyers and sellers and describe that as a "see-saw market." When the market begins to "see-saw" back and forth like that, it is a sign of a market that is on the verge of a change. Those types of markets are generally a nervous affair and anything can happen, which is not a good environment for investing. When the leaders continue to advance during the day, ending near the upper end of the day's price range, I interpret that as being a positive market, and expect continued buying momentum for the next day. The opposite is true when the leaders sell down and end near the lows of the day. I consider that to be a sign of negative market momentum.

MOMENTUM INVESTMENT EXITS

I generally begin to take profits when the trade goes over 10-percent because I feel it is best to trade safe rather than sorry. I teach traders everyday and I am constantly hit with the old "wish I had sold earlier" complaint as traders kept positions that were up 80-percent, but they wanted more. So they held, hoping for 100-percent, and wind up only getting 5-percent because of their own greed. Sell when the stock is climbing and don't allow incredible climbs by one or two trades after you sell to spoil your consistent record of profit-taking. Put greed on the back burner and take the money unless you feel very comfortable with the market and your momentum stock.

When you get signals of a market change, you have your choice to ride down the dip or take profits. I think it is wiser to note the winds of change and go with the flow. If the Nasdaq is at 5100 and you decide to hold the dip, your decision to hold will be a very difficult one to live with, laden with sleepless nights and sweaty palms, should that dip prove to be 2,000 points.

If the Nasdaq drops 2,000 points and you begin to see buying, look for opportunity, because even if the market should continue to dive a bit more, you are fairly safe in that some type of recovery is most likely close at hand. I love to buy when fear abounds. I often see traders sell with a large loss as the pain and fear overtakes them, only to find that was indeed the exact bottom. The key there lies in your ability to judge the signs of buying and your ability to look at the situation objectively, taking into account the principles of momentum. You have to be able to separate a dog from a good market participator that is simply down with the market. I began buying when the Nasdaq was 10-percent off the bottom and still dropping, and when it did bottom, I added more. The reason for this was the certainty that we were fairly close to a bottom. Many times the market can bottom and climb fast and high in one day, and I was determined not to miss out on such exceptional opportunity.

News events will drive the market as well as individual stocks. The feds, world events, and inflation are just some of the types of news that can drive a market up or down. When a news event hits the market unexpectedly, and I am in momentum trades, I will exit if they begin going against the direction I expected. Once a news event strikes, it can begin a whole new attitude of trading that may cause the market to change against my positions. I will also look for opportunity during bad news events such as the Mexican peso dropping overnight. I have found that bad news events create an over-reaction, and many good stocks get slaughtered along with the bad ones. This is the time to go shopping, once the dust clears a bit.

I normally watch my momentum play prior to the open, after the open, and during the day to make sure it is mirroring the leaders. I will want my trade to gap up with good volume much like the leaders, and I want them to get buying when the leaders climb, to not be sold over and above what I see with my leaders. For example, if my leaders move down $2 off the highs, I will want my momentum play to also move down about the same percentage. If I spot overselling during the day and my trade dips more than the leaders at the open or mid-day, I will suspect my trade is losing its upward potential. If the leaders go on a buying spree and my momentum trade does not, I take note and consider exiting the trade. Remember the reason you got into the trade in the first place. It had upward momentum and is expected to continue the trend. When the trend reverses, it is good to take your profits or losses whatever the case may be.

I began learning about momentum many years ago by doing hand tick charts and watching how each trade affects the movement of the prices of stocks under momentum. This taught me that each small movement a stock makes during the day becomes a clue to its larger trend. Momentum players have their finger on the pulse of the market like no others. We watch the small nuances that few are able to see because we are watching the movements of each individual stock very closely throughout each day. I took my dog out to the back yard one morning to do her business and when I got back my wife asked me if I saw the stool? "Heck, no!" I told her. She told me I would make a lousy nurse because the small changes of any health habits can signal upcoming problems and early detection is important to the health of the patient. Momentum players are much like nurses. We watch every little buying and selling wave as our leaders go through their daily routines.

Many times a stock that does not get the same buying wave that the leaders are having one day can experience a downtrend the next. The signs that traders may be losing interest can be subtle, so we have to stay aware and watch. Likewise, when a stock does not participate in the same selling wave as its counterparts, that can signal a very strong trend in subsequent trading days. By watching these subtle signals within the intraday behavior of our stock, momentum is understood and can be played by the astute momentum investor long-term as well as short-term.

PRE-MARKET GAPS

The general gapping of our leading stocks provides us with a very accurate indication for general market mood and confidence. The gaps reflect the mood for continuing momentum as the market opens and become a very good indication for subsequent market action. The following are the indications of positive and negative gaps, given both positive and negative markets.

General Market	Gapping	Indication for Macro-Momentum
Positive	Up	Indicates that momentum is continuing upward. Overnight and pre-market buying has occurred, indicating market confidence. Expectation at open would be limited or no profit-taking and early buying. Any stronger profit-taking and weaker climbs off the first bottoms could indicate a turn in momentum.

General Market	Gapping	Indication for Macro-Momentum
Positive	Down	Indicates that positive momentum could be turning. Overnight and pre-market selling has occurred, indicating nervousness or profit-taking. Expectation at open would be continued with profit-taking on gaps that slightly down, but possible early buying, especially on any larger gaps down, which become more attractive to bargain hunters. Bounces off the first bottoms may prove weaker if momentum is turning, and be stronger if momentum is to continue upward.
Negative	Down	Indicates that negative momentum is continuing. Overnight and pre-market selling has occurred, indicating continued nervousness. Expectation at open would be negative, but as upside potential grows, bargain hunters could come into the picture at any time. Climbs could occur very shallow or directly from open. First climbs will prove weak, followed by stronger selling, if momentum is to continue negative, but strong climbing would indicate a turn in momentum.
Negative	Up	Indicates that negative momentum could be turning. Overnight and pre-market buying has occurred, indicating bargain hunting and market confidence. Expectation at open would be initial profit-taking, but early buying off the first bottoms could occur. The amount of those first climbs will indicate whether the market is turning. Strong climbs would indicate that the market confidence shown in the gaps is being followed through on. If the first climbs are weak and followed by stronger selling, it would indicate short-lived confidence and continued negative momentum.

CLOSING COMBINATIONS

Where the market ends within its intra-day range is a sign of the general
market mood and direction going into the close. In a stable market, that
direction will carry forward the following day, amplified a bit more by
the overnight investor gaps. Likewise, in individual stocks, where that
stock ends within its intra-day range is also a sign of the ending interest
in that stock. For predictable movements, and highest potential, we look
to a combination of these ending ranges to guide our trading decisions.

Up = ending above mid-range point
Down = ending below mid-range point

Market	Stock	Implication
Up	Up	Micro-momentum and macro-momentum are upward-bound. Providing a stable market is present, the stock will most likely gap up the following morning and may continue upward.
Up	Down	Macro-momentum is ending positive, but your stock is not. That is a sign that your stock is not participating. Its weakness may continue the next day. It has broken from the macro-momentum and thus becomes unpredictable.
Down	Up	Your stock is showing more strength than the macro-momentum. The stock is not participating. If macro-momentum continues downward, your stock may be pulled down with it on the following day, unless it is an unpredictable exception.

Market	**Stock**	**Implication**
Down	Down	Both micro-momentum and macro-momentum are declining. Providing the market stays in that trend, your stock may gap neutral to negative the following morning and continue downward.

These methods and patterns tend to repeat themselves much like the short-term patterns discussed in the previous chapters. You must learn to track them daily as you did with dumpers, gainers, and news plays.

Let's trade the QQQ together, and let me explain how I apply momentum to my longer-term trading. Remember I am expecting a trend to begin and last for at least three days. If that does not occur, then I will lose money. Let's look at a daily chart of the Nasdaq composite and pick a day in which a trend begins. For our exercise, let's ignore all news events in the market and simply look at the chart in terms of pure momentum, remembering that a smart trader will be watching for changes in the winds of everyday trading and make more complex assertions based on the variables flowing in a dynamic market.

Following a two-day downturn in a climbing market, we had one day where the market ended at the high on 1-8-2001. Let's pretend we bought at the QQQ at the end of the day based on expecting the uptrending market to continue. On 1-9-01, the market gapped UP and ended the day above mid-range, indicating the upward trend was intact; we are still long the QQQ. The next day begins with a yellow alert because the market gapped DOWN. So if the market ends below mid-range, we EXIT. The market ended strong, confirming we still have an uptrending market and we are still long the QQQ. On 1-11-01, we receive another gap DOWN day and another yellow alert. If the market ends below mid-range, we exit the QQQ; it ends near the top again, and we are still long the QQQ and riding profits and a nice trend. On 1-12-01, the market gaps even and ends down, which is a yellow alert. If the market gaps DOWN, it would be two yellow alerts in a row, so we would exit. However, it gaps EVEN and we are nervous and may end the trade if the market ends below mid-range. It does not and we are still long our QQQ at the end of 1-16-01. On 1-17-01, the market gaps UP, indicating positive momentum. But the day ends near the low, and it would be another yellow alert. On 1-18-01, the market gaps UP, so we are OK and still long the QQQ and the day ends near the high. On 1-19-01, the market gaps UP but ends the day at the low for a yellow alert. The next day gaps DOWN, which is two yellow alerts, and we exit our QQQ trade.

These are the basics of following long-term momentum for as long as it lasts. You can reverse the procedure and do the same thing with negative momentum and follow some nice downtrends. If the market begins to go up one day and down the next and up the next, this method will lose money, but over the years that type of action does not occur very often.

It is my sincere desire to help struggling traders and I hope this book has provided a solid springboard from which you can take your own trading to new heights, stay at home, and raise your family.

EPILOGUE

In this book, we have discussed a myriad of topics ranging from the tools and tricks of the trade required to level the playing field with professional traders to advanced market dynamics. Although these topics are critical for a momentum trader to fully understand before entering the trading arena, they are only a start. Theory and methods, no matter how brilliant, are simply that, theory and methods. Nothing can beat the actual trading experience. Anyone can understand theory and methods; the true test of one's ability is putting these methods to practical use. I recommend you start slow, take one concept at a time, and let it build into the next. Before you trade actual capital, ensure you fully understand each concept and paper trade until you can prove to yourself that you can successfully and profitably trade them.

The education process is not a one-time event, nor is it something you can capture in an afternoon. It is an ongoing process. You must continually educate yourself. With each lesson, you graduate to higher and higher levels of proficiency and profitability. Find a mentor or a group of traders to discuss methodology and techniques. If you have troubles or questions, refer to the applicable chapters in this book or feel free to stop by the Mtrader.com or RealityTrader.com chat rooms to ask us directly yourself. We love to hear success stories as well as recommendations or new trading methodologies, so drop us a line if you have them at **Ken@mtrader.com** or **Chris@realitytrader.com.** Good luck and keep those stops!

GLOSSARY

All-or-none (AON):   An order that must be filled in its entirety or not at all.

Ask: Referred to as the "offer." It is the price at which a trader can buy shares of a stock.

Average down: Buying additional shares of a stock that one holds a position in and that has dropped in price since the earlier purchase.

Ax: The dominant Market Maker in a stock.

Bear market: A market that is on a consistent downward trend.

Bid: The price at which a trader can sell shares of a stock.

Big blocks: Big institutional buying resulting in large block buys.

Bull market: A market that is on a consistent upward trend.

Capitulation: Sellers and long players showing exhaustion after fast selling.

Chat room: An online chat forum where entry and exit criteria for stocks are discussed.

Closing price: The price which a security closes at.

Commissions: The fee paid to brokers for executing trades.

Daytrader strength: A measure of the amount of confidence daytraders have in a particular stock or the market in general.

Down-tick: A stock market transaction at a price lower than the preceding one for the same security.

Dumpers: Stocks that are down 20-percent or more from the previous day's close.

Earnings per share (EPS):   Net income for the past 12 months divided by the number of common shares outstanding, as reported by a company.

Electronic Communications Networks (ECN):   An ECN network's major brokerages utilized so that they can trade between themselves without having to go through a middleman.

Exchange: The marketplace in which shares, options, and futures on stocks, bonds, commodities, and indices are traded. Principal U.S. stock exchanges are the National Association of Securities Dealers (Nasdaq), New York Stock Exchange (NYSE), and the American Stock Exchange (AMEX).

Execution: The process of completing an order to buy or sell securities.

Float: The number of outstanding shares of a security available for public trading.

Front-running: The practice of trading ahead of others, commonly done by unscrupulous room leaders in chat rooms.

Gainers: Stocks that are up 20-percent or more from the previous day's close.

Gap: When a stock opens higher or lower than the previous day's close.

Historical market strength: Strength of the market in the recent past.

Hype: Touting the potential performance of a particular stock, not backed up by the facts.

In-betweeners: Trades that occur between the Bid and the Ask.

Initial Public Offerings (IPO):   A company's first sale of stock to the public.

Inside Ask: The best price at which a Market Maker will sell a particular stock.

Inside Bid: The best price at which a Market Maker will buy a particular stock.

Institutions: Entities with large amounts to invest, such as investment companies, mutual funds, brokerages, insurance companies, pension funds, investment banks, and endowment funds.

Level 1:   Real-time quotes of the best Bid and Ask prices for a given Nasdaq or OTCBB stock.

Level 2:   Real-time quotes of the Bid and Ask prices for each individual Market Maker for a given Nasdaq or OTCBB.

Limit order: When a trader places an order to buy or sell a stock at a set price. The trade occurs only at that price or a lower.

Market Maker: A broker that makes a market by providing liquidity to the market in a Nasdaq security by maintaining a firm quote on both the buy and sell side.

Market order: An order to buy or sell a stock at the going price.

Market strength: Strength of the overall market.

Moderator: A chat room leader who controls the room.

Momentum trader: A trader who enters and exits a stock as it drops or rises just after the momentum and direction shifts. Trades are held for seconds to minutes.

Moving average: Used in charts and technical analysis, the average of security or commodity prices constructed in a period as short as a few days or as long as several years and showing trends for the latest interval. As each new variable is included in calculating the average, the last variable of the series is deleted.

Open price: The price a stock opens at.

Oscillation: A stock that moves up and down intra-day, wavelike, within a price range.

OTC bulletin board: An electronic quotation system for unlisted, non-NASDAQ, over-the-counter securities.

Paper trading: Trading and tracking trades without using actual capital.

Price-to-earnings ratio (P/E):   The share price divided by earnings per share for a company's most recent four quarters.

Print: A real-time report of trades of a specific security.

Round trip: Entering and exiting a stock. Either a buy order and a sell order or a short order and a cover.

Scalper: A daytrader who enters and exits trades, quickly capturing small profits on each trade, such as .0625 or .125 of a point.

Sector strength: The strength of a particular sector of stocks.

Security Exchanges Commission (SEC):   A federal agency that is charged with regulating the U.S. financial markets.

Short: Borrowing shares of a security from a broker with the anticipation that the security will decrease in value. Also known as selling short.

Small Order Execution Service (SOES):   An automated execution system for bypassing brokers when processing small order agency executions of Nasdaq securities up to 1,000 shares.

Split: When a company splits their shares into a greater number of shares. A trader who owns 1,000 shares will own 2,000 after the split, at half the price, depending on the immediate action of the stock after the split.

Spread: The difference between the Bid and the Ask price.

Stochastics: A technical indicator that compares a stock's closing price to its price range over a given period of time. The belief is that in a rising market stocks will close near their highs, while in a falling market, they will close near their lows.

Stop loss: The practice of setting a specified exit price, limiting losses.

Stop order: An order to buy or sell at the market when and if a specified price is reached.

T-1 line: Extremely fast/high bandwidth connection.

Ticker: A scrolling display of current or recent security prices and/or volume.

Up-tick: A stock market transaction at a price higher than the preceding one for the same security.

RESOURCE LIST

EDUCATION

Chat Rooms: Online teaching forums specializing in teaching traders to develop their own disciplined and profitable trading programs. Features real-time discussion of trades as they occur during the market hours.

> **Mtrader.com**. Momentum trading instruction, daily e-mail advisory, chat room, online university, CD-ROMs, scanners available. Free trial.
>
> **RealityTrader.com**. Tape reading, daily e-mail advisory, Level 2 instruction, chat room, online training course, trading psychology CD's, scanners available. Free trial.
>
> **MainStreetInvesting.com**. Longer-term trading, momentum investing, e-mail advisory, educational material available.

Quotation/Execution Services: Services that provide real-time quotation and execution services.

> **MbTrading.com**. Execution/quotes, RealTick, Navigator, education, technical support.
>
> **Etrade.com**. Web-based broker with news, charts, quotes.
>
> **Abwatley.com**. Execution/quotes, RealTick.
>
> **Datek.com**. Execution/quotes.

Trading Information/Education: Web-based trading educational and informational sites.

> TheStreet.com
> Hardrightedge.com
> Siliconinvestor.com
> Nasdaq.com/reference/glossary.stm
> Whispernumber.com/
> Tradersworld.com/links.htm

ABOUT THE AUTHORS

Ken Wolff is CEO and founder of Mtrader.com, an Internet-based online teaching service that teaches traders how to develop their own successful and profitable trading programs. Ken is a popular speaker and broadcast commentator who has spent the last 10 years refining his high-percentage trading techniques. Ken founded Mtrader.com in 1997 after recognizing that the Internet was the most powerful forum for reaching a vast worldwide audience. Since 1997, Ken has taught literally thousands of traders to recognize and use the tools and methods previously only available to professional traders.

   Chris Schumacher is the former Head Trader at Mtrader.com and is currently the CEO and founder of RealityTrader.com. Chris founded RealityTrader.com based on his own tactics and techniques developed after years of teaching students online. Chris's methods are derived from his extensive experience with tape reading, trader psychology, and advanced execution systems. RealityTrader.com teaches students high-percentage Daytrading and SwingTrading methods while removing many of the common pitfalls that plague active traders.

   Jeff Tappan is the co-founder of Mtrader.com and was Ken Wolff's first online student in 1997. Prior to entering the daytrading arena, Jeff's expertise was primarily in recognizing potentially explosive small-cap stocks such as Iomega, Qualcomm, and Ion Laser Technology before they were recognized by the traders on the street. Jeff brings with him a unique understanding of trader psychology and market dynamics.

INDEX